Cooking in Piedmont

with

Roberto Donna

photography by Ted Boehm

FOOD CONCEPTS MARKETING CORPORATION
CLEVELAND, OHIO 1996

FIRST EDITION

10 9 8 7 6 5 4 3 2 1

LIBRARY OF CONGRESS CATALOG CARD NUMBER 97-60351
ISBN 0-9657242-0-4

Printed in the United States of America

Food Concepts Marketing Corporation
2530 Superior Avenue, 7th Floor
Cleveland, Ohio 44114
216-241-4949, Fax: 216-241-4320

Dedicated to my dear mother Anna,
and my father Giuseppe, who is no longer with us,
for their love and tradition.

To my sister, Loredana and her husband Silvano,
and children Edoardo and Federico.

"Tradition is fundamental in cooking – and in life.

I live my life based on certain traditions passed down from my family.

That tradition is the basis for my work."

Roberto Donna

In Ringraziamento
In Appreciation

Laurie Alleman
Ryan Allen
Mahe Bogdanovic
Al D'Alessandro
Enzo Fargione
Todd Gray
Cesare Lanfranconi
Jodi Lehr
Maureen Moxley
Michael Nayeri
Curtis Newton
Joyce Olson
Jean Louis Palladin
Regine Palladin
John Peca
Robert Pincus
Francesco Ricchi
Mario Sobbia
Jeanne Salvadori
Alan Savada
Lisa Sherman
Doug Smith
Elaine Tselepis-Sheetz

Sommario

Table of Contents

Chef Roberto Donna's cooking is reflective of the fresh and rich bounty of his native Piedmont Region in Northern Italy. Piedmont is known for its fresh produce, white truffles, game dishes, agnolotti, risotto and a rich and royal heritage of cuisine. Piedmont is a full, four-season region, nestled at the base of the Alps in the scenic Po Valley.

It was here, in Piedmont, where Donna was raised among a people of rich cultural heritage, with a hard-work ethic and a stern sense of pride in their Italian roots. The Piedmontese, Donna explains, are said to be "boujonaise" meaning "they do not move." Families establish themselves in the region and remain there to raise their families, passing on tradition for generations to come. In addition to its natural beauty, the Piedmont economy remains consistently strong due to the bountiful land and steady industry, offering its people good reason to stay true to their homeland.

Born and raised in Piedmont, Donna grew up in San Raffaele Cimena living in a duplex with his mother, father and older sister. On the opposite side of their duplex was a grocery store, run by Donna's mother. Next door to their home was a restaurant, a place where Donna would spend many hours learning the skills of a trade that would bring him much opportunity and success.

Donna's initial understanding of and interest in food began at age 6. On his first day at kindergarten, Donna recalls, "they served us boiled pasta with chicken stock, topped with Parmesan cheese. I did not like it and threw it away. I went home to my mother that day and I cried, I told her that I would not go back to school because I did not like the food." Donna pleaded with his mother to allow him to stay home from kindergarten, promising that he would stay out from under foot and spend his days working with the chefs at the restaurant next door.

Donna's mother agreed to the plan on a trial basis and he, in turn, remained true to his word. Every morning, Donna says, he ate breakfast, then headed next door to work in the kitchen. The two chefs took him under their wings, first giving him odd jobs to do around the kitchen. "When I was old enough to use a knife without cutting myself, they had me peeling potatoes," he says. And so Donna's introduction to food preparation began, at a tender young age.

The two Piedmontese chefs were truly an early influence on Donna's love for cooking. While his mother was too busy with the store to spend much time in the kitchen, their business introduced him to many different aspects of food. Their store, Donna says, carried everything from bread, to fresh meats, and cheese. In addition, Donna spent his summers in Asti with his grandparents who were vegetable gardeners. "It was there where I first developed my passion for fresh vegetables," Donna recalls. "Every day my grandfather would send me to the garden to gather the vegetables. Before every meal, we would eat the fresh-picked vegetables, dipping them in salt and olive oil."

Both in Asti and at home, food was at the center of family interaction and activity. Meal time was a special time for the Donna family. "Food became an important part of our lives because the only time our busy family was brought together on a daily basis was around the kitchen table," he says.

After taking his hiatus from kindergarten, Donna resumed school in the first grade, completing eight years, per Italian regulations. In Italy, after the eighth grade, students are required to choose a professional school at which to continue their education. Donna chose the culinary school, The Instituto Alberghiero di Torino "Colombatto," entering at age 13. He completed five years of training there, where he graduated with the highest marks earned by a student in the school's history.

Donna worked in various restaurants while attending culinary school, and upon graduating, went on to work in England and Switzerland before returning to Torino in Piedmont. Here, at Scudo di Savoia, a restaurant owned by Ernesto Bigio, Donna became head chef at age 16.

While working in Torino, he received a call from the vice president of the culinary school regarding a position at a restaurant, *Romeo and Juliet,* in Washington, D.C. Having no previous aspirations to travel to America, Donna agreed to spend one year at *Romeo and Juliet,* and left for the United States at age 19.

His experience with U.S. cooking was positive, he explains, as he was able to experiment and become familiar with many different kinds of foods, instead of specializing in one food type, the way many restaurants in Europe are structured.

While Donna's experience at *Romeo and Juliet* was positive, he was looking to expand his knowledge of food even further and, after one year, returned to Italy. Back at home, he found himself in a society that operated at a much slower pace than that to which he had grown accustom in the United States. He quickly found himself bored and was anxious for a new challenge. Three months later, he received a call

from the owner of *Romeo and Juliet*, offering him the head chef position, and the freedom to develop his own menu. He jumped at the chance and moved back to Washington D.C. where he worked at *Romeo and Juliet* until opening his flagship restaurant, *Galileo*, in 1984.

Since that date, Donna's four-star Galileo has won accolades from industry critics and has developed loyalty among diners from throughout the United States and Europe.

He has opened six other successful restaurants in the nation's capital, each with its own unique atmosphere and cuisine. During his years of work in the United States, Donna's cooking has evolved to incorporate new ideas and influences, while keeping its roots imbedded in traditional Piedmontese cuisine. The basis for Piedmont cooking is fresh vegetables and meats. That fresh influence is carried out through each of Donna's creations today.

In 1980, he recalls, American's did not identify carpaccio and risotto as Italian foods; they expected to eat cannelloni and spaghetti and meatballs at an Italian restaurant. But times have changed. The American people, he discovered, eventually grew comfortable with experimenting with new tastes. As people traveled more and learned more about other cultures and cuisines, their tastes became more sophisticated, Donna says. "It is our job as Italian chefs to offer people true Italian cuisine that one would find in Italy, not some dish that a magazine or a newspaper identifies as Italian cooking," he says.

While his cooking continues to evolve over time, Donna enjoys taking old Italian recipes and cooking them using today's modern techniques and tools. Preparing the dishes in this way is a challenge to Donna, as he tries to preserve the original flavors and textures of the food, as it was intended to be served hundreds of years ago. "Preserving that tradition is very important to me," he says.

Tradition is truly the cornerstone of Donna's success. The tradition and legacy of the hard-working people of Piedmont, coupled with the fresh and inviting cuisine of his homeland, have provided a framework that he has built upon to achieve his success.

Techniques

Bruciolo

"I like to use il bruciolo, a small stalk of rosemary inserted into a garlic clove, because it gives a good, fresh aroma of garlic and rosemary to the food without overpowering the dish.

The correct way to prepare bruciolo is to first cut a sprig of rosemary, no more than 5 inches in length. Blanch the rosemary in boiling water for 30 seconds; this will keep the leaves from falling off the rosemary stem during cooking. Insert the blanched sprig into a clean, peeled garlic clove. Be sure to insert the rosemary into the garlic at the heart of the clove.

When you are ready to prepare the recipe, place the bruciolo in the olive oil or butter when the fat is still cool. By placing it in the oil or butter before it is heated, the bruciolo will release its full aroma instead of searing or burning. When the garlic reaches a golden brown color, remove it from the pan. Having the rosemary and garlic cook side-by-side gives the food good flavor. The bruciolo is easy to remove from the dish, leaving behind the aroma and making the dish much more digestible.

I learned to cook with bruciolo from a chef who was also the vice president of my cooking school back in Italy. His name was Ernesto Bigio, a classical Piedmontese man with an excellent palate for food and wines, who was very proud of Piedmontese tradition. The first time I saw him use bruciolo, I was very interested. I liked the shape, the color and the smell when it started to cook in the pan. I was surprised to taste the flavor it left in the dish - good, sweet and not too strong."

Reconstituting Frozen Porcini Mushrooms

27 ounces frozen porcini mushrooms (or 2 lbs. fresh)
5 cloves garlic, cut once lengthwise
1 fresh rosemary sprig, cut into 3" lengths
3 fresh sage leaves
4 fresh thyme sprigs
1 teaspoon salt
2 teaspoons black pepper
1 ounce olive oil

Spread mushrooms in an even layer in the bottom of a baking dish. Add olive oil, and coat the mushrooms, herbs, salt and pepper and mix well. Bake uncovered in preheated oven at 400 degrees for 20 minutes. Stir at least two times. Remove dish from the oven; mushrooms should be firm to the touch. Remove herb sprigs.

The mushrooms are ready to be served as a side dish or used in a recipe. They can be stored in the refrigerator for four to five days. Allow the mushrooms to cool before putting them in a closed container to reduce moisture build-up.

Preparing Roasted Peppers

6 peppers (yellow or red)
2 ounces olive oil

Wash peppers using cold water. Place the dried peppers, whole, on a cookie sheet. Dribble each pepper with olive oil and turn to coat all sides of the pepper. Place the sheet in preheated oven at 450 degrees; after 10 minutes, pull out sheet and turn peppers. Continue to bake the peppers for 30 minutes, turning the peppers occasionally so that the skin on all sides of the pepper begins to wrinkle.

Remove the peppers from the oven and place them in a paper bag. The bag can be white or brown paper and should be free of ink. Roll the paper bag closed and let stand for 30 minutes. The moisture build-up in the bag will help prepare the skin for easy removal.

Take the peppers out of the bag and allow them to cool until they are comfortable to handle. Remove the pepper stem first, using your hands, and then scoop out the seeds and veins. Remove the outer, wrinkled skin. Never clean under running water since it will remove any flavor from the peppers.

Egg Wash

An Egg Wash is brushed on pasta dough to help seal the dough when making ravioli.

4 eggs
1/3 cup water

Combine eggs and water in mixing bowl and mix well using whisk. The wash can be applied on pasta using a cooking brush or your fingers.

For recipes that contain meat stocks or juices, vegetable stock can always be substituted to make the dish vegetarian.

Pasta Dough Basics

All of the pasta dough recipes in this book are made using a dough hook attachment on a mixer. You can also use your food processor with a dough hook to prepare pasta dough. When using the food processor, combine ingredients in bowl at once, then mix, increasing speed gradually to medium-high for 2 to 3 1/2 minutes. Mix dough at maximum speed for no more than 10 seconds. If you are mixing pasta dough by hand, double the advised mixing time.

If you choose to cut down on the number of eggs called for in a pasta dough recipe, substitute each egg with 1/4 cup water.

Fresh pasta dough can be stored in the refrigerator for 3-4 days. Wrap in plastic wrap.

Egg Yolk Dough (1 lb.)

3 1/2 cups all purpose flour
1 tablespoon salt
2 tablespoons olive oil
22 egg yolks

To prepare dough, combine ingredients in bowl and mix using dough hook attachment on mixer. Mix at low speed for 3 minutes. If dough is too stiff, add 1 teaspoon of water and mix briefly.

Place dough on floured surface. Add 1/4 cup flour and knead for 1 minute or until blended. If there are unmixed ingredients left in bottom of mixing bowl, add them and incorporate as you knead dough by hand. Wrap dough in plastic wrap and refrigerate for 2 hours.

Saffron Pasta Dough (1 lb.)

3 1/2 cups all purpose flour
1 tablespoon salt
5 eggs
1 tablespoon olive oil
2 teaspoons saffron threads (or 1 teaspoon saffron powder)

To prepare pasta dough, combine all ingredients in bowl and mix using dough hook attachment on mixer; mix at low speed for 3 to 5 minutes. Remove dough from bowl and knead slightly. Wrap dough in plastic wrap and refrigerate for 2 hours.

Tomato Pasta Dough (1 lb.)

3 1/2 cups all purpose flour
1 tablespoon salt
1 tablespoon olive oil
1 1/2 cup tomato paste
4 eggs

To prepare tomato pasta dough, combine ingredients in mixing bowl and mix using dough hook attachment on mixer or food processor; mix dough at low speed for 3 to 5 minutes. Remove from bowl and place on lightly floured surface. Add 1/4 cup flour and knead dough, mixing well for 1 minute. Wrap dough, lightly coated with flour, in plastic wrap and refrigerate for 2 hours.

Spinach Pasta Dough (1 lb.)

1 lb. spinach
4 eggs
3 1/2 cups all purpose flour
1 tablespoon olive oil

To prepare pasta dough, cook spinach in boiling water for 3 minutes; drain using a strainer, pressing down on spinach leaves to extract water. When spinach is drained and cooled, place in blender with 3 eggs and puree until smooth; set mixture aside.

Combine flour, olive oil, spinach puree and 1 egg in bowl and mix using dough hook attachment on mixer; mix at low speed for 3 minutes.

Place dough on floured surface. Add 1/4 cup flour and knead for 1 minute or until blended. If there are unmixed ingredients left in bottom of mixing bowl, add them and incorporate as you knead dough by hand. Wrap dough, lightly coated in flour, in plastic wrap and refrigerate for 2 hours.

Black Pasta Dough (1 lb.)

3 1/2 cups all purpose flour
1 1/2 tablespoons salt
1 tablespoon black ink from cuttlefish
5 eggs

To prepare black pasta dough, combine ingredients in mixing bowl, keeping 1/2 cup of flour on the side for later, and mix using dough hook attachment on mixer or food processor; mix dough at low speed, level 3, for 3 minutes. Remove from bowl and place on lightly floured surface. Add 1/2 cup flour and knead dough, mixing well for 1 minute. Wrap dough, lightly coated with flour, in plastic wrap and refrigerate for 2 hours.

Corn Pasta Dough (1 lb.)

2 3/4 cups all purpose flour
1 cup corn flour (cornmeal)
1 tablespoon salt
2 tablespoons olive oil
5 eggs

To prepare pasta dough, combine ingredients in mixing bowl and mix using dough hook attachment on mixer; mix at low speed for 5 minutes. Remove dough and place on lightly floured surface. Add 1/4 cup flour and knead dough until flour is blended. Wrap dough, lightly coated with flour, in plastic wrap and refrigerate for 2 hours.

How To Peel a Tomato

To prepare tomatoes, bring water to a boil over medium-high heat. Take tomato and remove core; using a sharp knife, mark an "X" on skin at opposite end of tomato.

Place tomato in boiling water for 1 1/2 minutes; remove from water and place in ice water bath. After tomato has cooled, remove from water, peel the skin away, using the "X" area as a starting point to grab skin tag.

Preparing Sweetbreads

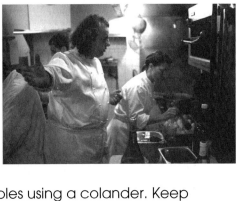

3 cups dry white wine
1 onion, peeled, finely chopped (1 cup)
1 carrot, peeled, finely chopped (1 cup)
2 celery stalks, cleaned, finely chopped (1 cup)
1/3 cup red wine vinegar
3 dried bay leaves
2 lbs. sweetbreads (veal neck and glands)

In a large sauce pan, combine 6 cups water and white wine. Add vegetables and bay leaves and cook over high heat for 10 minutes. Drain vegetables using a colander. Keep water.

Set water back over high heat and bring to a boil; add sweetbreads. After 8 minutes, drain sweetbreads using a colander. Place the sweetbreads in a small loaf pan and stack a second pan on top with a weight in the bottom to keep them tightly packed. This will allow the breads to keep their form, making them easier to slice. Place sweetbreads in the refrigerator for 5-6 hours. They are now ready to use in another recipe or store in the freezer for later use.

To prepare poached calf brain, bring the same water from the sweetbreads to a boil and add 10 ounce calf brain. Poach for 4 minutes and remove, draining water.

Fried Vegetables

Crispy Vegetables
For a very light, fried vegetable garnish, fry in grapeseed oil heated to 350 degrees. Wash vegetables in ice cold water to preserve color.

Crispy Artichokes
Three artichokes: peel off tough, outer leaves and stem; take artichoke hearts and cut in half, then cut in 1/16" slices. Fry in grapeseed oil for 30 seconds.

Crispy Leeks
Three leeks: using white stems only, split lengthwise; wash to remove dirt. Take split stems and cut very fine julienne. Fry in grapeseed oil for 30 seconds.

Crispy Basil
Take basil leaves and wash; cut leaves very fine julienne. Fry in grapeseed oil for 15 seconds.

Crispy Parsley
Take Italian parsley stems and wash; split stems and fry in grapeseed oil for 15 seconds.

Lobster Preparation

In order to render lobster meat for use in recipes, lobsters are first blanched in boiling water to remove the meat. To blanch a lobster, place whole in boiling water for 5 minutes. When lobster is removed from water, it will be bright orange in color. Allow the lobster to cool for 5-8 minutes. Keep the water for use in making stock.

After lobster is cooled enough to touch, it can be cleaned. Using a large, wide-blade knife, cut off tail first and drain liquid from inside. Turning lobster over on its back, take cooking scissors and carefully snip the membrane along the outer edge of both sides of the body. Remove body meat, piercing with a spear or skewer to keep meat in one long piece.

Pull off claws and remove meat by cutting away at shell and pulling out with your fingers. Cut down the length of the claw, all the way to the tip, to remove meat inside. If you want to keep the claw meat whole, use this technique, cutting carefully along the edge of the claw to preserve the shape of the claw meat. If you just want to extract the meat, crack the claw using cracker tool.

Vinaigrette Dressing

1 cup olive oil
1 cup red wine vinegar
1 cup balsamic vinegar
1 1/2 teaspoon salt
1 teaspoon black pepper

Mix ingredients together.

Have leftover dressing for use on salads or other vegetable dishes. The dressing can be stored for up to 60 days in the refrigerator.

Frog Leg Preparation, and Stock

4 frog legs
1 shallot, chopped (1/2 cup)
1/2 cup olive oil
1 cup dry white wine
5 cups chicken stock
1/4 cup butter
7 1/2 teaspoons salt
1 teaspoon black pepper
2 tablespoons of all purpose flour

To prepare frog legs, take each leg and cut off top of leg, leaving bottom 3 1/2 inches. Clean meat away from the bone; as you clean bone, pull the meat down to the base of the leg, forming a "ball" of meat at the base. Working with the tip of a small, flexible knife, continue to cut away at tendons and ligaments as you clean. The finished leg should have a base of meat with a clean bone protruding straight up from the center of that base. Take the top of the leg, which you chopped off earlier, and place in medium stock pot. Add shallots, 2 tablespoons olive oil and sauté over high heat for 3 minutes. Drain liquid and add one cup white wine. After wine has reduced by half, add chicken stock and simmer for 3 minutes.

Melt 1/4 cup butter in medium saute pan over medium heat. Take frog legs and sprinkle lightly with salt and pepper, then roll in flour. When butter is foamy, add frog legs, turning continuously as they saute to achieve a light golden brown color on all sides. When all legs are browned, remove from pan and place on baking sheet. Bake in preheated oven at 450 degrees for 5 minutes.

Polenta

4 cups water
3 tablespoons salt
5 ounces yellow Italian cornmeal, precooked

In a small sauce pan, bring 4 cups of water and salt to a boil over medium-high heat. Pour in cornmeal and stir briskly with a whisk. Reduce heat to low and simmer for 5 minutes.

Pour mixture into small loaf pan and allow to cool. Polenta can be sliced and served cold, grilled or sauteed.

Basil Puree

1 1/2 cup fresh basil leaves, packed
3/4 cup olive oil

Place basil leaves in blender or food processor; add half of the olive oil and begin blending allowing basil and oil to mix. Continue mixing, adding the remainder of the olive oil while blender is running, approximately 1 minute. Remove contents, cover and refrigerate for up to one week. May be frozen for up to 6 months.

How to Tie Meats

With standard cooking twine, begin at one end of meat to be tied, and hold leading end with forefinger, hand behind meat. Wrap meat slowly while rotating meat in the opposite direction of hand movement. Continue tying twine in a spiral with spaces between rows of about 1 inch. Twine should be fitted snugly enough to prevent meat from coming apart yet not so tight as to break surface. Do not tie too loosely as meat will shrink during cooking.

Cleaning Artichokes

Artichokes require some special attention and preparation before cooking. First, artichokes have sharp barbs on the ends of their leaves. The barbs must be removed before cooking and may be snipped using kitchen scissors. Artichokes also have a tendency to discolor when they are exposed to air. To keep the artichoke's color pale green, tie lemon slices to the cut surface to keep them from turning color. The tying will reduce the likelihood of the artichoke falling apart during cooking and will give the vegetable a neat, compact shape.

General Tips

• It is preferred that you use anchovy fillets preserved in salt; these fillets should be rinsed well under cold tap water before use. Remove bone and spine.

• In order to avoid a strong garlic aftertaste, you may modify the intensity of the garlic by following one of the procedures below.

Cut the garlic clove in half lengthwise and remove the "heart" in the center of the clove. The heart is the strongest part of the garlic.

In a small sauce pan, boil garlic cloves in 1 1/2 cups of milk for 20 minutes. A thick paste will form. Drain excess liquid away and add the paste to the anchovy mixture. Add 1/2 cup of heavy whipping cream to the finished mixture and boil for five minutes.

• Allow fried foods to set in warm area while frying other foods to accompany the dish. You may want to place them on a plate, set on the opened door of a warm oven.

• To prepare squid tentacles for decoration to accompany dish, place in small stock pot. Cover tentacles with water. Add 1 1/2 teaspoons salt and juice of 1/4 medium lemon. Bring to a boil for 20 minutes. Tentacles will be bright purple in color.

• When combining any liquid to flour, the mixing ingredient should be at a different temperature than the flour. For instance, combine room temperature flour with either warmer or colder water, but not room temperature water. The difference in temperature significantly aides ingredient dilution.

salse

A lot of sauces are used to serve with antipasti, mostly because they are made from the food that they are served with. The sauces are very natural, many stocks and reductions. In Piedmont, we do not make sauces to cover the food or the quality of the ingredients, we use the sauce to enhance the flavor and presentation of the food. I think that's what sauces should do.

We have sauces like Bagna Cauda that are a column of our cooking and a tradition with every family in Piedmont. It is a sauce that is usually eaten on Friday night because it takes two days to clean your palate from the taste of garlic, but it is a great sauce.

I tried to give you recipes for sauces that you will need to prepare a good Piedmontese meal. Of course they are not all of the sauces that exist in Piedmont, only a sampling. Everyone should have stock and glaze frozen in the freezer at home; that is what you need to make a simple recipes with full flavor and great results. The glazes take longer but a quick tomato sauce takes only 5 minutes. One of the most important things to remember when making tomato sauce is to never cook tomatoes for more than 30 minutes. Another suggestion for making sauce is not to prepare early and try to keep it warmed; it loses freshness. When sauce is finished, set it aside; re-heat just before you are ready to serve.

Brodo Di Manzo

Beef Stock

beef shank (12 ounces)
8 teaspoons salt
1/4 ounce black peppercorns
4 celery stalks, cleaned with leaves on
2 carrots, peeled, halved lengthwise
1 ounce fresh Italian parsley
2 onions, with skins on
3 garlic cloves
4 plum tomatoes, halved
5 fresh basil leaves
3 dried bay leaves

Clarification:
32 ounces ground beef
5 egg whites
1 onion, finely chopped (2 cups)
1 carrot, peeled, finely chopped (1 cup)
1/3 cup fresh parsley, chopped
3 celery stalks, rough cut
4 teaspoons salt
1/3 cup port wine
Beef stock (above)

Cut onions in half, leaving skins on, and place face-down on burner over medium-high heat. Allow onion to caramelize. When the white part of onions turn black, remove from burner using tongs.

Take celery and carrots and tie together with cooking twine, making a bouquet. Insert garlic cloves.

In a large stock pot, add meat, vegetable bouquet, onions, tomatoes and herbs. Add 6 quarts of water and place stock pot over high heat until contents come to a boil.

After stock begins to boil, reduce heat to low and continue to simmer for a total cook-time of 4 hours. In order to obtain a clear stock, skim the top of stock as it cooks removing any fat or other impurities.

The stock is ready to be used at this stage, or can be clarified, making the flavor more intense.

To clarify, first refrigerate the stock overnight at least 12 hours in an air-tight container. After the stock has been chilled, a layer of fat will form along the top; remove this layer using a spoon.

In a large stock pot, mix meat, vegetables and herbs using your hands to mix, making sure that ingredients are thoroughly blended. Add wine and beef stock and mix again. Place mixture over low heat for 2 1/2 hours.

The egg whites will act as a sponge, soaking up the beef. The meat and vegetables will rise to the top, leaving behind a very clear broth. When stock is fully cooked, remove from heat and pour through a fine colander lined with cheese cloth. The yield will be a richly- flavored clear broth.

Brodo Di Pollo
Chicken Stock

10 lbs. chicken bones
1 1/2 ounces fresh Italian parsley sprigs
2 dried bay leaves
1 ounce black peppercorns
3 tablespoons salt
10 plum tomatoes, halved
4 garlic cloves
1 ounce fresh basil leaves
1/2 ounce fresh thyme

Place chicken bones in large stock pot and cover with water. Place lid on pot and bring to a boil, approximately 30 minutes, over medium heat. Remove from heat and discard water, which contains impurities from bones. Cover bones with 2 1/4 gallons fresh water; add all other ingredients and cook uncovered over low heat. As stock boils, impurities will rise to the top. Continue to skim off impurities with a spoon or ladle as the stock cooks. Cook stock for 3 hours and remove from heat. Pour contents through strainer to yield clear stock.

Brodo D Anatra
Duck Stock

2 duck carcasses
1 onion, peeled, finely chopped (2 cups)
4 celery stalks, cleaned, finely chopped (2 cups)
2 carrots, peeled, finely chopped (2 cups)
3 cups dry red wine
4 tablespoons tomato paste
7 garlic cloves
5 fresh rosemary sprigs
15 fresh sage leaves
8 fresh thyme sprigs
8 plum tomatoes, halved

Place duck carcasses on baking sheet and bake in oven preheated to 450 degrees for 40 minutes. Remove from oven and discard fat and juices. Take duck bones and smash using meat mallet; set aside. Take baking pan and place over low heat, adding 2 cups of water. Using a spatula, scrape bottom of pan, loosening meat scraps. Empty contents of baking pan into large stock pot and add smashed bones. Add onions, celery and carrots and continue to cook for 2 minutes over low heat. Add wine, 16 ounces of water and tomato paste and increase heat to high. Add herbs and cook for 3 hours. Remove mixture from heat and pour contents through strainer to yield light duck stock.

Brodo D'Aragosta

Lobster Stock

4 lobster carcasses
6 quarts lobster water (techniques chapter)
6 celery stalks, rough cut (12 ounces)
3 carrots, peeled, rough cut (12 ounces)
2 onions, quartered (12 ounces)
3 teaspoons salt
1/2 teaspoon black peppercorns
1 ounce fresh Italian parsley, with stems
1/4 ounce fresh thyme
2 dried bay leaves
2 cups dry white wine

Combine all ingredients in a large stock pot and cook over high heat until mixture comes to a boil. After contents boil, reduce heat to medium-low and simmer for 20 minutes. Remove pot from heat and pour contents through a small colander or sieve. Using a spoon, press mixture, extracting juices; discard vegetable mixture. The recipe yields 6 quarts of stock.

Brodo Di Quaglie

Quail Stock

11 ounces quail
2 tablespoons olive oil
2 cloves garlic, halved
2 teaspoons salt
2 teaspoons black pepper
2 fresh rosemary sprigs
4 fresh sage leaves
10 fresh thyme sprigs
3 shallots, peeled, halved (5 ounces)
1 1/2 cups dry white wine
1 juniper berry, smashed
15 black peppercorns
1 dried bay leaf
2 cups chicken stock (sauces chapter)

Take whole quail and chop into small pieces using meat clever, only use bones, if possible. In a large stock pot, heat olive oil over medium heat. Add quail and cook until well browned, then add herbs. Cook for 5 minutes. Add wine and allow to reduce by half. Add chicken stock and bring mixture to a boil. After stock reaches a boil, reduce heat to low and simmer for 40 minutes.

Remove stock from heat and pour through fine sieve. Press down ingredients, using a spoon, to extract juices.

Brodo Di Cappesante

Sea Scallop Broth

1 ounce unsalted butter
1 shallot, chopped (1 ounce)
4 ounces of scallops or muscle from scallops
1 cup dry white wine
1/4 teaspoon salt

In a medium sauce pan, saute butter and shallots over medium heat for 1 1/2 minutes. Add scallop meat, salt and wine and cover pan, simmering over low heat for 6 1/2 minutes. Remove from heat and pour contents of pan through strainer or sieve. The recipe will yield 1 cup of broth.

Brodo Di Gamberetti D'Acqua Dolce

Crawfish Broth

25 ounces fresh crawfish
1/2 ounce fresh parsley
8 fresh thyme sprigs
3 fresh tarragon sprigs
4 celery stalks, finely chopped (2 cups)
1 onion, finely chopped (2 cups)
2 carrots, peeled, finely chopped (2 cups)
2 garlic cloves, smashed
2 1/2 teaspoons salt
20 black peppercorns
4 quarts cold water

Combine all ingredients in a large stock pot and cook over high heat, uncovered. Bring to a boil and reduce heat to low. Cook for 20 minutes. Remove from heat and strain mixture through a colander, extracting juices from crawfish and vegetables by pressing down firmly with your hand.

Brodo Di Piccione

Squab Stock

13 ounces squab bones, chopped
2 dried bay leaves
1 celery stalk, diced (1/4 cup)
1 carrot, peeled, diced (1/2 cup)
1 onion, diced (1/3 cup)
1 tablespoon salt
1 tablespoon peppercorns
2 juniper berries, smashed
5 fresh basil leaves
1 fresh rosemary sprig
6 fresh thyme sprigs
5 fresh sage leaves
5 plum tomatoes, halved
2 ounces fresh Italian parsley sprigs
2 leeks including stems and leaves, washed (7 ounces)
1 cup Madeira wine
1 onion, whole with skin
2 cups water

Clarification:
1 carrot, peeled (4 ounces)
2 celery stalks (4ounces)
1 onion (4-6 ounces)
6 egg whites
1 lb. ground beef

Take whole onion, with skin still on, and slice in half. Place face down on stove burner over medium heat to caramelize. When onion is blackened, remove from heat. Place in large stock pot along with all other ingredients. Cook with cover on high heat for 3 hours. Strain contents of pot through a sieve, yielding 2 quarts of stock. Set stock aside to cool.

To clarify stock, or bring out a more intense flavor, place vegetables and egg whites in food processor and puree until smooth. Blend beef in with mixture, by hand, mixing well. Add mixture to cooled stock and cook over low heat for 45 minutes. Strain through sieve to yield clarified consomme stock.

Fondo Di Pernice

Partridge Reduction

2 partridge carcasses
1/8 cup olive oil
5 fresh thyme sprigs
2 garlic cloves
5 fresh sage leaves
5 fresh rosemary sprigs
1 onion, finely chopped, (1 cup)
1 celery stalk, finely chopped (1/2 cup)
1 carrot, peeled, finely chopped (1/2 cup)
2 juniper berries, smashed
1/4 ounce black peppercorns
2 dried bay leaves
1- 5 ounce pig ear (5-6 pigs feet)
1 cup Madeira wine
5 cups beef stock (sauces chapter)

Chop partridge bones into small pieces using meat cleaver. In a large sauce pan, saute bones in olive oil until they become very brown and crispy. Drain oil from pan. Add vegetables and herbs and cook over high heat for approximately 5 minutes. Cut pig ear into 1/4" strips and add to mixture. Add wine and cook mixture over medium heat until wine has reduced by half.

In a large stock pot, add 5 cups beef stock and contents of sauce pan, after pan has deglazed. Cook over high heat until mixture is brought to a boil. After it boils, turn to low heat and simmer. As stock cooks, continue to skim impurities off the top. Total cook-time should be one hour and 30 minutes.

When sauce is finished cooking, remove from stove and pour contents through a strainer or sieve to yield reduction stock.

Fondo Di Coniglio

Rabbit Reduction

7 ounces rabbit shoulder, chopped
1/4 cup olive oil
4 fresh sage leaves
1 garlic clove, smashed
2 fresh rosemary sprigs
1 onion, peeled, finely chopped (1/2 cup)
1 celery stalk, cleaned, finely chopped (1/2 cup)
1 carrot, peeled, finely chopped (1/2 cup)
1/2 cup Madeira wine
3 cups rabbit stock (sauces chapter)
1/2 cup Marsala wine
1 tablespoon tomato paste

Heat olive oil in medium saute pan over medium heat. When oil is hot, add rabbit meat and saute for 1 minute. Add herbs and continue to saute until meat is browned, approximately 3 minutes. Drain oil and add onion, celery and carrots; cook until vegetables sweat and add Madeira wine. Continue to cook over medium heat until wine is completely reduced. Add 3 cups rabbit stock and bring mixture to a boil. After it reaches boiling point, reduce heat to low. Cook for an additional 7 minutes and add marsala and tomato paste. Continue to simmer for a total cook time of 48 minutes.

Remove stock from heat and pour through a strainer. Press down on mixture to extract juices. The recipe yields 1 cup of sauce.

Brodo Di Coniglio

Rabbit Stock

2 rabbits, cleaned
1 onion, finely chopped (1 cup)
2 celery stalks, finely chopped (1 cup)
1 carrot, finely chopped (1 cup)
4 teaspoons salt
1/4 ounce black peppercorns
4 fresh thyme sprigs
2 garlic cloves
3 fresh tarragon sprigs
5 fresh basil leaves
2 dried bay leaves
4 plum tomatoes, halved
1/2 ounce fresh Italian parsley

Chop rabbits into sections. Place into large stock pot, adding 4 quarts of water and all other ingredients. Place pot over high heat until mixture boils. After stock boils, reduce to low heat and simmer for a total cook-time of 2 hours and 20 minutes.

Remove stock from heat and drain through a large colander. Do not press mixture; allow stock to drain from contents of stock naturally.

Fondo Di Vitello

Veal Reduction

1 veal foot, mashed very well (1 1/2 lbs.)
6 lbs. veal bones
3 celery stalks, cut in 2" pieces
2 onions, peeled, quartered
2 carrots, peeled, cut into 2" pieces
3 fresh rosemary sprigs
8 fresh sage sprigs
10 fresh thyme sprigs
6 garlic cloves, smashed
2 cups red wine
20 cups veal stock (sauces chapter)
1/3 cup tomato paste
32 ounces veal, cubed
1 cup olive oil
1 bottle Madeira wine
1 bottle port wine

In a large, baking/roasting pan, spread veal bones in a single layer. Bake uncovered at 450 degrees for 45 minutes, turning every 15 minutes to allow bones to brown evenly. Remove pan from the oven and drain the fat from the bottom of the pan, leaving veal bones in the original baking pan. Add celery, onions and carrots and bake for an additional 40 minutes.

Remove pan from the oven; add rosemary, sage, thyme and garlic. Place pan over medium heat and add 2 cups of red wine. After the wine has reduced to half its original amount, add veal stock and tomato paste, veal foot; mix well. Transfer mixture to a large stock pot, cooking over low heat.

In a medium sauce pan, saute veal meat in olive oil over medium heat until meat becomes crispy. Add one cup of Madeira and one cup of port wine and return pan to heat. Cook until the veal juices and meat particles rise to the top; add the contents of the sauce pan to the original stock. Add the remainder of both bottles of wine and cook on low heat for 1 1/2 hours.

After stock has cooked down, drain and store in refrigerator overnight for at least 12 hours. All impurities will rise to the top, leaving a filmy layer of residue on the top of the sauce. This layer will be easily differentiated as the color will be slightly lighter than that of the sauce on the bottom. Remove the top layer with a spoon and discard.

The remaining stock will be approximately 8 cups of a jelly-like sauce. Pour stock into a medium saucepan and cook over high heat, allowing it to come to a fast boil. Reduce heat, keeping the substance at a boil. Skim the fat off of the top of the sauce as it rises. Continue to cook down until the sauce is reduced to half.

Pour the sauce through a colander to remove any impurities.

Sugo D' Arrosto

Roasted Meat Juice

19 ounces pork
22 ounces veal
17 ounces beef
3 fresh rosemary sprigs
6 garlic cloves
12 fresh sage leaves
6 fresh thyme sprigs
1/4 teaspoon salt
1/4 teaspoon black pepper
1/2 cup olive oil
1 cup dry red wine

Cut all meat in 2/3" pieces or cubes. All cuts of meat should be shoulder, neck or other cuts with a minimum of fat. In a large saucepan, heat olive oil and add meat; brown lightly over medium heat.

After meat is browned, pour contents of saucepan into a heavy, baking dish; add herbs, salt and pepper, and stir, coating meat with herbs. Bake in oven at 450 degrees for 30 minutes. Remove pan from oven and allow meat to sit for 10-15 minutes to extract juices. Using a colander, strain meat and set aside. Put baking pan back over medium heat to deglaze, adding red wine. Allow juices and meat particles to rise to top, stirring contents slightly. After wine has reduced by half, remove pan from heat and pour contents of baking pan through colander to yield juice.

Salsa Rossa

Red Sauce of Tomatoes, Peppers, Onions and Olive Oil

1/4 cup olive oil
2 cups plum tomatoes, peeled, seeds and juice removed
1 red onion, finely chopped (1 cup)
1 carrot, finely chopped (1 cup)
2 red peppers, cleaned, coarse cut
1 teaspoon crushed red pepper
3 teaspoons sugar
1 1/2 teaspoons salt
2 teaspoons black pepper
1/4 cup red wine vinegar

Combine all ingredients in a large sauce pan and mix well; cook uncovered over medium heat. When the mixture comes to a boil, reduce heat to low, stirring occasionally. Continue to cook uncovered over low heat. If the sauce becomes too dry, add tomato puree, 1/2 cup at a time, to keep the sauce dense and moist.

Continue to cook sauce for a total cook-time of 1 1/2 hours. Remove the pan from the stove and pour the contents into a blender. Puree the sauce for one to two minutes, until smooth. The sauce is ready to serve. To store the remaining sauce, empty into a bowl and allow it to cool. Pour a thin layer of olive oil over the top of the sauce to help preserve the flavor. Seal the bowl and store in the refrigerator.

Salsa Besciamella

Bechamel Sauce

3 ounces all purpose flour
4 cups milk
1/2 cup unsalted butter
2 tablespoons salt
1/8 teaspoon nutmeg
1 shallot, peeled (1/3 cup)
4 cloves

In a small sauce pan, place shallot with cloves inserted into side and bring to boil. Cover and let cool.

In a separate pan, melt butter over medium heat; when butter is completely melted, add flour and stir continuously to remove any lumps of flour. When the mixture is light golden brown in color, about 5 minutes, remove from heat and add to milk mixture. Cook for approximately five minutes, bringing mixture to a boil; remove shallot. Simmer for five minutes over low heat to bring out flavor of flour. Remove sauce from heat and pass through chinoise. Layer thin slices of butter on top to keep a skin from forming on the sauce.

Salsa Al Tartufo Nero

Black Truffle Sauce

1 shallot, peeled, chopped (1/3 cup)
2 tablespoons unsalted butter
2 fresh sage leaves
1 fresh thyme sprig
1/3 cup Madeira wine
1/3 cup sherry
1/2 cup black truffle peelings (or fresh black truffle, chopped)
1 cup veal reduction (sauces chapter)

In a small saute pan, heat butter and add shallots; saute over medium heat for 3 minutes and add sage and thyme. After 7 minutes, add Madeira and sherry. Continue to cook over medium heat until liquid has reduced by half. Add black truffle peelings and saute for an additional 2 minutes. Add veal reduction and cook for 4 minutes; reduce heat to low and simmer for 9 minutes. Remove from heat and pour contents of pan into blender. Puree at medium speed for 30 seconds. Add 1/2 ounce black truffles, julienned, if desired, and stir. Sauce is ready to be served.

Sugo Strafritto
Ragu of Chicken Liver and Kidney

1/4 cup olive oil
2 ounces salted pork, finely chopped
8 ounces chicken giblets
8 ounces chicken hearts
8 ounces chicken livers
1 onion, finely chopped (1 cup)
1 garlic clove, smashed
2 fresh sage leaves, finely chopped
2 cups tomato puree

Take chicken giblets and hearts and chop together, very fine. Finely chop chicken livers, separately, and set all meats aside.

In a large sauce pan, heat olive oil over low heat. Add onions, garlic and pork; saute until onions become translucent and garlic is golden. Remove garlic and add sage, giblets and hearts. Cover pan and simmer over low heat for 45 minutes, adding one ounce of water to mixture every 15 minutes.

After 45 minutes, add chicken livers and tomato puree; cook for an additional 15 minutes, covered, and remove pan from heat.

Salsa Di Capperi E Marsala
Sauce of Capers and Marsala

1/4 cup unsalted butter
1 shallot, peeled (1/2 cup)
4 fresh sage leaves
1/2 fresh rosemary sprigs
2 anchovy fillets
1/2 garlic clove, finely chopped
1 1/2 Marsala wine
1/2 cup veal reduction sauce (sauces chapter)
2 tablespoons capers, drained

In a small saucepan, saute shallots, anchovies and herbs in butter over medium-low heat until anchovy filets have melted and shallots become translucent, approximately 8 minutes.

Add wine and cook at medium heat until wine has reduced by half. Add veal reduction sauce and continue to cook for an additional 3 minutes. Pour contents of pan through strainer into the same size pan. Add capers to the strained stock and return it to cook over medium heat for an additional 12 minutes. Remove pan from heat and pour sauce again through strainer. The recipe will yield one cup of sauce.

Salsa Al Fegato D'Anatra

Sauce of Roasted Duck Liver

8 ounces duck liver
1 cup veal reduction (sauces chapter)
1/2 cup Madeira wine

Combine veal reduction and madeira in medium sauce pan. Cook over medium heat until mixture reaches a boil; boil for 45 seconds and add duck liver. Allow mixture to return to a boil, then reduce heat to low. Simmer for 7 minutes and remove from heat. Pour contents of pan into blender and puree until smooth. Transfer mixture back into pan and cook over medium heat. Allow mixture to return to a boil, approximately 2 minutes, and remove from heat.

Fonduta

Fontina Cheese Sauce

1 lb. Fontina cheese (16 ounces)
1/3 cup all purpose flour
3 cups milk
4 eggs

Remove skin from fontina cheese and break into small pieces or cubes. In a small sauce pan, place cheese cubes; add flour. Pour in milk; make sure milk is very cold. Mix well until all of the lumps of flour are broken apart. Set the pan in a warm area near or on top of a warm stove for 2 hours to allow cheese to become soft.

After 2 hours, place the sauce pan over medium heat, stirring contents continuously. Allow mixture to come to a low boil; when cheese has melted completely, remove pan from heat. Allow mixture to stop bubbling. Add four egg yolks and stir briskly with a whisk to ensure that egg yolk does not cook.

Look for the brown-labeled fontina cheese from Italy. It is the smoothest and best tasting of the fontina cheeses and will give this recipe a flavorful, rich taste. It is the perfect sauce for dipping crusty breads or serving over pasta and risotto. It also complements the flavor of fresh vegetables.

Use a double boiler for this recipe. It is important to cook the cheese sauce slowly and to mix in the egg yolks without allowing them to congeal.

This is a sauce that can be eaten by itself, with white truffle on top or with oven toasted bread. If you cannot find Italian Fontina, try Dutch Fontina. Of course it will not have the beautiful taste of the Fontina from Italy.

Salsa Verde

Green Sauce

4 anchovy fillets
1/2 ounce bread, torn into pieces
3 tablespoons red wine vinegar
1 garlic clove
1/2 egg white, hard boiled
1 teaspoon capers
1 gherkin
2 ounces fresh parsley, stems removed
1 cup olive oil

In a small mixing bowl, place pieces of bread. Any type of bread can be used for this recipe except sourdough. Add red wine vinegar allowing bread to soak up liquid. Set aside.

Combine all other ingredients in blender; add bread. Blend the mixture on high speed for approximately 30 seconds, until smooth.

Use the bold green sauce immediately to complement fish or pasta. To store, pour sauce into a bowl or storage container, covering with a thin layer of olive oil. Seal the container and store in the refrigerator.

This sauce can be used for many dishes. You can use to marinate salted anchovies that have been washed and de-boned. Marinate in sauce for two to three days; excellent dish.

Salsa Di Noci

Walnut-Honey Sauce

7 ounces walnuts
1 tablespoon red wine vinegar
1 cup honey
1 tablespoon Dijon mustard
1/2 cup chicken stock (sauces chapter)

Place chicken stock in small sauce pan and heat over medium-low heat until warmed through. Combine chicken stock and all other ingredients in blender and puree until smooth. The sauce is ready to be served over roasted pork or veal.

To make honey easier to work with, take jar of honey and place in boiling water for 50 seconds, or heat in microwave, causing honey to liquefy slightly.

Salsa D'Aragosta
Lobster Sauce

3 lobster carcasses
1/2 cup olive oil
1 head of garlic
7 fresh thyme sprigs
3 fresh tarragon sprigs
2 fresh rosemary sprigs
1/2 ounce fresh Italian parsley
4 onions, rough cut (1 pound)
5 carrots, peeled, rough cut (1 pound)
8 celery stalks, rough cut (1 pound)
1/2 teaspoon salt
1 teaspoon black pepper
2 1/2 cups sherry
3 tablespoons tomato paste

Chop lobster carcasses into small pieces using meat cleaver. Spread shells on a large baking sheet, covering them with 1/4 cup olive oil. Mix well to coat shells and place in oven. Bake at 450 degrees for 45 minutes, stirring contents thoroughly every 15 minutes. Remove shells from oven and set aside in separate bowl. Set pan aside.

In a large stock pot, heat 1/4 cup olive oil. Take one full head of garlic and cut in half through width of head; place head into heated oil, face down. Add vegetables, herbs, salt and pepper and cook over medium-high heat for 5 minutes. Add roasted shells and cook for an additional 2 minutes. Add sherry and cook.

While the sherry is reducing, take baking pan from lobster shells and place over medium heat, adding white wine to deglaze pan. Using a spatula, stir the wine mixture, deglaze of meat and juices. After two minutes, remove from heat.

When sherry is reduced, add the reduction from baking pan, tomato paste and one gallon of water to the stock pot. Turn heat to high until stock comes to a boil. When mixture boils, reduce heat to low and continue to simmer for a total cook-time of 3 hours. Allow stock to set after removing from heat. A layer of oil will form on top. Skim oil off before storing. The recipe yields 8 cups of sauce.

To reduce the sauce for an even more pungent, rich-tasting sauce, return the 8 cups of sauce to a stock pot and cook over high heat until it boils. After the sauce boils, reduce to low heat, simmering for a total cook-time of 3 hours. The yield will be 2 1/2 cups of sauce.

Salsa Al Madeira

Madeira Sauce

1 ounce unsalted butter
2 shallots, chopped (2/3 cup)
1 teaspoon fresh rosemary, chopped
8 fresh sage leaves
4 cups Madeira wine
2/3 cup veal reduction (sauces chapter)

In a small saucepan, saute shallots, rosemary and sage in butter over medium heat for 5 1/2 minutes. Add wine and allow alcohol to burn off and liquid to reduce by about half. Expect to see a flame until alcohol has dissipated. After 12 minutes, add veal reduction and continue to cook over medium heat. After 3 minutes, remove sauce from heat. Pour contents of pan through strainer; help to extract liquid by pushing down on mixture with spoon. The sauce should yield 1 cup.

Salsa Maionese

Mayonaise Sauce

2 egg yolks
1/2 teaspoon salt
3 1/2 tablespoons lemon juice
1/2 tablespoon Dijon mustard
9 ounces olive oil

In a medium mixing bowl, combine egg yolk, salt, 2 tablespoons lemon juice and mustard; begin to stir using whisk. To keep sauce from separating, it is important to continuously stir the sauce in the same direction. Add 2 tablespoons olive oil and mix; add an additional 1/3 cup of oil and continue to mix well. Add remaining lemon juice; stir briskly. Slowly add remaining olive oil. Continue to stir mixture until ingredients are fully blended into a creamy sauce.

Always make sure that the ingredients are the same temperature and stirred in the same direction or the sauce will break down. Always store in the refrigerator.

Agliata

Garlic Bread Sauce

5 garlic cloves
2 slices white bread, crust removed (1/2 ounce)
2 ounces walnuts
1 cup chicken stock (sauces chapter)
1 teaspoon salt
1 teaspoon black pepper

Combine all ingredients in blender; puree until smooth. Serve sauce over pasta or boiled meats.

Salsa Al Marsala

Marsala Sauce

1/2 shallot, peeled, chopped (1/4 cup)
2 tablespoons unsalted butter
3 fresh sage leaves
1 fresh rosemary sprig
2 cups Marsala wine
1 tablespoon tomato paste
1 cup veal stock (sauces chapter)

In a medium saute pan, heat butter, shallots and herbs. Saute over medium heat for 1 1/2 minutes and add Marsala. Bring mixture to a boil, allowing alcohol to cook down and liquid to reduce by half. Bring heat to low, add tomato paste and allow sauce to simmer. After 25 minutes the sauce should be reduced to 1 cup of liquid; add veal stock and cook for an additional 15 minutes, then remove from heat. Filter sauce, pouring through a strainer. The sauce yields 1 cup.

Salsa Del Pover Uomo

Sauce of the Poor Men

1/4 cup unsalted butter
1/2 cup olive oil
12 anchovy fillets
2 garlic cloves, finely chopped
1 cup veal stock (sauces chapter)
2 teaspoons unseasoned bread crumbs

In a large saucepan, cook butter, olive oil and anchovies over medium heat. Stir continuously; allow the butter and oil to get very hot, melting the anchovies. When mixture is fully melted and slightly thickened, add veal stock and bread crumbs. Increase heat to high and bring mixture to a boil for 30 seconds until done.

This sauce can be personalized by adding more or less anchovies or garlic.

Salsa Al Rosmarino

Rosemary Sauce

1/2 teaspoon fresh rosemary, chopped
2 tablespoons unsalted butter
1/2 cup veal reduction (sauces chapter)

Combine ingredients in small sauce pan and cook over high heat until mixture reaches a boil. Allow mixture to boil for 1 minute and remove from heat. Sauce is ready to be served, complementing both pork and beef dishes.

Salsa Di Salsiccia E Porri

Sausage and Leek Sauce

1 ounce olive oil
1 lb. pork sausage
8 leeks, finely sliced (20 ounces)
1 cup dry white wine
1 pint heavy whipping cream
1 cup veal stock (sauces chapter)

In a large, medium-weight sauce pan, brown sausage in olive oil over medium heat. Using a wooden spoon, continuously break up the meat as it cooks, avoiding large chunks. Cook approximately 16 minutes or until meat is lightly browned. Add leeks and cook over medium heat for five minutes. Reduce heat to low; add white wine and cover pan. Allow the meat to stew in the wine.

After 20 minutes, add veal stock and cover. When stock and wine have reduced by half, add whipping cream. Simmer for five minutes until done.

Chicken stock may be substituted in place of veal stock.

Salsa Alla Salvia

Sage Sauce

1 1/2 ounces unsalted butter
20 fresh sage leaves
1/4 cup veal reduction (sauces chapter)
1/2 cup heavy whipping cream

In a small saucepan, saute butter and sage over medium heat for 2-3 minutes, or until the mixture is lightly bubbling. Simmer sauce for 2 minutes. Add veal reduction sauce and bring mixture to a boil. After the sauce boils, add whipping cream and allow to boil again. Remove sauce from heat and serve.

Salsa Passata Di Pomodoro

Tomato Sauce Puree

1/2 cup olive oil
1 onion, finely chopped (1 1/2 cups)
1 garlic clove, cut in half lengthwise
5 cups tomato puree
7 fresh basil leaves, torn into small pieces
1 1/2 teaspoons salt
2 teaspoons black pepper

In a large saucepan, saute onions and garlic in olive oil over medium heat until the onions become clear. Add tomato puree, basil, salt and pepper. Continue to cook over medium heat for 25 minutes.

Ragu' Di Salsiccia

Sausage Meat Sauce

1 lb. beef shoulder
1 lb. pork shoulder
5 ounces olive oil
1 fresh rosemary sprig, blanched
7 fresh sage leaves
3 fresh thyme sprigs
2 garlic cloves, cut lengthwise
1 onion, finely chopped (1 cup)
1 celery stalk, finely chopped (1/2 cup)
1 carrot, peeled, finely chopped (1/2 cup)
2 1/2 teaspoons salt
4 teaspoons black pepper
6 cups plum tomatoes, pureed, juice and seeds removed

Spread out a single piece of cheesecloth. In the center, stack the rosemary, sage, thyme and garlic. Tie the herbs together in the cloth, creating a bouquet of spices.

Cut beef and pork into chunks and grind together using the meat grinding attachment on a food processor or mixer. Set ground meat aside. In a large saucepan, heat olive oil over medium heat. When oil is hot, add ground meat; turn heat to high to brown the meat. Add the spice bouquet.

Continue to brown the meat, stirring as needed. When the meat is completely browned, drain the majority of the fat, using a colander, leaving some fat in the bottom of the pan. Return the pan to the stove and add onions, celery and carrots to the browned meat. Cook over high heat for five minutes, stirring contents.

Add red wine and reduce to medium heat. Cook until wine is reduced to half its original amount. When the wine is initially added to the sauce, it will have a bitter smell. After it has combined with the meat juices and reduced, it will have a sweet aroma. Add salt, pepper and tomatoes and reduce to low heat. The total cook-time should be 1 1/2 hours. Remove the spice bouquet before serving.

Adding salt and pepper extracts moisture from the meat. In this recipe, the salt and pepper are added after the meat is browned, allowing a greater amount of moisture to be extracted from the meat, making it brown faster and more thoroughly. The more the meat is browned, the more intense the flavor.

The wine used in this recipe should be dry-tasting drinking wine; do not use cooking wine.

Salsa Di Pomodori E Peperoni

Tomato and Roasted Pepper Sauce

1 onion, peeled, finely chopped (1/3 cup)
2 ounces olive oil
2 garlic cloves, smashed
8 fresh basil leaves
2 teaspoons salt
1 teaspoon black pepper
3 cups tomato puree
3 peppers, roasted (11 ounces)

In a medium sauce pan, saute onions, herbs, salt and pepper in olive oil over medium heat for 2 1/2 minutes. Add tomato puree and bring mixture to a boil, approximately 5 minutes. After it reaches a boiling point, reduce heat to low. Simmer for 20 minutes and add roasted peppers torn into large pieces. After five minutes, remove sauce from heat and pour contents into blender. Puree on high speed until smooth. Serve sauce over pasta.

Salsa Veloce Di Pomodoro

Quick Tomato Sauce

34 ounces plum tomatoes, peeled, juices and seeds removed
2 garlic cloves, chopped
14 fresh basil leaves, torn into small pieces
1/2 cup olive oil
3 teaspoons salt
3 teaspoons black pepper

To serve as a cold sauce, combine ingredients together in a bowl, mix well and serve over pasta or with fish. To serve hot, combine ingredients in a large sauce pan and cook for five minutes over medium heat.

For a different flavor, use bruciolo in the recipe. Place bruciolo in pan first to brown then quickly add tomatoes and saute. You will get a beautiful aroma of garlic and rosemary.

Bagna Caoda

Bagna Cauda Sauce

15 garlic cloves
15 anchovy fillets, oil drained (6 ounces)
1 cup olive oil
1 1/2 cup walnuts, finely chopped

In a small, heavy sauce pan, combine all ingredients and bring to a boil over medium heat. It is preferred that you use anchovy fillets preserved in their own salt; these fillets should be rinsed well under cold tap water before use. After the mixture reaches the boiling point, with 3/8" bubbles, reduce the heat to low and allow sauce to simmer, uncovered, stirring occasionally. The garlic and anchovies should not be browned.

Continue to cook the mixture for 50 minutes, then remove from stove and allow to cool. Pour the sauce into a blender and blend at medium speed until smooth.

In order to avoid a strong garlic aftertaste, you may modify the intensity of the garlic by following one of the following procedures:

Cut the garlic clove in half lengthwise and remove the "heart" in the center of the clove. The heart is the strongest part of the garlic.

In a small sauce pan, boil garlic cloves in 1 1/2 cups of milk for 20 minutes. A thick paste will form. Drain excess liquid away and add the paste to the anchovy mixture.

Add 1/2 cup of heavy whipping cream to the finished mixture and boil for five minutes.

Pesto Di Rucola

Pesto of Arugula

3 garlic cloves
1 cup olive oil
1 teaspoon salt
1 teaspoon black pepper
1 lb. arugula, cleaned
1/3 cup grated Parmesan cheese
1/4 cup pine nuts, toasted

Combine garlic, olive oil, salt and pepper in blender; puree for 1 minute on high or until garlic is blended. Add arugula, cheese and pine nuts and puree until smooth.

The sauce is ready to serve over pasta. It can be stored for up to 4 weeks in the refrigerator, topped with 3 tablespoons olive oil and covered in the freezer until ready to use.

antipasti

There is a saying in Piedmont that "antipasti destroys your meal" because of its size and richness. When you look at the list of appetizers in Piedmont you will understand. It contains recipes for Pepperoni Bagna Cauda, Tongue with Red Sauce, Bollito Misto, Flan, Fontina and so forth. In this book I tried to give you the ones that are the most important and those which I prefer. They are all traditional, full-bodied dishes.

Some of these recipes have evolved or have come from different courses. For example, Bollito Misto, which is found in the Meat and Game Chapter in this book, used to be served as an appetizer. I think it was moved to a main course today because our stomachs are not strong enough to digest this kind of heavy food.

More than any other region in Italy, Piedmont has many traditional appetizers in its cooking. Piedmont appetizers are based with meat, eggs, cheese, sauces such as Salse Rosa and Mayonaise with White Truffle. Some of the recipes you will find in the antipasti section of this book, you might find as main courses in restaurants. If you serve these dishes in large portions they can be enjoyed as a main course.

Focaccia Di Ceci

Stuffed Roasted Onion "Cesare Giaccone"

4 onions (2 1/2 lbs.)
1 1/2 tablespoons sage sauce (sauces chapter)
4 fresh sage leaves

Stuffing:
5 ounces gorgonzola cheese, chopped
1 cup Bechamel sauce (sauces chapter)
1/4 cup milk
1/3 cup Parmesan cheese
2 fresh sage leaves, finely chopped

Serves: 4
Complexity: • • •
Preparation Time: 1 Hour, 15 Minutes
Italian Wine: Bramaterra,
Red at least four years old, full
bodied, velvety, slightly bitter at
the finish.

To roast onions, place whole onions, with skin on, on baking sheet. Bake in preheated oven for 1 hour and 40 minutes. Remove from oven and set aside to cool. After onions are cooled enough to touch, peel off outer layer of skin, leaving remaining browned skin; cut off top end of onion, approximately 1/8" and set cap aside. Scoop out inner layers of onion, leaving 3 layers on sides. If the bottom side of the onion has a hole, slice one piece of an inner layer and place over hole to close off bottom of onion. Take pulp and use to make cold onion salad (antipasti chapter).

To prepare stuffing, combine gorgonzola, Bechamel and milk in a medium sauce pan and place over medium heat. Stir mixture as it cooks for 7 minutes, then remove from heat. Pour mixture into mixing bowl and blend using whisk. Add Parmesan cheese and mix well, ensuring that there are no lumps in mixture. Add sage and continue to mix well. When mixture is blended, place bowl inside a second mixing bowl filled with ice water to cool.

Rub unsalted butter on baking sheet and place onions on sheet. Fill pastry bag with chilled gorgonzola sauce; fill onion shells with mixture. Place tops on onions and place in preheated oven at 375. Bake for 8 minutes and remove.

Serve each onion with 2 teaspoons sage sauce; garnish with sage leaves.

I got this idea from Cesare Giaccone, at the restaurant "Dei Cacciatori." He is one of the best chefs we have in Italy. I want to thank him for giving me the idea. I know this recipe is different from his original, but this is my interpretation and I did not want to copy his recipe completely.

Focaccia Di Ceci

Chick Pea Focaccia

1 lb. chick peas, soaked in water 24 hrs.
8 fresh sage leaves
2 onions, peeled, finely chopped (2 cups)
1 tablespoon salt
1 teaspoon black pepper
1/4 cup olive oil
1 fresh rosemary sprig
3 eggs
1/2 cup grated Parmesan cheese
1/4 cup unseasoned bread crumbs

Serves: 4
Complexity: • •
Preparation Time: 2 Hour, 10 Minutes
Italian Wine: Barbera Del Monferrato,
Red, young with a fragrant grape flavor.

In a large sauce pan, combine chick peas, 2 sage leaves, 1 cup onion and spices; add 6 ounces water and place over high heat until mixture comes to a boil, approximately 7 minutes; reduce heat to low and simmer for 1 hour and 20 minutes. Remove from heat and pour contents of pan through strainer; remove sage leaves. Allow peas to cool.

In a medium sauce pan, combine olive oil, remaining onions, 6 sage leaves and rosemary; cook over medium low heat for 9 minutes, stirring mixture as it cooks.

Combine contents of pan and chick peas in food processor; add eggs and blend for 2 minutes. Add cheese and continue to blend for an additional 4 minutes, until mixture becomes creamy.

Coat the bottom and sides of a 12 1/2" round baking pan with olive oil. Pour bread crumbs into pan and the turn pan to coat evenly. Spread focaccia mixture evenly in pan. Sprinkle with 1/2 tablespoon olive oil and bake in preheated oven at 350 degrees for 25 minutes.

I put this dish in the book in honor of my mother. She loves this dish. I could not do a Piedmont cookbook without this recipe, or my mother would be very upset. I remember when I was young, we would drive around for hours to find the pizzeria that would make this dish for her. Thank you, Mama.

Uovo In Camicia Al Tartufo Nero
Soft Poached Egg in Black Truffle Sauce

2 tablespoons red wine vinegar
1 1/2 teaspoons salt
4 eggs
6 tablespoons black truffle sauce (sauces chapter)

Serves: 4
Complexity: ● ● ● ●
Preparation Time: 15 Minutes
Italian Wine: Barbaresco,
Red, four years old, full bodied and
early in maturity.

Prepare black truffle sauce. In a small sauce pan, combine 3 cups water, red wine vinegar and salt over medium heat. When mixture reaches a boil, add egg and poach for 2 minutes. Remove from liquid with slotted spoon and set on cutting board. Using a sharp knife, trim around outer edge of egg, leaving egg yolk framed with even border of egg white. Repeat process for each egg.

Serve each poached egg over 1 1/2 tablespoons black truffle sauce.

Variation: Use 2" baking ring for poaching egg to keep egg in perfect, round form. To use form, rub inside of ring with unsalted butter. Place ring in boiling water and place egg inside ring.

Uovo In Camicia Di Fontina
Egg with Fontina Cheese

12 ounces fontina cheese
4 eggs, poached
2 eggs, beaten
1 cup all purpose flour
1 1/2 cups unseasoned bread crumbs
5 cups oil, canola or vegetable oil

Serves: 4
Complexity: ● ● ● ●
Preparation Time: 1 Hour, 20 Minutes
Italian Wine: Arneis,
Young with a pronounced fruitiness.

Heat oil in large sauce pot over high heat. Take block of fontina cheese and place in boiling water for 15 - 25 seconds. Remove and place on sheet of plastic wrap. Fold wrap over cheese and roll with rolling pin; roll until cheese is spread into a thin, even layer. Remove plastic wrap.

Poach each egg in boiling water, 1 1/2 minutes per egg, and remove from water using a slotted spoon. Allow egg to cool, then place on cheese sheet. Fold cheese over egg; press down around outside of egg to seal cheese; carefully cut around egg, trimming excess cheese. First roll cheese-wrapped egg in flour; then dip in egg, coating both sides evenly; then roll in bread crumbs. Place breaded egg in refrigerator for 5 minutes to chill; remove and place in heated oil. Fry for 30 seconds and remove, placing on baking sheet layered with paper towels to absorb excess oil.

Make sure when you put the cheese in hot water that you don't allow it to get too soft or it will melt. You need it soft enough to stretch it around the egg.

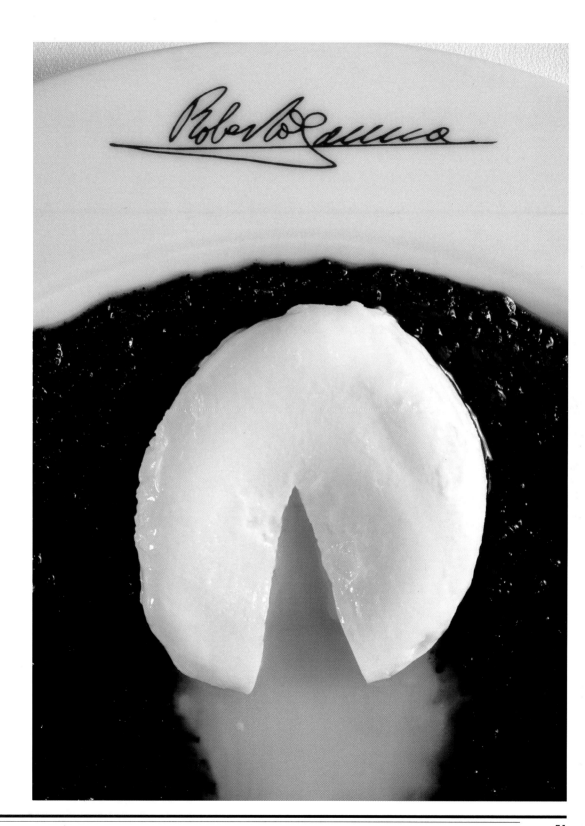

Vitello Tonnato

Veal in Tuna Sauce

20 ounces veal (shoulder or leg) tied in cooking twine
1 carrot, peeled, cubed (4 ounces)
2 celery stalks, cleaned, cubed (4 ounces)
1 onion, peeled, cubed (4 ounces)
3 cups dry white wine
1 tablespoon black peppercorns
2 tablespoons salt
6 fresh basil leaves
2 dried bay leaves
5 plum tomatoes, halved
1 ounce fresh Italian parsley sprigs

Sauce:
2 tablespoons capers, drained
2 anchovy fillets
6 ounce can tuna packed in oil, drained
1/2 cup dry white wine
mayonaise sauce (sauces chapter)

Serves: 6
Complexity: •••
Preparation Time: 1 Hour, 30 Minutes
Italian Wine: Arneis,
White, fresh and fruity.

Have your butcher tie the veal meat with cooking twine, salami-style.

In medium stock pot, combine vegetables, herbs, salt and pepper; add 8 cups water and place over high heat until mixture comes to a boil, approximately 7 minutes. After it reaches the boiling point, reduce heat to low and add veal meat. Simmer for 1 hour and 20 minutes. Remove veal and set aside. The stock can be filtered, using a strainer and set aside for use as veal stock.

Prepare mayonaise sauce; set aside. Combine sauce ingredients in blender and puree until smooth. Add pureed mixture to mayonaise sauce and stir using whisk.

After veal is completely cooled, slice and serve over bed of sauce.

Veal can be roasted in an oven and thinly sliced. Always cook until the meat is pink.

Insalata Di Coniglio Con Lardelli

Rabbit Salad

14 ounces rabbit fillet
1/2 teaspoon salt
1/2 teaspoon black pepper
5 ounces white bread, crusts removed
4 ounces pancetta, cut into 1" pieces
1/2 cup olive oil
4 bruciolo (techniques chapter)
4 teaspoons fresh sage, finely chopped
4 teaspoons fresh rosemary, finely chopped
16 sweet and sour cippolini onions (vegetables chapter)
lettuce leaves, cleaned
2 tomatoes, dried

Dressing:
2 anchovy fillets
2 tablespoons balsamic vinegar
1/4 cup olive oil
1 teaspoon red wine vinegar
1/4 teaspoon salt
1/4 teaspoon black pepper

Serves: 4
Complexity: ● ● ● ●
Preparation Time: 30 Minutes
Italian Wine: Grignolino,
Red with a fine density and with a
line of bitterness at the finish.

Season rabbit fillets with salt and pepper and set aside.

Cut bread into 20 croutons, 3" x 3/4", and set aside.

Heat olive oil in medium sauce pan over medium heat. When oil is hot, add bruciolo; saute for 1 minute. Add rabbit fillets and saute lightly on each side, until fillets are golden brown in color; add pancetta. After rabbit and pancetta have cooked for 5 minutes, remove rabbit from heat and set aside. Set pan aside.

Combine chopped sage and rosemary. Place bread in original sauce pan and place back over medium heat, adding chopped herbs. When bread is lightly browned on both sides, approximately 30 seconds, remove from heat. Remove toasted pancetta from pan.

To prepare dressing, combine ingredients in small mixing bowl and mix well, using whisk.

Prepare cippolini onions. To serve, slice rabbit fillets and place on plate with cippolini onions, toasted bread croutons and crisp pancetta, dressed with 1 tablespoon of sauce. Garnish dish with lettuce and diced tomatoes.

Insalata Russa

Russian Salad

2 carrots, peeled, diced (3 ounces)
1 potato, cleaned, peeled, diced (6 ounces)
4 ounces green beans, diced
3 1/2 ounces turnips, peeled, diced
3 ounces peas
1 tablespoon salt

Sauce:
1/3 cup gherkins, diced
1/4 cup capers, drained
4 ounces tuna, drained, diced
3 anchovy fillets, chopped
1 cup mayonaise sauce (sauces chapter)

Serves: 4
Complexity: • • •
Preparation Time: 1 Hour, 40 Minutes
Italian Wine: Erbaluce Di Caluso,
White, drink at one year old with
this dish when the wine has a
fine line of fruitiness.

In a large sauce pan, bring 8 cups water with salt to a boil over high heat. Add carrots and cook for 5 minutes, then add remaining vegetables. Cook for 12 minutes, remove from heat and drain. Allow vegetables to cool. In a large mixing bowl, combine sauce ingredients and mix well. Add cooled vegetables and mix well.

To serve, place 2" ring or form on each serving plate. Pour mixture into form; allow to set briefly and remove form. Garnish dish with sliced hard boiled eggs, if desired.

Peperoni Ripieni "Alla Carlina"

Stuffed Roasted Peppers "Carlina Style"

8 red or yellow roasted peppers (12 ounces) (techniques chapter)
2 tablespoons olive oil
Stuffing:
6 ounces tuna in oil
8 anchovy fillets
1/2 ounce fresh Italian parsley
1 garlic clove
4 ounces potato, peeled, boiled, pureed
4 gherkins (1/2 ounce)
1 tablespoon capers, drained
1/3 cup olive oil
1 egg, hard boiled

Serves: 4
Complexity: ● ● ●
Preparation Time: 1 Hour, 30 Minutes
Italian Wine: Erbaluce Di Caluso,
well balanced white with
a light bouquet.

Prepare roasted peppers and set skins aside.

Combine ingredients for stuffing in food processor and blend until smooth. Place 1/4 cup stuffing on opened pepper skin and roll pepper around filling. Refrigerate stuffed peppers for 2 hours. Remove after chilled. To serve, slice each pepper and sprinkle lightly with olive oil.

We use potatoes to prepare the filling in this recipe. If you do not wish to use boiled potatoes, use the white part only of bread, soaked in milk.

Frittata Rognosa

Flat Omelette "Rognosa Style"

7 ounces hard salami, cubed very fine or processed through meat grinder
1/4 cup olive oil
1 garlic clove, smashed

Frittata batter:
12 eggs
3/4 cup grated Parmesan cheese
1 teaspoon salt
1 teaspoon black pepper
1 tablespoon fresh mint, finely chopped
3 tablespoons fresh Italian parsley, finely chopped
3 fresh sage leaves, finely chopped
1 ounce arugula, finely chopped
1 garlic clove, smashed, finely chopped

Serves: 4
Complexity: ● ●
Preparation Time: 25 Minutes
Italian Wine: Dolcetto D'Ovada,
Red, drink in the first year not to
acidic with a light bitter finish.

To prepare frittata batter, combine ingredients in large mixing bowl and mix well using a wooden spoon. Add salami and continue to stir until mixture is well blended. Set aside.

Place a 10" non-stick saute pan over medium heat. When pan is hot, add olive oil and garlic clove; saute until garlic turns golden brown in color; remove garlic and discard. Add frittata batter and reduce heat to low; stir mixture as it slowly begins to cook.

After 4 minutes, remove pan from heat and place in preheated oven; set at 350 degrees and bake for 13 minutes. Remove from oven and cover pan with lid. Holding lid, turn pan upside down to remove frittata, placing it on side of lid; use lid to flip cake back into pan to cook other side of frittata. Place over low heat for one minute to brown underside.

To serve, flip frittata out of pan and onto serving plate. Slice and serve warm.

Lingua Di Vitello In Salsa Rossa

Veal Tongue in Red Sauce

Serves: 4
Complexity: ● ●
Preparation Time: 2 Hour
Italian Wine: Arneis Del Roero,
White, one year old when it reaches
maximum freshness and fruitiness.

1 lb. prepared veal tongue (techniques chapter)
1/2 cup red sauce (sauces chapter)
2 tablespoons olive oil

After allowing tongue to cool in stock for 1 hour, remove from liquid. Pull away outer layer of skin and slice tongue in half, lengthwise. Take the half piece and slice very thinly, on an angle; 1/2 tongue serves 1 person.

Combine red sauce and olive oil in a small mixing bowl; stir with a whisk. Pour one tablespoon of sauce over sliced tongue and serve.

Frittatine Di Spinaci Della "Nonna Rita"

Spinach Frittata "Nonna Rita Style"

20 ounces spinach, cleaned
1/3 cup grated Parmesan cheese
8 eggs, beaten
1 teaspoon salt
1 teaspoon black pepper
1/4 cup olive oil

Serves: 4
Complexity: •
Preparation Time: 25 Minutes
Italian Wine: Erbaluce Di Caluso,
Fresh white with a bouquet of
field flavor.

In a large stock pot, bring water to a boil over medium heat. When water comes to a boil, add spinach and cook for 3 1/2 minutes. Pour contents through strainer and press down on spinach to extract excess water. After spinach is drained, remove from sieve and chop finely; place in mixing bowl. Add cheese, eggs, salt and pepper and mix well using a wooden spoon.

In a large, non-stick saute pan, heat olive oil over medium heat. When oil is hot, add 1/4 cup of batter. Fry cakes in oil; as they cook, use a spatula to push hot oil over top of cake to cook the top side. Continue to cook, flipping cake once to achieve a golden brown color on both sides, then remove from pan. Place fried cakes on baking sheet layered with paper towels to absorb oil. Serve cakes hot or cold.

This is a dish that my lovely grandmother who I love very much, used to prepare for me every Sunday when I went to visit her in Asti. She used to make 20 or 30 for me. I would go crazy eating them. Thank you, Nonna.

Farinata

Chick Pea Flat Bread

8 ounces chick pea flour
1-2 teaspoons salt
1/2 cup olive oil
1 teaspoon fresh rosemary, chopped

In a medium mixing bowl, combine chick pea flour with 3 cups water; mix with whisk until lumps are dissolved. Pour mixture through strainer to remove any hidden lumps and add salt. Mix again and cover with plastic wrap; allow to set for 4 hours.

After 4 hours, remove layer of foam off top of batter using a spoon. Add olive oil and mix with whisk.

Coat bottom and sides of 2- 12 1/2" round baking pans with olive oil. Pour 2 cups of batter into each pan. Sprinkle chopped rosemary over top and bake in preheated oven for 13 minutes.

Remove bread from oven; remove from pan. Fold in half, then fold in half again, making a pie shape. Cut and serve bread warm.

Rape Farcite Di Cacio Cotte Al Forno

Roasted Turnip with Cacio Cheese

4 turnips, peeled (12 ounces)
2 teaspoons salt
4 fresh rosemary sprigs
4 ounces cacio cheese
1/2 pig ear, poached, julienned (techniques chapter)
2 tablespoons unsalted butter
1/4 cup veal meat juice (sauces chapter)
1/4 teaspoon fresh rosemary, chopped

Serves: 4
Complexity: ● ● ●
Preparation Time: 1 Hour, 10 Minutes
Italian Wine: Nebbiolo, Red, 4 or 5 years old, with a full body.

Take peeled turnips and shave edges to form each turnip into a rounded, barrel shape. In a medium stock pot, place turnips in 2 quarts of water with salt. Bring to a boil over medium heat. When water reaches boiling point, reduce heat to low and simmer turnips for 46 minutes; remove pot from heat. Place turnips on towel and allow to cool. When turnips are cool enough to handle, slice into 1/8" slices, 7 slices per turnip.

Slice cacio cheese into 14 even slices and set aside.

Take turnip and cheese slices and build a tower, alternating layers beginning with a turnip slice. After the tower is 7 layers tall, insert a skewer through the center of the tower, piercing each layer.

Rub bottom and sides of baking dish with unsalted butter. Place turnip towers in the dish and bake in preheated oven set at 350 degrees for 6 minutes. Remove from oven and press down on tower to compact layers. Remove from pan with spatula and carefully remove skewer. Take rosemary stem and insert it in the hole made by the skewer.

Place a small sauce pan over medium heat. When pan is hot, add butter; when butter foams, add pig ear and saute for 30 seconds. Add meat juice and chopped rosemary. Cook for an additional 2 minutes and remove from heat.

To serve, place turnip tower in center of serving plate and garnish with 2 tablespoons of sauce around base.

This is a Piedmontese recipe that I found in a very old cookbook. They used to prepare this dish in a small pot and put it under the ashes until the cheese was melted.

Lattughine Ripiene Con Vegetali E Ricotta
Stuffed Lettuce Leaves

12 bib lettuce leaves, blanched
1/4 cup veal reduction (sauces chapter)

Stuffing:
1/4 cup olive oil
3/4 cup zucchini, cleaned, finely chopped
1/3 cup yellow pepper, cleaned, finely chopped
1/3 cup red pepper, cleaned, peeled, finely chopped
3 shallots, peeled, finely chopped (1/3 cup)
1/2 garlic clove, smashed, finely chopped
1/4 teaspoon black pepper
1/2 teaspoon salt
1 cup ricotta cheese
1/4 cup Parmesan cheese

Sauce:
3 ounces fava beans
1 ounce pancetta, chopped
1 tablespoon shallots, peeled, chopped
1 tablespoon unsalted butter
1/2 cup chicken stock (sauces chapter)

Serves: 4
Complexity: • • • •
Preparation Time: 35 Minutes
Italian Wine: Pinot Bianco,
A dry and austere white.

To prepare lettuce, place leaves in salted boiling water for 3-4 seconds. Remove with tongs and cool in bowl of ice water. When cooled, remove leaves from water and lay flat on a towel to absorb water.

To prepare stuffing, heat large, heavy sauce pan over medium heat. When pan is hot, add olive oil, vegetables, egg, garlic, salt and pepper. Saute mixture for 2 minutes; remove from heat and allow to cool for 5-10 minutes. After mixture is cool, place in mixing bowl and add cheeses; mix well. Set aside.

Take blanched lettuce leaf and place 1 tablespoon of filling in center. Wrap leaf, sides first, and then ends, forming a roll. Repeat for each leaf.

In a small sauce pan, combine shallots, butter and pancetta; saute over low heat for 1 minute and add fava beans and chicken stock. Cook for 5 minutes and add rolls. Add veal reduction and saute rolls for 2 minutes each, turning to heat on all sides. Remove rolls from heat and serve with fava bean sauce.

Zucchini Ripieni Al Sapore Di Amaretto

Stuffed Zucchini with Amaretto Cookies

4 zucchini, cleaned (1 1/4 lb.)
1 teaspoon salt
2 dried bay leaves
3 cloves
2 cups dry white wine

Stuffing:
2 ounces veal
8 ounces ground beef
2 tablespoons olive oil
1 onion, peeled, finely chopped (1/2 cup)
1 garlic clove
8 amaretto cookies
1/4 cup grated Parmesan cheese
1 potato, peeled, boiled, pureed (1/4 cup)

Serves: 4
Complexity: ••
Preparation Time: 35 Minutes
Italian Wine: Cortese Dei
Collo Totronesi,
White with a delicate bouquet and
a light almond flavor.

Take zucchini and cut in half, lengthwise. Using a melon scoop, clean out inside of zucchini, setting pulp and shells aside, separately.

In a medium stock pot, combine 4 cups boiling water, salt, bay leaves, cloves and wine. Place over medium heat and bring mixture to a boil. When it reaches the boiling point, add zucchini shells; reduce heat to low and simmer for 9 minutes. Remove shells from water.

To prepare stuffing, in a medium sauce pan, saute olive oil, onions and garlic over medium heat until onions begin to sweat, approximately 1 minute. Add meat and saute for 4 minutes. Add zucchini and cook an additional 3 minutes; remove from heat. Pour contents of pan into food processor and add cookies, Parmesan cheese and potato puree; blend well until smooth. Pour into pastry bag.

Coat surface of baking sheet with unsalted butter. Place zucchini shells on sheet and fill each shell with stuffing mixture, using pastry bag. Sprinkle each with Parmesan cheese and place in preheated oven at 400 degrees. Bake for 12 minutes and remove; serve as an appetizer or vegetable to accompany a main dish.

Orecchie Di Maiale In Agro

Pig Ear Salad

4 pig ears, cleaned (3 1/2 ounces per ear, cleaned)
8 gherkins, julienned (2 ounces)
1 red onion, peeled, julienned (4 ounces)
1/4 cup olive oil
4 teaspoons red wine vinegar
4 teaspoons fresh Italian parsley, finely chopped
1/8 teaspoon salt
1/8 teaspoon black pepper

Serves: 4
Complexity: • • •
Preparation Time: 2 1/2 Hours
Italian Wine: Freisa,
Dry and intense red, with
perfume of raspberry or violets.

To poach pig ears, place in large stock pot, covering with 1 gallon of water and 1 teaspoon salt. Bring to a boil over high heat. After boiling for 2 hours, pig ears will be tender; remove from water. To clean, remove cartilage from middle of the ear and peel off outer layer of skin, using thin, sharp knife. Slice pig ears, julienne style.

Combine all ingredients in medium mixing bowl; mix well. Allow pig ears to marinate in the mixture for 1 hour. Toss lightly and serve.

If you choose to store salad in the refrigerator, allow it to return to room temperature before serving.

Make sure salad is served at room temperature, not cold.

Asparagi Con Intigolo Di Tartufi Neri

Asparagus with Black Truffle Dressing

25 asparagus stalks, trimmed (1/2 lb.)
1 ounce black truffle shavings, chopped

Vinaigrette Dressing:
1 cup olive oil
1/4 cup red wine vinegar
1/2 cup balsamic vinegar
1 1/2 teaspoon salt
1 teaspoon black pepper

Serves: 4
Complexity: • • •
Preparation Time: 15 Minutes,
12 Hours Refrigeration
Italian Wine: Favorita,
A young white fresh wine
with a vegetable finish.

Place 6 cups water and salt in medium stock pot. Bring water to a boil and add asparagus. Cook in boiling water for 2 1/2 minutes and remove. Place asparagus in ice water bath to cool. After spears are chilled, drain water.

Mix vinaigrette dressing. Chop black truffle and mix with 1 ounce dressing; allow to set for 12 hours in refrigerator.

To serve, cut asparagus spears in half and build "log cabin" of asparagus, alternating spears as you build the structure. Top with vinaigrette/truffle dressing. Save leftover dressing for use on salads or other vegetable dishes. The dressing can be stored for up to 60 days in the refrigerator.

I like to make this dressing 2-3 days in advance to let black truffles marinate inside the sauce, giving it a better flavor.

Torretta Di Carne Cruda

Raw Beef "Piedmont Style"

24 ounces beef tenderloin, finely diced
1 cucumber, cleaned, thinly sliced (6 ounces)
3/4 cup Parmesan cheese, shredded
1 cup button mushrooms, diced

Dressing:
5 tablespoons lemon juice (2 lemons)
1 cup olive oil
1 teaspoon salt
2 teaspoons black pepper
6 tablespoons fresh Italian parsley, chopped
1 garlic clove, smashed, finely chopped

Serves: 4
Complexity: ● ● ● ●
Preparation Time: 30 Minutes

In a medium mixing bowl, combine ingredients for dressing; mix well using a whisk. Take 1/4 of the sauce and set aside. Add beef to remaining mixture and blend well, using hands.

Use a ring or form 3" wide x 1 1/2" high to mix ingredients for this recipe. Place the ring on serving plate. Take 10 cucumber slices and layer along bottom of mold; add 1/2 teaspoon of mixture, top with 3 teaspoons mushrooms; push down to compact. Add 1 1/2 teaspoons of mixture, then add a second layer of cucumbers, ten slices, and press down. Add meat, forming a 2 1/2" layer. As you add meat, slide form up to mold meat; press down on meat to compact. Add 3 tablespoons of cheese and continue to slide form off top, leaving a colorful, compacted layer of vegetables and meat. Repeat process for each serving.

Make sure to put enough dressing in between layers of meat, vegetable and cheese as you build the tower.

Insalata Di Cipolle Al Forno

Roasted Onion Salad

12 ounces onions, roasted, quartered (antipasti chapter)
1/4 teaspoon salt
1/4 teaspoon black pepper
1/2 tablespoon red wine vinegar
2 tablespoons olive oil
1 teaspoon fresh Italian parsley, chopped

Serves: 4
Complexity: ● ● ●
Preparation Time: 1 Hour

Prepare roasted onions and cut into quarters.

Place in large mixing bowl and add vinegar, olive oil, parsley, salt and pepper; mix well. Serve salad chilled.

Tonno Di Coniglio
Tuna of Rabbit

25 ounces whole rabbit, cleaned with bones
2 celery stalks, cleaned (4 ounces)
1 carrot, peeled (2 1/2 ounces)
1 onion, peeled (5 ounces)
2 leeks, cleaned, with stems removed
1 1/2 tablespoons salt
1 tablespoon black peppercorns
1 ounce fresh Italian parsley
2 dried bay leaves

2 garlic cloves, thinly sliced
13 fresh sage leaves
1/2 cup olive oil

Serves: 6
Complexity: ● ●
Preparation Time: 1 Hour, 30 Minutes
48 Hours to reset before eating
Italian Wine: Arneis,
Fresh and fruity, will work well with
sage in the dish.

In a large stock pot, combine celery, carrot, onion, leeks, peppercorns, parsley stems, bay leaves and salt. Add 16 cups water and place over high heat until mixture reaches a boil; reduce heat to low, add whole rabbit, ensuring that rabbit is covered with liquid. Simmer for 1 hour. Remove rabbit and set aside. Pour contents of stock pot through strainer to yield rabbit stock; discard vegetables.

Pull meat away from bones, keeping in large pieces, and set aside; discard bones or use to make rabbit reduction (sauces chapter).

In a large mixing bowl, place 2 sage leaves and a few slices of garlic. Layer with rabbit meat. Build a third layer of 3 sage leaves and a few garlic slices; top again with meat slices. Add 3 sage leaves and garlic slices, again, topped with meat and kidneys. Top with garlic slices and 5 sage leaves. Place towel over bowl and press down to compact. Remove towel and cover with 1/2" olive oil. Cover bowl in plastic wrap and refrigerate for 2 days. Continue to add more olive oil as it is absorbed by the meat. After 48 hours, remove from bowl and serve chilled.

This is an old recipe from my country. This recipe was developed because it could be prepared 2-3 days in advance. They could prepare it and let it set. When they came back from their days in the country it would be ready to serve. This dish is actually better eaten 2-3 days after is has been cooked. Be sure the meat is cooked until it comes off the bones cleanly. Add oil a little at a time. You can remove original sage leaves and replace with fresh leaves as you add oil and allow to set because the leaves can become brown from staying in the refrigerator.

Capunet Alla Fonduta

Stuffed Cabbage Leaves

4 cabbage leaves
1 cup fonduta sauce (sauces chapter)
2 tablespoons unsalted butter

Filling:
1 1/2 cups milk
8 ounces chestnuts, peeled

12 ounces mild Italian sausage meat
1/4 cup olive oil
1 onion, peeled, finely chopped (1/2 cup)
2 fresh sage leaves, chopped
1/4 cup black truffle peelings (optional)
2 ounces white bread, without crust
1/2 cup milk

Serves: 4
Complexity: ● ● ● ●
Preparation Time: 35 Minutes
Italian Wine: Nebbiolo,
Red, drink young with this dish,
with enough acid to counter the fat
of the fontina cheese.

Blanch cabbage leaves in salted boiling water for 30 seconds; remove from water and lay flat on towel to dry.

In a small sauce pan over medium heat, combine chestnuts and milk. When mixture reaches a boil approximately 10 minutes, reduce heat to low and simmer for 14 minutes; remove from heat. Drain milk from nuts, passing mixture through a strainer. Set prepared chestnuts aside.

In a large saute pan, heat olive oil, onion and sage over medium heat for 2 minutes; add sausage and black truffle peelings, if desired. Break sausage meat up with wooden spoon as it cooks. After 4 minutes, add chestnuts and remove mixture from heat, continuing to mix well.

Place bread in mixing bowl and add milk. Allow bread to absorb milk, then remove soaked bread and squeeze off excess milk. Pass bread through meat grinding attachment on a food processor or mixer. Take half of chestnut mixture and pass through meat grinder. Combine remaining chestnut mixture with ground mixtures and blend well, using hands. Divide into four equal parts.

To prepare rolls, place 1/4 filling mixture in center of poached cabbage leaf. Fold leaf around mixture, pulling up sides first, then taking top leaf and fold it in; next fold in bottom leaf, rolling over top. Repeat for all rolls.

Coat the bottom and side of baking dish with unsalted butter. Place rolls with seam-side down in bottom of pan. Rub tops with butter and place in preheated oven, set at 350 degrees; bake for 14 minutes.

To warm fonduta sauce, place prepared sauce in small mixing bowl or pot and place over top of larger pot of boiling water. Add milk as needed to regain creamy consistency.

After 14 minutes, remove rolls from oven. To serve, place each roll on a bed of 1/4 cup warmed fonduta sauce.

Filletti D'Anatra Alla Canavese

Duck Fillets Salad

8 ounces duck fillets
1/4 cup olive oil
4 garlic cloves, smashed
4 teaspoons fresh rosemary, chopped
8 ounces porcini mushrooms, heads only
4 ounces mache lettuce
4 tablespoons vinaigrette dressing (sauces chapter)
1/2 teaspoon salt

Cheese sauce:
3 ounces toma cheese
(or mascarpone cheese)
1/2 cup heavy cream
1/4 teaspoon black pepper

Marinade:
4 garlic cloves, sliced
4 tablespoons fresh rosemary, chopped
1 teaspoon salt
1 teaspoon black pepper
1/2 cup olive oil

Serves: 4
Complexity: • • • •
Preparation Time: 35 Minutes,
1 Hour Marinate
Italian Wine: Grignolred,
Dry with a good acidity to stand
up to the dressing.

Vegetable garnish:
1 carrot, peeled, cut into 3/4" pieces (4 ounces)
4 garlic cloves
1/2 cup olive oil
1/2 teaspoon sugar

To prepare marinade, combine ingredients in pan; mix well. Place duck fillets in marinade sauce and mix to coat evenly. Allow fillets to marinate for 1 hour.

To prepare cheese sauce, take toma cheese and remove outer layer of skin; break up cheese into cubes. Place cheese and cream in blender and puree for 30 seconds. As soon as the mixture becomes thick and pasty, stop mixing as it will take the form of butter if it is blended too long. Empty mixture from blender into small mixing bowl and add pepper; mix to blend and set cheese mixture aside.

To prepare vegetable garnish, combine carrots, garlic, olive oil and sugar in a medium saute pan; place over medium heat and stir. When mixture takes light color, after approximately 4 minutes, add 1/4 cup water and cover pan. After 5 minutes, remove lid. If there is still liquid in pan, continue to cook until it has completely reduced. When all liquid has dissipated, remove carrots and set aside.

In a separate saute pan, heat olive oil, garlic and rosemary over medium heat for 1 minute. Add mushrooms and season with pinch of salt and pepper. Saute mushrooms 30 seconds on each side and remove from heat. Set mushrooms aside.

Place pan with oil back over medium heat. Place marinated fillets in pan; saute fillets 30 seconds each side and remove from heat. Place fillets on baking sheet layered with paper towels to absorb oil.

To serve, place lettuce in center of plate, surrounded by fillets. Slice 1 mushroom and place over lettuce; add other mushrooms, carrots and garlic to garnish. Pour vinaigrette dressing over lettuce. Using 2 teaspoons, form cheese sauce into egg shape and place on side of plate. Drizzle with olive oil.

Sformato Alla Portoghese

Portuguese Pudding with Chicken Livers

4 cups stock
1 cup semolina flour
12 ounces chicken livers
4 ounces chicken hearts
1/2 cup olive oil
8 fresh sage leaves
1 teaspoon salt
1 teaspoon black pepper
1 1/3 cups Marsala sauce (sauces chapter)

Serves: 8
Complexity: ● ● ●
Preparation Time: 15 Minutes,
Italian Wine: Nebbiolo,
Red, 4 to 5 years old, full bodied
with good tannin to stand
up to the liver.

To prepare semolina, place chicken stock in medium sauce pan over medium heat. Bring to a boil, then add semolina flour. Reduce heat to low and stir briskly with a whisk. After 7 minutes, remove from heat and pour mixture into 1-cup molds.

In a small saute pan, heat olive oil, sage leaves and spices over medium heat. After 1 minute, add chicken livers and hearts and increase heat to high; after 3 minutes, remove from heat. Remove hearts, cut in half and set aside. Discard oil and place pan back over medium-high heat, adding marsala sauce; cook until mixture comes to a boil, then remove from heat.

After semolina has set, remove from molds and place on serving plate. For each serving, slice chicken heart and place over top of semolina mold. Place liver around base of mold, pouring marsala sauce over each.

Tartra' Con Fegato D'Anatra

Flan with Roasted Duck Liver

Cream Mixture:
3 cups heavy whipping cream
1 cup milk
5 fresh sage leaves
1 teaspoon fresh thyme, chopped
1 teaspoon fresh rosemary, chopped
1 garlic clove
1 teaspoon black pepper

Onion Mixture:
1/4 cup unsalted butter
1 onion, peeled, finely chopped (2 cups)
1 teaspoon salt

8 eggs, slightly whipped
1/3 cup grated Parmesan cheese
1 teaspoon salt
1 teaspoon black pepper

Duck liver:
12 ounces duck liver
1/2 teaspoon salt
1/2 teaspoon black pepper
6 fresh thyme sprigs
4 fresh sage sprigs
2 fresh rosemary sprigs

Serves: 6
Complexity: ● ● ● ●
Preparation Time: 1 Hour
Italian Wine: Arneis,
White with good balance
and an herbal flavor.

To prepare flan, combine cream mixture ingredients, except pepper in medium sauce pan. Place over medium heat and cook until mixture reaches a boil; remove from heat and add pepper. Cover and allow to set for 2 hours. After 2 hours, take cream mixture and pass through strainer to remove herbs. Discard herbs and set sauce aside.

To prepare onion mixture, in a small saute pan, melt butter over low heat. When butter foams, add onions and cover pan. Cook for 3 minutes and remove from heat. Add one teaspoon salt and allow onion mixture to cool for 5 minutes.

In blender, combine whipped eggs and cooled onion mixture; puree for 30 seconds, froth will form on top. Pour contents of blender into bowl with cream mixture and mix well using whisk. Add Parmesan cheese and 1 teaspoon each of salt and pepper and continue to blend to make flan mixture.

Take 1/2 cup flan cups or ramakins and brush inside with butter. Pour flan mixture into each cup, filling to 1/8" from top. Place filled flan cups in baking dish and fill with water until it reaches 2/3 height of cups. Bake in 300 degree oven for 20 minutes; after 20 minutes, cover pan with aluminum foil and continue to bake for an additional 10 minutes. Remove from oven and allow to cool in pan with water for 15 minutes.

To prepare duck liver, combine ingredients in medium sauce pan. Set over medium heat and saute for 1 1/2 minutes on each side; remove from heat. Place pan in preheated, 350 degree oven. Bake for 15 minutes and remove. Remove livers from pan and wrap in towel.

To serve, unmold flan and place in center of a serving plate. Slice sauteed duck livers in half and place around base of the flan. Spoon duck liver sauce over livers and flan.

Bastoncino Alle Olive Nere

Bastoncino with Black Olives
2 cups all purpose flour
2 tablespoons active yeast
1 tablespoon salt
5 ounces pitted sun dried olives, finely chopped
rock sea salt
5 tablespoons olive oil

Mix salt and flour in mixing bowl, using dough hook attachment on mixer. Dissolve yeast in 1 1/2 quarts warm water; add to dry mixture. Mix at medium speed for 7-8 minutes. Place dough in flour-dusted bowl and allow to rise until two times its original size. Push down dough, forming a long, tubular shape. Leave in a warm area again, allowing dough to double its original size. Brush the dough with olive oil and sprinkle with sea salt. Bake at 350 for 40 minutes.

Polenta Piccante Con Le Uova Di Quaglia "Al Paletto"

Spicy Polenta with Quail Eggs

4 cups polenta (techniques chapter)
12 quail eggs
1 teaspoon olive oil

Sauce:
1/2 cup bagna cauda sauce (sauces chapter)
1/2 teaspoon crushed red pepper
1/2 tablespoon tomato paste

Serves: 6
Complexity: • • •
Preparation Time: 1 Hour, 25 Minutes
Italian Wine: Barbera D'Alba,
Red at least three years old, round
to the palate with a light nutty finish.

Prepare polenta.

Open quail eggs using a knife to break the shells. Place eggs in bowl and set aside.

In a small sauce pan, combine bagna cauda sauce, crushed red pepper and tomato paste. Place over medium heat and stir with whisk until paste is well blended with mixture; remove from heat.

In a small, non-stick saute pan, heat olive oil. When oil is hot, add eggs and cook over medium heat for 30 seconds, until egg whites are cooked.

For each serving, place soft polenta in a bowl, top with 3 quail eggs and crown with sauce.

zuppe

Soup in Piedmont has always been a very important part of a meal. It was the only one-dish meal. We always have some meat or fish inside so you get full from one course. I took old soup recipes and cooked them almost in the same way as they were once prepared, but I just changed the presentation of the dishes. I have made them more eye-appealing. There really was no work to be done on the actual recipes; they have remained the same for many years. Soups in Piedmont are seasonal; they reflect the season in which they are made based on what is readily available. Some of the soups take me back to my childhood. My grandmother used to prepare pumpkin soup in the fall.

In this book I have included all very hearty, rustic soups that I have made more elegant. I hope I achieved the goal.

Cisra'

Chick Pea Soup with Sweet Garlic Toasted Bread

14 cups water
8 ounces salted pork, cubed (techniques chapter)
20 fresh sage leaves, chopped
2 teaspoons salt
2 garlic cloves, sliced
1/4 cup olive oil
2 dried bay leaves
3 teaspoons dried marjoram
1 onion, peeled, finely chopped (1 cup)
1 lb. chick peas, soaked
2 heads garlic
4-8 slices white bread

Serves: 8
Complexity: • •
Preparation Time: 3 Hours
Italian Wine: Barbera D'Asti,
Red to be enjoyed in the first or
second year, very tannic with
a good grape flavor.

Place chick peas in large mixing bowl and cover in cold water; soak beans uncovered overnight.

In a medium stock pot, combine olive oil, sliced garlic cloves, sage and salted pork; place over high heat and saute for 2 minutes. Add bay leaves, marjoram, onions and salt. Saute until onions become translucent. Drain and add soaked chick peas and 14 cups fresh water. Keep pot over high heat until mixture reaches a boil, approximately 30 minutes, then reduce heat to low. Simmer over low heat for a total cook-time of 2 1/2 hours.

Remove pot from heat and pour half of stock pot contents into food processor; puree until smooth. Pour pureed mixture back into original soup mixture in stock pot and mix well.

Take 2 heads of garlic with skins on and wrap in aluminum foil. Bake in preheated oven for 20 minutes. Remove from oven and unwrap heads from foil. Place small slices of bread under broiler to make bread lightly crispy. Remove 1 clove of garlic and peel off skin. Rub baked clove over bread, coating lightly.

To serve, pour soup in bowls and drizzle a hint of olive oil over top of soup, making a spiral design. Add coated bread slices crowned with whole garlic cloves as garnish.

This recipe dates back to 1525. It used to be called "soup of red chick peas." At that time, they thought chick peas were an excellent cure for liver disease. We do know that they are a good source of protein.

Buseca

Tripe Soup

1 1/2 lbs. tripe, julienned (3/8" wide)
10 celery stalks, cleaned, tops removed, diced 1/4", save leaves
1 onion, peeled, chopped
1/2 cup olive oil
6 ounces salted pork, chopped (techniques chapter)
2 garlic cloves, smashed
1 tablespoon salt
1 1/2 teaspoons fresh ground black pepper
11 ounces shiitake mushrooms, julienned
2 dried bay leaves
1 teaspoon dried marjoram
8 cups water
2 Idaho potatoes, peeled, cubed (1 lb.)
1/2 ounce fresh Italian parsley
1/2 ounce celery leaves
1/4 ounce fresh basil
2 teaspoons fresh ground black pepper

Serves: 6
Complexity: ● ●
Preparation Time: 2 Hour
Italian Wine: Barbera D'Asti,
Red to be enjoyed in the first or
second year, very tannic with a
good grape flavor.

In a large stock pot, heat 1/4 cup olive oil; when oil is hot add garlic cloves. Saute for 1 minute and add salted pork; continue to saute over medium heat. After 1 minute add celery, onions, mushrooms, salt and pepper. Sweat vegetables for approximately 3-4 minutes; add tripe, bay leaves, marjoram and 8 cups water. Increase heat to high and bring mixture to a boil. After it reaches boiling point, approximately 8 minutes, reduce heat to low and simmer for one hour. Add potatoes and cook an additional 30 minutes over low heat.

Combine parsley, celery leaves and basil, and 1/4 cup olive oil and basil in blender. Puree until smooth.

Serve soup with drops of puree and freshly ground black pepper.

Zuppa Di Trote

Trout Soup

8 whole trout fillets (4 reserved)
12 ounces Italian tomatoes, peeled, juice drained
1 carrot, peeled, finely chopped (1 cup)
2 celery stalks, cleaned, finely chopped (1 cup)
2 onions, peeled, finely chopped (1 1/2 cups)
1/8 teaspoon red pepper, chopped
1/3 cup olive oil
1 teaspoon fresh thyme, chopped
10 fresh basil leaves
1/3 cup fresh Italian parsley, chopped
2 teaspoons salt
1 teaspoon black pepper
2 dried bay leaves
1/8 teaspoon dried marjoram
4 cups water
4 tablespoons all purpose flour (for dredging)
2 tablespoons olive oil

Spread:
toasted bread
1 garlic clove, finely chopped
1 egg yolk
1/2 teaspoon tomato paste
1/3 cup olive oil
juice of half a lemon (1/4 cup)
1/4 teaspoon salt

Serves: 8
Complexity: • • • •
Preparation Time: 1 Hour 35 Minutes
Italian Wine: Gavi Di Gavi,
Dry white with a full body to match
the tomato base.

In a large stock pot, combine all ingredients, except for trout fillets and spread. Place pot over medium heat until mixture comes to a boil, approximately 15 minutes, then reduce heat to low and simmer for 1 hour.

For the trout fillets, you may either purchase 4 cleaned trout from your fish monger or fillet the fish yourself, removing the head, spine and skin. Cut fillets into chunks. Add to soup after it has cooked for 20 minutes. Add any other meat scraps from fish.

After soup has cooked for 1 hour, remove bay leaves. Empty contents of stock pot into food processor and blend for 1 minute. Empty the contents of the food processor into a blender, a few cups at a time, and puree until smooth. After all of soup is pureed, place back in stock pot over medium heat.

Take remaining 4 trout fillets, cut them into even pieces and sprinkle lightly with salt. Roll the fillets evenly in bleached flour. In a medium saute pan, heat 2 tablespoons olive oil. When oil is hot, add fillets and saute until lightly golden brown on both sides.

To prepare spread for toasted bread, combine the spread ingredients in a blender or food processor; puree until smooth. The mixture should have a creamy consistency. Toast a few slices of bread under broiler and spread mixture on bread.

To serve, pour soup into bowl. Set toasted bread with spread on top of soup; layer with sauteed trout fillets.

This soup grew out of Piedmontese chefs' inventiveness. They did not have any seafood, so they used vegetables and trout to make stock. I suggest you saute the trout in very hot oil until it is golden in color; that will assure the success of the dish.

Zuppa Di Piccione

Squab Soup

3 ounces squab breast
1 tablespoon olive oil
2 fresh sage leaves
1/4 teaspoon fresh rosemary, chopped
1/8 onion, peeled, finely chopped (1 tablespoon)
1/8 celery stalk, cleaned, finely chopped (1 tablespoon)
1/8 carrot, peeled, finely chopped (1 tablespoon)
1 cup Madeira wine
1/4 cup heavy whipping cream
4 cups squab stock (sauces chapter)
4 squab livers
4 squab kidneys
4 squab hearts
4 teaspoons unsalted butter
4 slices bread
12 ounces cacio cheese
6 ounces calf's brain, sliced into 12 medallions
1/2 teaspoon salt
1/2 teaspoon black pepper
2 tablespoons fresh Italian parsley, chopped

Serves: 8
Complexity: ● ● ●
Preparation Time: 30 Minutes, 12 Hours to rest
Italian Wine: Arneis,
A white with good acidity and fruitiness.

In a small sauce pan, combine olive oil, 2 sage leaves, rosemary and chopped vegetables. Place over medium heat and saute. When onions become translucent, add squab breasts. Turn meat as it cooks, lightly browning each side. After 3 1/2 minutes, add Madeira. Continue to cook over medium heat for an additional 3 1/2 minutes and remove from heat. Remove meat and set sauce aside. Take squab meat and grind using meat grinding attachment on a food processor or mixer. In blender, combine ground meat with sauce and cream. Puree for 15 seconds. Place in covered container and refrigerate for 12 hours.

In a medium sauce pan, simmer squab stock over medium heat. Meanwhile, take 12 slices of calf's brain and lightly coat in flour. Saute in 2 teaspoons butter over medium heat for 30 seconds on each side. Remove and set aside. Take bread and cut 1" round croutons, 3 for each soup serving. Saute lightly in butter until golden brown on both sides. Set aside.

In a small saute pan, heat 2 teaspoons butter. Saute squab hearts, kidneys and livers, sprinkling lightly with salt and pepper. After 2 minutes, remove from heat and wrap in towel to absorb blood.

Remove meat mixture from refrigerator after 12 hours.

To serve, heat squab stock and pour in bowl, place three croutons on each serving. On each crouton, place sauteed slices of calf's brain and top with thin slices of cacio cheese; place 1 heart, one kidney and 1 liver on each. Take refrigerated mixture and, using 2 teaspoons, form into egg shape. Alternate croutons with egg-shaped mixture to garnish the dish. Sprinkle freshly chopped Italian parsley over top.

Crema Di Riso Tartufata

Cream of Arborio with White Truffle

4 tablespoons unsalted butter
1 onion, peeled, finely chopped (1/2 cup)
1/2 cup arborio rice
1 cup dry white wine
3 cups veal stock (sauces chapter)
2 cups heavy whipping cream
4 tablespoons white truffle oil

Parsley Flan:
1 3/4 cup heavy whipping cream
1/4 cup Bechamel sauce (sauces chapter)
3/4 cup milk
1/2 bunch fresh Italian parsley
1 fresh rosemary sprig
1 fresh sage sprig
2 garlic cloves
1 tablespoon grated Parmesan cheese
1 teaspoon salt
1/2 teaspoon white pepper
2 eggs, beaten

Serves: 8
Complexity: • • • •
Preparation Time: 1 Hour
Italian Wine: Chardonnay,
Rich and barriqued with a full body.

In a small sauce pan, combine cream, Bechamel, milk, parsley and herbs. Place over medium heat and bring to a boil. After mixture reaches boiling point, reduce heat to low and simmer for 4 minutes. Remove from heat and allow to cool for 2 hours. After sauce is cooled, pour into blender and puree for 30 seconds; remove and pass sauce through strainer. Add cheese, salt, pepper and eggs; mix well. Prepare 1" diameter flan molds with butter generously coating inside, bottom and all sides. Pour mixture into molds, filling 1/4" from top. Place filled molds in bottom of baking dish. Fill dish with water, 1/2 the height of flan molds. Cover pan with aluminum foil and bake at 300 degrees for 35 minutes. Remove molds from water and turn upside down to remove flan.

To prepare soup, saute butter and onions over medium heat in a medium sauce pan. When onions become translucent, add arborio and wine. Cook until wine reduces, approximately 7 minutes. Add veal stock and reduce heat to low. Simmer for 25 minutes and remove from heat. Pour contents of pan into blender and puree for 1 minute. Add heavy whipping cream and puree until smooth. Add white truffle oil and blend.

To serve, place flan in center of soup bowl and pour soup around flan, filling to 2/3 its height. Garnish with fried parsley, refer to techniques chapter.

I got the idea for this soup from Jean-Louis Palladin. I think it is a soup that deserves high marks as a culinary example of Piedmontese cuisine. It is excellent. When you prepare, start with less arborio that the recipe calls for to make sure you get a nice consistency. More rice can be added later to thicken. If it is too thick, add stock.

Tufeja Con Il "Prete"

Bean Soup

9 garlic cloves
30 fresh basil leaves
7 fresh rosemary sprigs
1 cup olive oil
1 pork skin bellies
3 teaspoons salt
1 onion, peeled, finely chopped (2 cups)
1 1/2 lbs. cranberry beans, soaked

Serves: 8
Complexity: • • •
Preparation Time: 3 Hours 30 Minutes
Italian Wine: Nebbiolo,
A red, to be consumed young with
this dish for the tannin.

Combine 6 garlic cloves, leaves from 4 rosemary sprigs, basil and olive oil in blender; puree until smooth. Roll out 3 pork belly skins and sprinkle with salt and pepper. Add puree mixture and spread evenly over belly skin. Roll skin from end to end, creating a "jelly roll." Using cooking twine, securely tie roll like salami.

In a 4-quart cast iron pot, combine onions, cranberry beans, and pig rolls with 12 ounces of water. Take the rosemary leaves from the remaining sprigs and 3 garlic cloves and chop finely together. Add herbs to pot and cover. Bake at 350 degrees for 3 hours, the oven does not need to be preheated. Remove pot from oven and remove rolls; set aside. Using a hand blender, mix soup for 2 minutes.

To serve, pour soup in bowl and garnish with slice of pork belly roll.

I used to cook this in Italy in a terracotta container, and put inside the wood-burning oven which was outside of the house. In small towns in Italy, they would have one wood-burning oven in the town to share. Every Sunday one person after the other would bake their bread, then they would bring clay pots down with beans inside. They would bake overnight and they would pick them up the next morning. Many of the country workers would eat the soup for breakfast.

Zuppa Di Castagne

Chestnut Soup

5 ounces salted pork, julienned (techniques chapter)
1/4 cup olive oil
2 onions, peeled, julienned (11 ounces)
19 ounces chestnuts, peeled
6 cups veal stock (sauces chapter)
2 dried bay leaves
4 fried sage leaves (techniques chapter)

Rabbit Sausage:
2 rabbit sausages (4 ounces; available at gourmet stores)
3 fresh rosemary sprigs
3 fresh sage leaves
2 garlic cloves
2 tablespoons olive oil
1/4 teaspoon salt
1/8 teaspoon black pepper

Serves: 8
Complexity: ••
Preparation Time: 1 Hour 20 Minutes
Italian Wine: Chardonnay,
Light on the barrique with a fine
acidity to contrast the fat in soup.

In a medium sauce pan, combine olive oil, salted pork and onions and cook over medium heat for 3 minutes. Add chestnuts and continue to cook for an additional 9 minutes; add veal stock and bay leaves. Cook until mixture reaches a boil, then reduce heat to low. Simmer mixture for a total cook-time of 1 hour and remove from heat. Remove bay leaves and pour contents of pan into blender, puree until smooth.

To prepare rabbit sausage, take sausage, still in casings, and place in baking pan. Add olive oil, salt, black pepper and herbs. Mix well to coat sausage; bake for 4 minutes in a preheated 400 degree oven. Remove sausage from oven.

To serve, pour soup in bowl and garnish with slices of roasted rabbit sausage and fried sage leaves.

This soup is excellent if you use fresh chestnuts, but you may also use frozen chestnuts. If you use canned chestnuts, be sure that they are not packed in water; these have no flavor.

Zuppa Di Rape Con L'Olio Di Bietole Rosse

Turnip Soup With Beet Oil

4 cups beef stock (sauces chapter)
1 ounce olive oil
1 roasted head of garlic (techniques chapter)
4 slices bread
2 tablespoons unsalted butter

Turnip Flan:
1 3/4 cups heavy whipping cream
1/4 cup Bechamel sauce (sauces chapter)
3/4 cup milk
2 turnips, diced (3 ounces)
1 fresh thyme sprig
1 garlic clove
1 tablespoon grated Parmesan cheese
1 teaspoon salt
1/2 teaspoon white pepper
2 eggs, beaten

Beet Oil:
3 beets (8 ounces)
pinch salt
pinch black pepper
1 3/4 cup olive oil

Serves: 4
Complexity: ••••
Preparation Time: 45 Minutes,
2 Hours to cool
Italian Wine: Chardonnay,
Light on barrique and well balanced.

To prepare turnip flan, in a small sauce pan, combine cream, Bechamel, milk, turnips and herbs. Place over medium heat and bring to a boil. After mixture reaches boiling point, reduce heat to low and simmer for 4 minutes. Remove from heat and allow to cool for 2 hours. After sauce is cooled, pour into blender and puree; remove and pass sauce through strainer. Add cheese, salt, pepper and eggs; mix well. Take flan molds and rub butter generously inside, coating bottom and all sides. Pour mixture into molds, filling 1/4" from top. Place filled molds in bottom of baking dish. Fill baking dish with water, 1/2 the height of flan cups. Cover pan with aluminum foil and bake in preheated oven at 300 degrees for 35 minutes. Remove molds from water, turn upside down to remove flan.

To prepare beet oil, place beets in baking dish and coat with olive oil; mix well to coat beets. Place in preheated oven and roast for 1 hour. Remove from oven and allow beets to cool. Peel beets and place in blender; add olive oil and puree. Cover and refrigerate for up to 14 days.

To prepare soup, simmer beef consomme over medium heat. Take bread slices and cut three 1-inch-round croutons for each serving. In a medium saute pan, heat olive oil and saute croutons until lightly browned on both sides. Take roasted garlic and remove cloves. Place one clove on top of each crouton and spread evenly with a knife.

To serve, place turnip flan in soup bowl and pour beef consomme around the flan, covering 2/3 of its base. To garnish, add croutons with garlic spread and drop beet oil along perimeter of bowl.

Zuppa Di Latte E Riso

Cream of Butternut Squash Soup with Arborio

2 tablespoons unsalted butter
1 onion, peeled, finely chopped (1 cup)
1 butternut squash (16 ounces)
1 cup arborio rice
4 cups milk
1 cup chicken stock (sauces chapter)
1/4 cup olive oil
2 tablespoons salt

Serves: 6
Complexity: •
Preparation Time: 30 Minutes
Italian Wine: Cortese Di Gavi,
Dry white with a good fruity bouquet.

*To make this soup a vegetarian dish, substitute 1 cup of milk for the chicken stock.

To prepare butternut squash, take vegetable and cut off bulb at base of stem. Take trunk and set aside. Using the bulb, cut in half and remove seeds and outer skin. Dice squash and set aside.

In a medium stock pot, combine butter and onions and cook over medium heat until onions become translucent, approximately 2 1/2 minutes. Add squash and continue to saute over medium heat for 2 1/2 minutes.

Add arborio, 2 cups milk and chicken stock. After 12 minutes, reduce heat to low and add 1 cup of milk and 1 1/2 teaspoons salt. After a total cook-time of 30 minutes, remove from heat and add 1 cup milk. Pour contents into blender and puree until smooth. Transfer pureed mixture back into stock pot, adding 1 cup milk and 1 tablespoon salt; mix well. Keep over low heat until served.

Remove the peel from the trunk of the butternut squash and slice into 3/8" pieces. Over medium heat, warm olive oil in a medium saute pan. When oil is hot, add squash slices and saute until golden brown on both sides. After sauteed evenly on each side, remove squash slices and place on baking sheet layered with paper towels to absorb oil. Sprinkle lightly with the remaining salt.

To serve, pour soup into bowls and garnish with sauteed slices of butternut squash.

This soup is also good if you puree it in a blender and serve as cream soup with sauteed croutons.

Minestra Di Fave

Fava Bean Soup

2 ounces olive oil
6 ounces prosciutto, julienned
1 onion, peeled, finely chopped (1 cup)
1 garlic clove, smashed
3 ounces Boston lettuce, julienned
3 cups chicken stock (sauces chapter)
1 lb. fava beans, cleaned
3 teaspoon semolina flour
1 cup Parmesan cheese

Serves: 8
Complexity: • •
Preparation Time: 35 Minutes
Italian Wine: Cortese Di Gavi,
Dry white with a good fruity bouquet.

In a medium sauce pan, warm olive oil over medium heat. When oil is hot, add prosciutto, onions and garlic and saute for 2 minutes. Add lettuce and continue to saute mixture over medium heat for an additional 3 1/2 minutes. Add chicken stock and cook until mixture reaches a boil, then add fava beans. Allow mixture again to reach a boil, then reduce heat to low. Add semolina flour and Parmesan cheese and incorporate into soup.

After 25 minutes total cook-time, fava beans are cooked and soup is ready to be served.

risotti

Risotto is a very traditional Piedmont dish. It has been a dish prepared for more than 1,000 years for Piedmontese people. It has become increasingly more popular in Piedmont during past years. It used to be prepared only on holidays or Sundays.

Use carnaroli arborio. The carnaroli arborio is shorter and thicker and gives the dish a thicker and creamier consistency. In this book, I present most traditional risotto dishes prepared in Piedmont, as well as some of mine that I really like.

When you make risotto, it takes a maximum of 13-15 minutes after arborio has been toasted. Toasted means cooking just one minute in the pan with olive oil and onion. Add arborio to the pan and toast it lightly. After preparation, make sure there is no other liquid than the oil in the bottom of the pan. You can keep the arborio that way for up to one hour before continuing to prepare the dish. Toasting the arborio is the only step which you can do in advance. Another suggestion, if you have other dishes to prepare, set toasted arborio aside in a non-stick pan. This way, when you stir, the arborio will not stick to the pan and break. Just move the pan lightly to stir or shuffle arborio.

Cook the arborio over medium heat. Add one ladle of stock at a time and let it completely reduce. This will give more flavor to the arborio and you can control it; you don't want to have too much liquid inside the dish. At the end, when you add butter and Parmesan cheese to the arborio, always remove the pan from the heat because the heat will melt the butter and it will melt too quickly. After it is stirred completely is should not be too thick; if you move the pan quickly, the risotto should move like a wave on the sea. When you have leftover risotto, you can make small risotto fritters sauteed in olive oil or use a non-stick pan and pour a very thin layer of arborio in the bottom of the pan; saute until it is crunchy on both sides. Make the cake crunchy on the outside; inside it will be moist.

Risotto Con Le Rane

Risotto with Frog Legs

2 tablespoons olive oil
1/3 cup unsalted butter
2 onions, peeled, finely chopped (2/3 cup)
1 lb. arborio rice
1 cup dry white wine
1 cup quick tomato sauce (sauces chapter)
10 fresh basil leaves, finely chopped
5 cups frog leg stock (sauces chapter)
2/3 cup Italian parsley, finely chopped
3 1/4 ounces grated Parmesan cheese
1/4 cup heavy whipping cream

4 frog legs (techniques chapter)
4 shallots, chopped (1/2 cup)
1/4 cup olive oil
1 cup dry white wine
5 cups chicken stock (sauces chapter)
1/4 cup unsalted butter
1/2 teaspoon salt
1 teaspoon black pepper
2 tablespoons all purpose flour

Serves: 4
Complexity: ••••
Preparation Time: 45 Minutes
Italian Wine: Arneis,
a fresh white with a nice round
bouquet and herbaceous.

Prepare frog legs (techniques chapter).

Empty oil from pan and add tomato sauce, first chopping sauce on cutting board to reduce size of vegetable chunks. Continue to cook over medium heat, adding basil, 2 teaspoons chopped parsley and 3 tablespoons frog leg stock. Cook for 5 minutes. In a large saute pan, heat 2 tablespoons each of olive oil and butter; after butter foams, add onions. Saute until onions become translucent. Add arborio and toast for 30 seconds, stirring continuously. Add white wine and allow to reduce completely.

After wine has dissipated, add 5 cups hot frog leg stock 1 cup at a time and continue to cook over medium heat for a total cook-time of 15 minutes. Remove from heat and add 1/3 cup butter, Parmesan cheese, parsley and cream; mix well

Serve risotto dotted with red sauce and breaded frog legs in the center. Garnish with fresh herbs.

Risotto Alla Pernice

Risotto With Partridge

2 partridges
1 teaspoon salt
1 teaspoon black pepper
3 fresh rosemary sprigs, 1 split in half
1 sage sprig, split in half
1 garlic clove, halved
1 ounce salted pork
1 lb. arborio rice
1/4 cup olive oil
1 onion, peeled, finely chopped (1/2 cup)
1/2 teaspoon fresh rosemary, finely chopped
2 cups sparkling Italian wine
4 cups chicken stock (sauces chapter)
3/4 cup unsalted butter, sliced
6 ounces grated Parmesan cheese
1/4 cup partridge reduction sauce (sauces chapter)

Serves: 4
Complexity: •••
Product Availability: •••
Preparation Time: 1 Hour
Italian Wine: Dolcetto Di Diano D'Alba, A nice vivacious red, to be drunk young.

Take 2 cleaned partridge and sprinkle salt and pepper inside cavity of each; put halves of split rosemary, sage and garlic in each. Take salted pork and 2 rosemary stems and chop together very finely. Mix together using the back of a spoon to form a paste-like consistency. Divide the paste in half and coat the breasts of each partridge.

In a medium sauce pan, heat 2 tablespoons olive oil; add partridge. Cook over medium heat for 3 minutes. Keeping in same pan, transfer partridge to preheated oven to bake for 20 minutes.

In a separate large saute pan, heat 2 tablespoons each of olive oil and butter; after butter foams, and 1/2 teaspoon chopped rosemary. Saute over medium heat until onions become translucent. Add arborio and toast for 30 seconds, stirring mixture as it cooks. Add 1 cup sparkling wine and cook until completely reduced. Add a second cup over partridge in oven.

When wine has dissipated, add 4 cups hot chicken stock, 1 cup at a time. As technique is described in the risotto chapter introduction. After 15 minutes, arborio is cooked. Remove from heat and add butter and Parmesan cheese. Mix well. After 20 minutes, remove partridge from oven and shave breast meat. Display meat over risotto. Add bones to partridge reduction sauce; heat sauce and place 1 tablespoon of sauce over each breast.

Wild partridge can be substituted with quail, pheasant or guinea hen and can be prepared in the same way. The cooking time is the only thing that has to be adjusted.

Risotto All'Aragosta

Lobster Risotto

4 lobsters (1 lb. of meat, sliced)
1 lb. arborio rice
1/4 cup olive oil
1 onion, peeled, finely chopped (1 cup)
2 celery stalks, cleaned, finely chopped (1/2 cup)
4 tablespoons basil puree (techniques chapter)
1 1/2 cups dry white wine
1/2 cup tomato puree
1 tablespoon tomato paste
2 cups lobster stock (sauces chapter)
4 ounces fresh fava beans
1 teaspoon salt
1 teaspoon black pepper
1 cup unsalted butter, sliced (1/2 lb.)

Serves: 4
Complexity: • • •
Preparation Time: 45 Minutes
Italian Wine: Gavi Di Gavi,
Dry white with a good acidity
to cut the sweetness of the dish.

In a large sauce pan, heat olive oil over medium heat. Add onions and saute until onions begin to sweat. Add 2 tablespoon basil puree and arborio to pan; toast arborio, stirring as it cooks, for 2 minutes.

Add wine and continue to cook until wine is completely reduced. After wine has dissipated, add tomato puree and tomato paste. Cook until reduced by half and add 2 cups hot lobster stock, salt and pepper and continue to cook down mixture, stirring well. Add fava beans and an additional 3 cups of hot stock. After cooking for 10 minutes, add lobster meat. Cook for 1 minute; remove from heat. Add butter and 2 tablespoons basil puree. Mix well and serve topped with lobster pieces.

Make sure your stock is very good, not fishy. If you cannot make lobster stock from the lobster shells, I suggest cooking with a very light chicken stock. Also, do not overcook lobster. The risotto with lobster has always been one of the preferred dishes at Galileo.

Risotto Agli Asparagi

Risotto with Asparagus

1 lb. arborio rice
2 lbs. asparagus
2 tablespoons olive oil
1/2 cup unsalted butter
1 onion, peeled, finely chopped (1/2 cup)
1 cup dry white wine
7 cups chicken stock (sauces chapter)
2/3 cup grated Parmesan cheese

Serves: 4
Complexity: • • •
Preparation Time: 40 Minutes
Italian Wine: Favorita,
A particular white with a
hint of asparagus flavor in it,
drink young.

Take asparagus and cut bottom 1 1/4" inches of stem; cut off tips and set aside; chop the remainder of stem into 1/3" pieces. In a small stock pot, place chopped asparagus stems with 5 cups chicken stock. Cook over medium heat until tender. Remove from heat and drain asparagus. Puree in blender until smooth.

In a large sauce pan, heat olive oil and 2 tablespoons butter over medium heat. When butter foams, add onions and saute until onions become translucent. Add arborio to pan and toast arborio, stirring as it cooks, for 30 seconds.

Add wine and continue to cook until wine is completely reduced. After wine has dissipated, add 2 cups hot chicken stock; cook for 2 minutes and add asparagus tips and puree. After 15 minutes, risotto is cooked. Remove from heat and add 1/3 cup butter and Parmesan cheese. Mix well and serve.

The recipe calls for puree; but if you are in a hurry, you can cook onions in olive oil, add arborio with chicken stock and add chopped asparagus all at once 7 minutes before the end. You will have good results, but not like the results I have intended for this dish.

Risotto Al Gorgonzola E Pistacchi

Risotto with Gorgonzola Cheese and Pistachios

1 lb. arborio rice
1/4 cup olive oil
1 onion, finely chopped (1 cup)
1 1/2 cups dry white wine
2 cups chicken stock (sauces chapter)
14 ounces gorgonzola cheese
1 teaspoon salt
1 teaspoon black pepper
1 cup unsalted butter, sliced (1/2 lb.)
3 ounces pistachio nuts, chopped
8 ounces grated Parmesan cheese

Serves: 4
Complexity: • • •
Preparation Time: 1 Hour
Italian Wine: Dolcetto Di Diano D'Alba,
Dry red and slightly almond with a
good fruity nose.

In a large sauce pan, heat olive oil over medium heat. Add onions and saute until onions begin to sweat. Add arborio to pan and toast arborio, stirring as it cooks, for 2 minutes.

Add wine and continue to cook until wine is completely reduced. After wine has dissipated, add hot chicken stock, salt and pepper and continue to cook down mixture, stirring well. After 7 minutes, add gorgonzola cheese, cut into pieces. Continue to stir mixture as it cooks for an additional 4 minutes. Remove from heat and add butter, pistachios and Parmesan cheese. Mix well and serve.

I suggest that you add very little stock at a time. As the gorgonzola melts you do not want to have too much liquid. When you add the gorgonzola to the rice, make sure that the rice is thick, then you can control the end result.

Risotto Ai Gamberi D'Acqua Dolce E Carciofi

Crawfish Risotto with Artichokes

12 ounces cooked crawfish
4 fresh artichoke hearts, sliced
42 asparagus spears, remove bottom 1 1/2", chopped (1 1/4 lbs.)
1 lb. arborio rice
2 tablespoons olive oil
1 onion, peeled, finely chopped (1/2 cup)
1 garlic clove, smashed
1 cup dry white wine
1 cup tomato puree
5 cups crawfish broth (sauces chapter)
1 teaspoon salt
3 ounces unsalted butter, sliced
2/3 cup grated Parmesan cheese
1/3 cup chopped fresh Italian parsley

Serves: 4
Complexity: ● ● ●
Preparation Time: 40 Minutes
Italian Wine: Arneis,
A fresh white with a good
flavorful bouquet.

In a large sauce pan, heat olive oil over medium heat. Add onions, artichokes and garlic and saute until onions become translucent; remove garlic. Add salt and arborio to pan; toast arborio, stirring as it cooks, for 30 seconds.

Add wine and continue to cook until wine is completely reduced. After wine has dissipated, add tomato puree and 5 cups hot crawfish broth, one at a time; continue to cook down mixture, stirring well. Add asparagus. After cooking for 15 minutes, add crawfish. Cook for 1 minute; remove from heat. Add butter, Parmesan cheese and parsley. Mix well and serve.

Risotto Al Parmigiano

Parmesan Risotto

1/4 cup olive oil
1 onion, finely chopped (1/2 cup)
1 lb. arborio rice
1 cup dry white wine
4 1/2 cups veal stock (sauces chapter)
1 cup fonduta sauce (sauces chapter)
1/4 cup unsalted butter, sliced
1/2 cup Parmesan cheese, shredded
2 tablespoons grated Parmesan cheese
1 teaspoon veal reduction (sauces chapter)

Serves: 4
Complexity: •
Preparation Time: 25 Minutes
Italian Wine: Dolcetto D'Ovada,
Dry red with a soft round bouquet,
2-3 years old.

To make a twill, or cup, for the fonduta sauce, first take flan cups or molds and rub butter on the outside of the cups. Turn the molds upside down on an even surface. In a small, non-stick saute pan, dust a fine layer of grated Parmesan cheese, approximately 2 tablespoons. Place pan over low heat and allow cheese to cook very slowly, allowing the bottom side to get light golden brown in color. While the cheese cooks, continuously lift the cheese with a spatula to ensure that it does not stick or overcook. Remove pan from heat as needed and continue to lift cheese from underneath. Do not flip the cheese. When it is cooked lightly and evenly, remove from pan and place, with light side down over the inverted flan cup. Gently press the cheese around the cup. Allow the cheese to cool, then remove cheese from flan mold. Fill the twill, or cup, with warmed fonduta sauce. To ensure that the fonduta sauce does not separate as it is warmed, place the sauce in mixing bowl or pan and place in a larger pot of boiling water.

Heat olive oil in a large sauce pan over medium heat. When oil is hot, add onions and cook until onions become translucent, approximately 3 1/2 minutes. Add arborio to pan and toast for 4 1/2 minutes, stirring as it cooks. Add white wine and cook until completely reduced, approximately 2 minutes. When wine has dissipated, add hot veal stock. After 12 minutes total, risotto is cooked. Remove from heat.

To serve risotto, add butter and 1/2 cup Parmesan cheese and mix well.

Risotto Al Nero Di Seppia

Black Risotto With Cuttlefish

4 ounces cuttlefish, cleaned and deboned
3/4 cup olive oil
1 onion, peeled, finely chopped (1/2 cup)
1 cup dry white wine
4 2/3 cup chicken stock (sauces chapter)
1 lb. arborio rice

Marinade:
1/4 cup olive oil
1 teaspoon fresh thyme
1/2 teaspoon salt
1/2 teaspoon black pepper
1 garlic clove, thinly sliced

Serves: 4
Complexity: • • •
Preparation Time: 35 Minutes
Italian Wine: Chardonnay,
Light on the barrique but with full body.

Combine marinade ingredients. Slice raw cuttlefish fillets in half and place in marinade; stir to coat evenly. Allow fillets to marinate for 20 minutes.

Heat olive oil in a large sauce pan over medium heat. When oil is hot, add onions and cook until onions become translucent, approximately 3 1/2 minutes. Add arborio to pan and toast for 4 1/2 minutes stirring as it cooks. Add white wine and cook until completely reduced, approximately 2 minutes. When wine has dissipated, add hot chicken stock. After 10 minutes add cooked cuttlefish. After 12 minutes total, risotto is cooked. Remove from heat. Add 1/8 cup olive oil and stir for 1 minute.

Heat a small saute pan over medium heat and place marinated filets, along with marinade juices, in pan, searing each filet on both sides. Cook filets for 50 seconds remove.

Risotto Con Porcini E Salsiccia Di Coniglio

Porcini Risotto with Rabbit Sausage

1/4 cup olive oil
1 onion, peeled, finely chopped (1/2 cup)
1 lb. arborio rice
4 cups veal stock (sauces chapter)
14 ounces porcini mushrooms (2 cups)
1 cup dry white wine
1 tablespoon fresh sage, chopped
1 tablespoon fresh rosemary, chopped
1/2 cup tomato puree
1/2 ounce Italian parsley, chopped
2 tablespoons unsalted butter, sliced
2 tablespoons grated Parmesan cheese
4 rabbit sausages (meat & game chapter)

Serves: 4
Complexity: ● ● ●
Preparation Time: 35 Minutes
Italian Wine: Barbaresco,
Four years old with a light
touch of acidity in it and
slightly tannic.

Heat olive oil in a large sauce pan over medium heat. When oil is hot, add onions and cook until onions become translucent, approximately 3 1/2 minutes. Add arborio to pan; toast arborio for 30 seconds, stirring as it cooks. Add white wine and cook until completely reduced, approximately 2 minutes. When wine has dissipated, add hot veal stock. After 7 minutes, add mushrooms, sage and rosemary. After cooking an additional 5 minutes, add tomato sauce. After 15 minutes total, risotto is cooked. Remove from heat and add parsley, butter and Parmesan cheese.

Prepare rabbit sausage. Serve risotto topped with slices of roasted rabbit sausage.

Porcini mushrooms can be substituted with portobello, white button mushrooms, or any kind of wild mushroom. If you use white button mushrooms, I suggest that you add one ounce dried porcini or other dried mushrooms that have been soaked in warm water to give the dish more flavor.

Risotto Al Tartufo Bianco
White Truffle Risotto

1/4 cup olive oil
1 onion, peeled, chopped (1/2 cup)
1 cup dry white wine
4 1/2 cups veal stock (sauces chapter)
1 lb. arborio rice
1/4 cup unsalted butter, sliced
1/3 cup grated Parmesan cheese
4 tablespoons white truffle oil
1 white truffle, if desired

Serves: 4
Complexity: • • •
Preparation Time: 25 Minutes
Italian Wine: Chardonnay,
Classical method with a good acidity

Heat olive oil in a large sauce pan over medium heat. When oil is hot, add onions and cook until onions become translucent, approximately 3 1/2 minutes. Add arborio to pan; toast arborio for 4 1/2 minutes stirring as it cooks. Add white wine and cook until completely reduced, approximately 2 minutes. When wine has dissipated, add hot veal stock. After 12 minutes total, risotto is cooked. Remove from heat.

Add butter, cheese and white truffle oil and mix well for 1 minute. Before serving, slice fresh white truffle over top, if desired. White truffle oils vary in taste from one to the next. The more expensive the oil, the richer and more pungent the taste. When cooking this recipe, add truffle oil to taste, based on your own preference and the strength of the oil.

Panissa

Risotto with Beans, Cabbage, and Pork

1/2 cup olive oil
1 onion, finely chopped (1/2 cup)
2 celery stalks, cleaned, finely chopped (1/2 cup)
1 carrot, peeled, finely chopped (1/2 cup)
1/4 head cabbage, sliced (7 ounces)
1 1/4 ounces salted pork, chopped (techniques chapter)
2 leeks, stems only, peeled, finely chopped (5 1/2 ounces)
3 1/2 ounces pinto beans
4 1/2 ounces mild Italian sausage (in casing), chopped
5 ounces mild Italian sausage meat (without casing)
1 lb. arborio rice
1 cup dry red wine
2 1/2 cup vegetable stock (sauces chapter)

Serves: 4
Complexity: ••
Preparation Time: 40 Minutes
2 Hours to cook beans
Italian Wine: Lessona,
Dry and tannic red to be
consumed young.

Place pinto beans in medium sauce pan. Cover with 5 cups water and place over high heat until water boils. After it reaches a boiling point, reduce heat to low and simmer beans for 2 hours. Drain beans through a strainer.

In a small stock pot, combine 1/4 cup olive oil, vegetables, salted pork and sausage, in casing, and place over medium heat. After 10 minutes, add 5 cups water. Cook an additional 30 minutes and remove from heat. Pour contents of pot into food processor and puree mixture.

In a large sauce pan, heat 1/4 cup olive oil over medium heat. When oil is hot, add sausage meat, without casing. Brown meat for 5 minutes, breaking up with wooden spoon as it cooks. Add arborio to pan and toast for 4 1/2 minutes. Add red wine and allow wine to cook down until reduced, 2 minutes. Add drained beans; add 1 cup vegetable puree at a time until 2 1/2 cups have been added to mixture. After 15 minutes total cook-time, risotto is cooked. Remove from heat; mix well for 1 minute and serve.

pasta

Pasta in Piedmont is an important part of the meal and a very important social moment for the family. Usually during the week in Piedmont we eat dried pasta and on Sunday we eat fresh pasta. It can be tagliatelle, tagliarini or angolotti. Angolotti means "brine" which means pinch in Piedmontese. An angolotti is made rounder and is pinched on the side.

The reason I say it is important for the family is because usually on Saturday night after dinner, everybody cleans dishes and my grandmother or mother prepares the fresh pasta and we all help. Anglotti was a special kind of pasta to make because we would all participate; someone would roll out the dough, someone else brushes it with egg, another person is in charge of filling. It gets the entire family involved. After we are finished, everybody goes to sleep and when we wake in the morning my mother and grandmother are already up making the ragu and sauces for the pasta, preparing the meal for the day. It is a beautiful memory for me. That's why I have many fresh pastas in this chapter. I also tried to remember to put in a few dried pastas for use everyday.

Raviolo Aperto Alle Cappesante E Funghi
Open Raviolo with Mushrooms and Sea Scallops

4 ounces black pasta dough (techniques chapter)
4 ounces egg pasta dough (techniques chapter)

Filling:
10 ounces chanterelle mushrooms, cleaned
11 ounces shiitake mushrooms, cleaned
1 fresh rosemary sprig
1 garlic clove, smashed
1/4 cup olive oil

8 sea scallops (14 ounces)
1/4 cup olive oil
1 teaspoon salt
1 teaspoon black pepper
1/2 cup dry white wine
20 fresh basil leaves, chopped
1/4 cup unsalted butter

Serves: 4
Complexity: ● ● ● ●
Preparation Time: 50 Minutes
2 Hours for dough
Italian Wine: Gavi Di Gavi,
Fruity and fresh but with a good
flavor to match the mushrooms.

Prepare pasta dough and refrigerate as per recipe instructions. First take chilled black pasta dough and feed through pasta maker, beginning with setting #1 and graduating to setting #6. Cut pasta into 4 1/2" x 4 1/2" squares. Clean pasta maker to ensure no black dough is left in roller, then feed egg dough through in the same fashion. After pasta is passed through at #6, lay noodle out flat and place 1 fresh Italian parsley leaf in center; fold pasta noodle in half and pass through at #7 setting. Cut into 4 1/2" x 4 1/2" square. Repeat process, making inlay of parsley leaf in each white noodle. Place noodles in salted boiling water; cook for 25 seconds and remove from water. Place on towel and pat dry.

To prepare filling, first heat 1/4 cup olive oil in large saute pan; when oil is hot, add rosemary and garlic and saute over medium heat for 1 minute; add mushrooms and saute for an additional 4 minutes. Remove from heat and discard garlic and rosemary.

Take scallops and cut each horizontally into 3 even slices. Set scallops aside. In a medium saute pan, heat 1/2 cup olive oil over medium heat. When oil is heated, add sliced scallops; sear scallops, browning evenly on both sides. When scallops are browned, remove pan from heat and drain oil; add mushrooms, white wine, salt, pepper and basil. Cook until wine is reduced by half its original amount. Remove pan from heat and add butter; mix well.

For each serving, lay black noodle down on serving plate, layer with scallop mixture, and top with white noodle with parsley leaf inlay.

This recipe is not my invention. I give credit once again to Gualtiero Marchesi. He invented this recipe. I just use different ingredients for preparing the sauce and the stuffing. I thank him for the recipe.

Tagliarini Neri Al Ragu' Di Cappesante Ed Asparagi

Black Tagliarini with Sea Scallops and Asparagus

1 lb. Black Pasta Dough (techniques chapter)

Sauce:
4 ounces salted pork, sliced (techniques chapter)
60 asparagus spears (14 ounces)
16 ounces bay scallops
1/2 cup olive oil
1 teaspoon salt
1 teaspoon black pepper
1/2 cup dry white wine

Serves: 4
Complexity: • •
Preparation Time: 1 Hour, 25 Minutes
Italian Wine: Gavi Di Gavi,
White with a fruity and fresh flavor.
Buy a vintage, no more
than a year old.

To prepare sauce, first take asparagus and cut off bottom 1 1/2" of stems and discard. Cut off tips and set aside. Chop remaining stems and set aside separately.

In a large saute pan, heat olive oil, salted pork and chopped asparagus stems over medium heat. After 1 1/2 minutes, add asparagus tips. Continue to cook for 3 minutes and add scallops, salt, pepper and wine. Cook until wine is reduced, approximately 4 minutes. Remove sauce from heat.

To prepare pasta, take chilled black dough and pass through pasta maker, beginning at setting #1 and graduating to setting #6. Feed sheet of dough through the linguine pasta cutting setting. Place cut pasta on floured baking sheet.

Cook pasta in salted boiling water for 30 seconds and remove. Drain pasta and toss with scallop sauce. Pasta is ready to serve.

Rigatoni Ripieni Ai Broccoli Con Salsa D'Aragosta
Stuffed Rigatoni In Lobster Sauce

48 rigatoni noodles
   (cook a few extra in case of breakage)
2 broccoli heads, remove stems,
   saving florets (30 ounces)
6 tablespoons grated Parmesan cheese
9 teaspoons unsalted butter
6 ounces lobster meat
1 shallot, finely chopped (2 teaspoons)
6 tablespoons lobster sauce (sauces chapter)

Serves: 4
Complexity: ● ● ● ●
Preparation Time: 40 Minutes
Italian Wine: Favorita,
Dry white, acidic enough to cut the
sharpness of the sauce.

Bring water and 2 teaspoons salt to a boil in a medium stock pot. When water reaches boiling point, add rigatoni noodles and cook for 12 minutes. Remove from water and drain using a colander. Run under cold tap water. Then place colander in a larger bowl of ice water, allowing rigatoni to be immersed in cold water. Set aside.

In a separate stock pot, bring salted water to a boil and add broccoli florets. Cook for 4 minutes and drain using colander. Push down on vegetables using your hand or a spoon to extract water. Place cooked broccoli in a blender or food processor. Add 2 tablespoons Parmesan cheese and puree. Pour contents into pastry bag. Take cooled rigatoni noodles and stuff each with broccoli filling. Set aside.

In a large frying pan, melt 1 teaspoon butter and place stuffed rigatoni in a single layer at bottom of pan. Top with 1 teaspoon melted butter and 1 tablespoon cheese. Place pan in preheated oven at 350 degrees for 3 minutes.

Cut lobster meat in pieces, keeping claws whole to use as garnish, if possible. In a small sauce pan, saute 1 teaspoon butter and shallots over medium heat for 30 seconds; add lobster. Saute for an additional 30 seconds. Add 5 tablespoons of lobster sauce to shallot sauce and warm through for 30 seconds.

To serve, place rigatoni on platter and top with lobster sauce. Garnish with whole lobster claw brushed with melted butter.

I got the idea for this recipe from a dinner I had in New York cooked by Gualtiero Marchesi. He cooked rigatoni with lobster sauce. I decided to stuff it with broccoli and to make it crusty on top. Make sure to get a nice gratin on top of the rigatoni before you serve them.

Ravioli D'Aragosta Nel Suo Sugo

Lobster Ravioli

Dough:
3 eggs
2 cups all purpose flour
1/2 cup semolina flour
2 teaspoons salt
1 tablespoon olive oil

Filling:
4 ounces lobster meat, diced
1 ounce black truffle peelings
1/4 teaspoon salt
1/4 teaspoon black pepper
3 ounces baked potato, peeled, chopped
1 tablespoon fresh Italian parsley, chopped
1 egg

Sauce:
1 ounce butter
1 cup lobster reduction (sauces chapter)
2 1/2 teaspoon fresh thyme

Serves: 4
Complexity: ••••
Preparation Time: 1 Hour,
2 hours, for dough
Italian Wine: Gavi Di Gavi,
Dry white, one year old in the
peak of its fruitiness.

To make dough, combine ingredients and mix in food processor or mixer with dough hook attachment. If this attachment is not available, mix using your hands. After dough is initially folded, knead further, using your hands on lightly floured surface. Wrap dough in plastic wrap and store in refrigerator for 2 hours. This will give dough greater elasticity.

To make filling, mix lobster meat, truffles and salt and pepper in medium mixing bowl. Add potato and parsley and continue to mix well, using wooden spoon. Set aside. The potato will absorb some of the water from the lobster meat and, due to its starch, will help to bind other ingredients.

Take chilled dough and roll slightly on lightly floured surface. Using a pasta maker, electric or manual, begin to feed dough through at #1 setting. Continue to re-feed dough, increasing setting to #6, which will allow noodle to become wider and thinner as it is passed.

Combine 1 egg and 2 tablespoons water in small mixing bowl and beat with a whisk. When dough is rolled into an even, thin noodle, brush lightly with egg mixture. Place 1/2 ounce of filling, walnut-sized spoonfuls, in a row, lengthwise down the center of the dough, leaving 1 1/4" in between each. Fold dough over top of filling. Press down with fingertips, lightly sealing dough fold along outside edges. Continue to press dough around each filling pocket, releasing any air bubbles that have formed in between layers.

Using ravioli cutter, cut edges of ravioli, forming sealed, scalloped edges. If a ravioli cutter is not available, use a sharp, thin-blade knife. After cutting all ravioli, place on baking sheet dusted with semolina. Check each ravioli again for air pockets. Use a needle to puncture dough, and push gently, releasing air. It is important to remove air from ravioli pockets because air will cause ravioli to fill with water, making filling soggy. Cook ravioli in salted boiling water for 2 1/2 minutes.

To make sauce, combine ingredients in small sauce pan over medium heat. Saute for approximately 1 minute, or until sauce is warmed and dense in consistency.

Serve ravioli topped with reduction sauce.

Conchiglie Con Salsa Di Pesce Spada

Seashell Pasta with Swordfish Caper Sauce

This dish makes use of leftover swordfish. Other fish such as tuna and halibut can be substituted. When freezing swordfish, keep fillets hole and cut after they have thawed.

10 ounces seashell pasta
12 ounces swordfish, cubed in 1/4" pieces
4 anchovy fillets, chopped (fresh or canned)
1 garlic clove, smashed, finely chopped
4 tablespoons olive oil
1 teaspoon tomato paste
3 tablespoons capers, drained
1 tablespoon Calamata olives, pitted and quartered
1/4 teaspoon salt
1/4 teaspoon black pepper
1/4 teaspoon red pepper, crushed
12 fresh basil leaves, finely chopped

Serves: 4
Complexity: • •
Preparation Time: 20 Minutes
Italian Wine: Gavi Di Gavi,
Dry white with a strong body
enough to stand the acidity
of the capers.

Prepare seashell pasta in salted boiling water, cooking for 10 minutes. Remove from heat, drain and rinse with cool water. Set aside.

In a medium sauce pan, heat olive oil over low heat. Add anchovies and garlic and saute; add tomato paste. Cook for 1 1/2 minutes. In a separate bowl, combine fish, capers and olives; mix well. Add fish mixture to anchovy mixture along with salt, pepper, basil and crushed red pepper. Saute for an additional 5 minutes and remove from heat. Add pasta and serve.

Tagliarini Al Ragu' Di Carne

Egg Tagliarini with Meat Sauce

Serves: 4
Complexity: •
Preparation Time: 10 Minutes,
2 Hours in Dough
Italian Wine: Grignolino,
A slightly bitter finish, good to cut
the sweetness of the sauce.

1 lb. egg yolk dough
1 teaspoon unsalted butter
1 fresh sage leaf
3/4 cup bolognese meat sauce

To prepare pasta, take chilled egg yolk dough and pass through pasta maker, beginning at setting #1 and ending with #6. Fold sheet in half and pass through #6 setting a second time. On a lightly floured surface, take pasta sheet and fold in half; fold in half again; then roll, length to length, creating a "jelly roll." Cut slices 1/8" thick from roll. Unroll the slices to reveal a long pasta noodle that is thinner than fettucine. Place cut pasta on floured baking sheet. Place pasta in salted boiling water for 40 seconds, then remove from water.

In a medium sauce pan, combine butter and sage leaf over medium heat; when butter foams, add pasta and toss; remove from heat. The pasta can be served as is, or topped with meat sauce.

Macaron Del Fret con Salsa di Porcini e Ghiandole di Vitello

Hand Made Rigatoni In a Sausage Ragu

1 lb. egg pasta dough (techniques chapter)

Sweetbreads Sauce:
12 ounces sweetbreads, diced
10 ounces porcini mushrooms, roasted
1/4 shallot, finely chopped (4 tablespoons)
2 tablespoons unsalted butter
1/4 cup olive oil
4 teaspoons fresh rosemary, chopped
4 cups tomato puree
2 teaspoons salt
2 teaspoons black pepper

Serves: 4
Complexity: ● ● ●
Preparation Time: 45 Minutes
Italian Wine: Primaticcio,
Young red, fresh and lively
with a good acidity.

Prepare egg pasta dough; after dough has chilled for 2 hours in refrigerator, remove and allow to soften at room temperature.

When dough is soft and pliable, take 1/4 ounce, 1/2 tablespoon, of dough and place on lightly floured surface using fingers, roll dough into a small, 4" long cylinder. Take a knitting needle, coated in flour, and lay along top of cylinder, lengthwise. Press down and roll needle back and forth briskly, 3 to 4 times. Slide pasta off needle, creating a hollow, cylinder-shaped pasta noodle. Place noodles on a floured baking pan. To prepare sauce, combine butter, olive oil, shallots and rosemary in medium sauce pan; saute over medium heat for 2 minutes. Add mushrooms and sweet bread and cook for 1 minute; add tomato puree and salt and pepper. After cooking an additional 4 minutes, remove sauce from heat.

To cook pasta, place in 3 quarts boiling water with 2 teaspoons salt; cook for 3 1/2 minutes and drain. Add cooked pasta to sweet bread sauce and toss. Pasta is ready to serve.

If you do not have a knitting needle, use a pencil to make macaroni. Use the pasta the same day you make it, because if it gets too dry, it will be difficult to cook.

Calhiette

Baked Potato, Sausage and Fontina Cheese Dumpling

2 medium Idaho potatoes, cleaned, peeled, boiled (1 1/2 lbs.)
4 ounces mild Italian sausage meat, without casing
3 tablespoons onion, peeled, finely chopped
1 tablespoon olive oil
1/4 cup milk
1 egg
2 tablespoons grated Parmesan cheese
pinch nutmeg
1/4 cup all purpose flour
1/2 teaspoon salt
1/2 cup unsalted butter
6 ounces fontina cheese, sliced

Serves: 4
Complexity: • • •
Preparation Time: 1 Hour
Italian Wine: Dolcetto,
Fruity, red with a vivacious finish.

Take boiled potatoes and pass through food mill to yield 15 ounces potato puree; set aside.

In a small saute pan, combine sausage meat, onion and olive oil and cook over high heat for 10 minutes, breaking up sausage as it browns. Add milk and cook until milk reduces completely. Remove from heat and pour contents of pan into food processor; blend for 8 seconds and set aside, allowing mixture to cool.

In a large mixing bowl, combine potato puree, egg, cheese, nutmeg, flour and salt; mix well. When sausage mixture has cooled, add to potato mixture along with 2 tablespoons flour. Mix ingredients well.

Using 2 teaspoons, shape 1 spoonful of dough into long, egg-shaped dumplings. Continue to form remaining dough in same fashion, placing finished dumplings on floured baking sheet.

Place dumplings in boiling salted water for 1 minute, until they rise to the top; remove from water and place in small sauce pan. Add butter and saute lightly over medium heat for 30 seconds. Transfer contents of pan into baking dish and cover with layer of fontina cheese slices. Bake in oven preheated to 400 degrees for 5 minutes. Remove baking dish from oven and pasta is ready to serve.

Work in the potato with the flour when the potato is still hot. Add the flour a little at a time; if you put too much flour, the dough will be tough.

Tagliatelle Alla Carlo Umberto

Tagliatelle "Carlo Umberto Style"

1lb. egg yolk dough (techniques chapter)
3 1/2 cups all purpose flour
1 tablespoon salt
2 tablespoons olive oil
22 egg yolks

Pasta Sauce:
12 ounces sausage
1/2 cup olive oil
2 cups Barolo wine

8 ounces fonduta sauce (sauces chapter)
1/2 cup all purpose flour

Serves: 4
Complexity: ••
Preparation Time: 45 Minutes
Italian Wine: Arneis,
Delicate, white fresh and with
herbed finish.

To prepare pasta, take chilled dough and feed through pasta maker, beginning with #1 setting and graduating to #6. Pass through at the #6 setting twice. Feed dough through the cutting setting for fettucine noodles. Set noodles aside on a floured baking sheet.

For sauce, heat olive oil in medium sauce pan over medium heat. When oil is hot, add sausage and saute until browned, breaking up meat as it cooks using a wooden spoon. After meat is browned, 5 minutes, add wine and cook for 2 minutes or until wine is completely reduced. Remove from heat.

Place prepared pasta in boiling salted water for 40 seconds. Remove and toss pasta noodles in sauce. To serve, place pasta with sauce on serving plate; top each serving with 1/4 cup fonduta sauce.

Agnolotti Di Brasato Di Bue Con Il Suo Sugo

Red Wine Braised Beef Agnolotti

1 lb. spinach pasta dough (techniques chapter)

Meat filling:
1/4 cup olive oil
16 ounces beef, cubed (shoulder or neck)
2 fresh sage leaves
2 garlic cloves, smashed
1 tablespoon fresh rosemary, chopped
1 clove ground cinnamon
1 dried bay leaf
1 onion, peeled, finely chopped (1/2 cup)
1 carrot, peeled, finely chopped (1/2 cup)
2 celery stalks, cleaned, finely chopped (1/2 cup)
2 cups Barolo wine
1 teaspoon salt
1 teaspoon black pepper
1 egg
1/4 cup grated Parmesan cheese
2 tablespoons unsalted butter

Serves: 4
Complexity: ● ● ● ●
Preparation Time: 1 Hour
Italian Wine: Dolcetto D' Asti,
Dry red with a velvety consistency,
well balanced with a low acidity.

To prepare meat filling, heat olive oil in medium sauce pan over medium heat. When oil is hot, add meat and increase heat to high; saute meat, adding herbs and spices. Cook for 2 minutes and add vegetables; saute for 6 minutes and add wine. Continue to cook mixture for an additional 6 minutes and remove from heat; pass contents through a strainer to drain meat juice. Do not press down on meat to extract juice, rather, allow meat to drain naturally. Set meat juice aside.

Pass meat through meat grinding attachment on a mixer or food processor; pass through a second time to achieve a finely ground mixture. Place ground meat in mixing bowl and add egg and cheese; mix well using hands. Set meat filling aside.

After spinach pasta dough has chilled for 2 hours, remove from refrigerator. Take dough and pass through pasta maker, beginning with #1 setting and graduating to #6.

Make sure to reduce beef sauce until it coats the back of a spoon. Lay dough on lightly floured surface. Take meat filling and place 6 1/2"-balls along sheet, spacing evenly apart.

Take egg wash (techniques chapter) and brush around outside of filling ball. Take dough sheet and fold in half, draping over filling. Using fingers, press down around the circumference of each filling pocket to seal the pasta dough. Using a ravioli cutter, trim dough around filling pockets, leaving 1/2" of dough framing each pocket. Poke hole in filling pocket with a needle if necessary to remove any air bubbles.

Cook ravioli in salted boiling water for 2 1/2 minutes and remove.

Pour meat juice in small sauce pan and add butter; cook over medium-high heat until mixture reaches a boil, then remove from heat. Toss cooked ravioli in meat juice and serve.

Cook pasta for 3 1/2 minutes in boiling salted water. Remove from water.

To prepare sauce, heat olive oil in medium sauce pan over medium heat. When oil is hot, add herbs and saute for 5 seconds; add tomato puree and spices. After 2 minutes, add butter and stir with whisk; remove sauce from heat.
To serve, place pasta over bed of sauce.

Make sure to make a hole with a needle to release the excess air in pocket. Make sure to reduce beef sauce until it coats the back of a spoon.

Capellini Di Grano Al Sugo Strafritto
Corn Capellini with Double Fried Sauce

Serves: 4
Complexity: • •
Preparation Time: 10 Minutes
2 Hours refrigeration
Italian Wine: Grignolino,
Dry, red with enough acidity
to cut the sauce.

1 lb. corn pasta dough (techniques chapter)
strafritto sauce (sauces chapter)

Take chilled dough and pass through pasta maker, beginning at setting #1 and graduating to setting #5. Feed sheet of dough through the linguine pasta cutting setting. Place cut pasta on floured baking sheet.

Prepare strafritto sauce.

Cook pasta in salted boiling water for 30 seconds. Remove from water and drain. Top pasta with strafritto sauce and serve.

Carbonara Monferrina Di Tagliatelle E Asparagi

Carbonara "Monferrina" Style

1 lb. egg pasta dough (techniques chapter)

Sauce:
2 ounces pancetta, chopped
20 asparagus stalks, cleaned (7 ounces)
3 ounces salted pork (techniques chapter)
1/2 teaspoon black pepper
1 egg yolk
1/2 cup grated Parmesan cheese
3/4 cup heavy whipping cream
2 tablespoons vegetable stock (sauces chapter)

Serves: 4
Complexity: ● ● ●
Preparation Time: 15 Minutes
Italian Wine: Favorita,
Dry slightly acidic,
with a light asparagus flavor.

Prepare egg pasta per recipe. Take chilled egg dough and pass through pasta maker, beginning with #1 setting and graduating to #6. Take pasta sheets and feed through pasta cutting setting for fettucine. Set cut pasta aside on floured baking pan.

To prepare sauce, take asparagus stalks and cut off bottom 1 1/2" of stem and discard. Cut tips and set aside; take remaining middle stems and chop finely; set aside separately.

Take pancetta, chopped asparagus stems and salted pork and grind together, using meat grinding attachment on mixer or food processor. Set aside.

Combine ground mixture, vegetable stock and pepper in large, covered sauce pan over low heat. After 4 minutes, add asparagus tips. In a separate bowl, combine Parmesan cheese and cream; add to sauce pan. Cook mixture for an additional 3 minutes and remove from heat.

Cook pasta in salted boiling water for 45 seconds. Remove pasta from water and drain. Toss pasta with asparagus sauce; add egg yolk, mix well and serve.

This is a dish that the countrymen from Monferrato, an area in Piedmont, would prepare in May because they could use wild asparagus which grew at the perimeter of the woods. Today we cannot find wild asparagus, but we use regular asparagus and get the same result, which is very tasty.

Penne In Salsa Piccante

Penne in a Spicy Sauce

1 lb. penne pasta

Sauce:
15 plum tomatoes, peeled, seeded (21 ounces)
3 ounces capers, drained
15 anchovy fillets, chopped
1 garlic clove, finely chopped
1/2 teaspoon salt
1 teaspoon black pepper
1 teaspoon Worchestershire sauce
1/2 cup olive oil
10 fresh basil leaves, chopped

Serves: 4
Complexity: ●●●
Preparation Time: 1 Hour
Italian Wine: Grignolino,
Red with a well building
flavor to contrast the spicy sauce.

Place tomatoes in food processor and blend for 3 seconds. Place chopped tomatoes in large mixing bowl and add remaining sauce ingredients; mix well.

Prepare pasta, cooking in salted boiling water for 11 minutes. When pasta is almost cooked, pour sauce into pan and place over medium heat for 3 minutes, to warm slightly. Drain pasta when finished cooking and toss with sauce. Pasta is ready to serve.

Lasagnette Croccanti

Crunchy Lasagne

1 lb. egg pasta dough (techniques chapter)

6 ounces mild Italian sausage meat (without casing)
2 tablespoons olive oil
1 fresh sage leaf, finely chopped
2 ounces fontina cheese, sliced
4 ounces shiitake mushrooms,
   julienned (techniques chapter)
4 tablespoons grated Parmesan cheese
2 tablespoons veal stock (sauces chapter)
1/4 cup rosemary sauce (sauces chapter)

Serves: 4
Complexity: ● ● ● ●
Preparation Time: 1 Hour
Italian Wine: Dolcetto Di Dogliani,
Fruity and round to cut the flavor
of the sausage.

Take chilled pasta dough and feed through pasta maker, beginning with setting #1 and graduating to setting #6. Lay pasta on lightly floured surface and cut into 4″ x 4″ squares, 4 pasta sheets per serving. Cook pasta in salted boiling water for 35 seconds. Remove from water and lay on dry towel to cool.

In a large saute pan, combine sausage meat, olive oil and sage; saute until meat is browned, breaking up sausage meat as it cooks. After 2 minutes, remove from heat and allow to cool.

Rub unsalted butter on bottom and sides of baking dish. Lay pasta sheets in single layer along bottom of pan; top each sheet with browned sausage meat, then a layer of fontina cheese slices. Add a second layer of sausage on each; top sausage with mushrooms and sprinkle with Parmesan cheese. Place baking dish under broiler for 4 minutes; remove and bake in oven preheated to 400 degrees for 6 minutes. Remove dish from oven.

To serve, remove baked pasta sheets with spatula. Place first sheet on serving plate; place second sheet diagonally on top. Build 4 pasta sheet layers, each alternating in direction. Drizzle warmed sauces over top.

Be sure to make this very crunchy; do not be afraid to let it gratinee in the oven.

Cannelloni Alla Barbaroux

Cannelloni "Babaroux" Style

Cannelloni shell:
3 eggs
3 tablespoons all purpose flour
1/4 teaspoon salt
1/4 teaspoon black pepper

Filling:
5 ounces prosciutto
pinch nutmeg
10 ounces roasted veal, cubed (use leftover piece from roast
   or use 14 ounces veal shoulder)
2 cups olive oil
2 garlic cloves
2 fresh sage leaves
2 fresh rosemary sprigs
1 cup dry white wine
1 egg
1/4 cup grated Parmesan cheese
2 1/2 cups Bechamel sauce (sauces chapter)
2 teaspoons grated Parmesan cheese

Serves: 4
Complexity: • • •
Preparation Time: 1 Hour
Italian Wine: Barbera D'Asti,
Well balanced red with a hint of
acidity, good with the cannelloni.

To prepare cannelloni filling, place large saute pan over medium heat. Add olive oil and herbs; saute until herbs are browned, then remove herbs from pan and discard. Add veal meat and saute, browning meat evenly on all sides. After cooking meat for 5 minutes, add wine; place pan in oven preheated to 450 degrees and bake until wine is reduced, 15 minutes. Remove pan from oven and set veal meat aside. Take veal and prosciutto and grind together, using meat grinding attachment on a mixer or food processor. In a medium mixing bowl, combine ground meat with nutmeg, egg and cheese; mix well using hands. Pass blended mixture through meat grinder a second time. Set filling mixture aside.

To prepare cannelloni shell, combine eggs, flour, salt and pepper in mixing bowl; mix well using whisk. If the mixture is lumpy, pass through a strainer to yield a creamy and smooth batter.

Take a 7 1/2" non-stick saute pan and place over high heat; when pan is hot, coat lightly with olive oil; remove pan from heat. Add 2 tablespoons of batter mixture; spread evenly by tilting pan. Place pan briefly over heat, 20 seconds; when crepe is very lightly browned, remove from heat and flip crepe in pan. After 5 seconds, remove from pan. Repeat method for remaining batter.

Take filling mixture and add 1 cup bechamel sauce; mix well. Fill pastry bag with filling mixture. Lay crepes flat and, using pastry tube add filling, making one, tube-shaped row of filling across center of crepe. Roll crepe around filling, making long, tube-shaped rolls. Cut off edges of crepes to make tubes even in length.

Rub bottom of a baking dish with unsalted butter. Line crepes in bottom of pan in single layer. Pour 1 1/2 cups Bechamel sauce over top; sprinkle with 2 teaspoons Parmesan cheese. Bake in oven, preheated to 400 degrees, for 8 minutes. Remove from oven and serve.

Lasagnette Del Pastore

Large Noodle with Tomato and Ricotta Cheese

1 lb. saffron pasta dough (techniques chapter)

Ricotta Mixture:
2 garlic cloves
8 fresh sage leaves
2 teaspoons fresh rosemary, chopped
4 teaspoons fresh Italian parsley, chopped
8 ounces ricotta cheese
2 teaspoons salt
3 teaspoons black pepper
2 cups chicken stock (sauces chapter)

Sauce:
16 plum tomatoes, peeled, seeded, chopped (24 ounces)
1/2 cup olive oil
2 garlic cloves, chopped
4 tablespoons fresh Italian parsley, chopped
1 onion, peeled, finely chopped (1/2 cup)
1 carrot, peeled, finely chopped (1/2 cup)
2 celery stalks, cleaned, finely chopped (1/2 cup)
2 tablespoons basil puree (sauces chapter)
1 1/2 teaspoon sugar
1/4 cup red wine vinegar
1 teaspoon salt
1 teaspoon black pepper

Serves: 4
Complexity: ••
Preparation Time: 20 Minutes
Italian Wine: Chardonnay,
Full body with some acidity but
not barriqued.

Take chilled dough and, using 4 ounces of dough at a time, feed through pasta maker beginning with setting #1 and graduating to #6. Take the sheet of pasta dough and fold in half once; then again; fold a third time; and finally a fourth. Cut roll into 1" pieces. Unroll each and cut the ribbons into 5" pieces. Place cut pasta on floured baking sheet.

To prepare sauce, combine olive oil and garlic in medium sauce pan; saute over medium heat for 1 minute. Add onions, carrots, celery, basil puree and parsley; cook for 2 minutes. Add tomatoes, sugar, vinegar and salt and pepper; cook an additional 7 minutes and remove sauce from heat.

Combine garlic, sage, rosemary and parsley; chop all herbs finely together. In a medium mixing bowl, combine chopped herbs with ricotta cheese, salt and pepper and hot chicken stock. Mix well.

Cook pappardelle pasta in salted boiling water for 45 seconds. Remove from heat and drain. Combine drained pasta with ricotta mixture. To serve, top with tomato sauce.

Tagliatelle Con Asparagi E Tartufo Nero

Fettuccine with Asparagus and Black Truffle

1 lb. egg pasta dough (Techniques chapter)

Sauce:
20 asparagus stalks, cleaned (7 ounces)
2 tablespoons olive oil
1 garlic clove, thinly sliced
1/4 teaspoon salt
1/4 teaspoon black pepper
1/2 cup chicken stock (sauces chapter)
1 1/2 ounces black truffle peelings

Serves: 4
Complexity: •
Preparation Time: 15 Minutes,
2 Hours for dough refrigeration
Italian Wine: Favorita,
Soft white with a light
asparagus finish.

To prepare sauce, take asparagus stalks and cut off bottom 1 1/2" of stem; discard. Cut off tips and set aside; dice remaining stems and set aside separately.

In a large sauce pan, saute olive oil and garlic clove over low heat for 1 minute; add diced asparagus stems and salt and pepper. Cover and cook for 3 minutes. Uncover pan, add chicken stock and increase heat to medium. After 5 minutes, add asparagus tips and black truffle peelings; cook for 2 minutes; remove from heat.

Take chilled egg dough and pass through pasta maker, beginning with #1 setting and graduating to #6. Take pasta sheets and feed through pasta cutting setting for fettucine. Set cut pasta aside on floured baking pan.

Cook pasta in salted boiling water for 45 seconds; remove from water and drain. To serve, toss pasta with sauce.

Ravioli Di Fonduta In Salsa Di Salvia
Ravioli of Fonduta in Sage Sauce

1 lb. tomato pasta dough (techniques chapter)

Filling:
3 cups fonduta sauce, chilled (sauces chapter)

Sauce:
1/4 cup unsalted butter
3 fresh sage leaves
1 cup veal meat juice (sauces chapter)
1 cup egg wash (techniques chapter)

Serves: 4
Complexity: •••
Preparation Time: 50 Minutes
Italian Wine: Cortese Del Monferrato, White fresh and fruity with a touch of bitterness and well balanced.

To prepare ravioli, take refrigerated dough and feed through pasta maker, beginning at #1 setting and graduating to #6. Take sheet of pasta dough and lay flat on lightly floured surface. Place 6 spoonfuls of fonduta sauce, 1 tablespoon for each filling pocket, in a row, evenly spaced along pasta sheet. Brush around each filling pocket with egg wash. Fold pasta sheet over filling. Using fingers, press down around each filling pocket to seal pasta dough and release air bubbles. Using ravioli cutter, cut ravioli into square pieces, leaving an even frame of dough around each filling pocket. If necessary, insert needle into pocket to release any air bubbles that may have formed inside. Set ravioli on a floured baking sheet.

To prepare sauce, combine butter, sage and veal juice in a small sauce pan over medium-low heat. Simmer until sauce is warmed through.

To cook ravioli, place in salted boiling water and cook for 2 1/2 minutes. Remove from water and drain. Serve ravioli topped with warmed sage sauce.

When you close ravioli, make sure to insert needle and press down on pocket to release air. If you do not release the air, the filling will become very watery and your ravioli will be soggy.

Rotolo di Pasta con Spinaci

Pasta and Spinach Roll

Spinach Roll Dough:
1 lb. spinach, cleaned, drained
3 1/2 cups all purpose flour
1 tablespoon salt
1/4 cup unsalted butter, melted
5 eggs

Filling:
2 lbs. fresh spinach, cleaned, drained
1 onion, peeled, finely chopped (1/2 cup)
1/4 cup olive oil
1/2 tablespoon salt
1/2 tablespoon black pepper
2 tablespoons grated Parmesan cheese

1/2 cup sage sauce (sauces chapter)

Serves: 4
Complexity: ● ● ● ●
Preparation Time: 1 Hour
Italian Wine: Cortese Di Gave.
Dry white with a light fruity bouquet.

To prepare dough, first cook spinach in salted boiling water for 3 minutes. Remove from heat and drain through colander lined with cheese cloth. Press down on spinach leaves to remove excess water. After spinach cools, lift out cheese cloth and wring spinach inside cloth, extracting all excess liquid. Combine spinach, flour, salt, butter and 4 eggs in mixing bowl. Mix using dough hook attachment on mixer; mix on low speed for 1 1/2 minutes. If dough seems stiff, add fifth egg and continue to mix for an additional 1 1/2 to 3 1/2 minutes. Remove dough from bowl and place on lightly floured surface. Knead dough, adding 1 cup flour, for 1 minute. When dough ingredients are well blended, cover in plastic wrap and place dough in refrigerator for 2 hours.

To prepare filling, cook spinach using preparation method outlined above. Set aside. In a medium saute pan, saute olive oil, onions and salt and pepper for 2 minutes over medium heat. Remove pan from heat and pour contents into blender; add spinach and puree mixture until smooth, not liquefied. Set aside.

Take chilled pasta dough and pass through pasta maker, beginning on setting #1 and graduating to #6. Lay pasta noodle on flat, lightly floured surface. Roll slightly with a rolling pin to spread noodle to 10 1/2" x 8". Carefully remove noodle from floured surface and place on towel, again, laying flat. Spread pureed spinach mixture over noodle using spatula. Spread mixture evenly, 1/8" thick, leaving 1/4" of pasta noodle around edges. Sprinkle Parmesan cheese over top of filling. To form the roll, first fold one end of the noodle over the filling and slightly roll dough to form a long, cylinder shape, rolling from width to width. After the roll form is started, using the towel as a guide, drag towel using both hands, pulling the noodle and rolling the roll at the same time. When roll is completed, tie with kitchen twine using method outlined in techniques chapter.

Place roll in salted boiling water for 8 minutes, then remove. Cut roll into 1 1/2" slices. Serve spinach roll slices topped with sage sauce.

Ravioli Di Patate E Porri Alla "Guido"

Potato and Leek filled Ravioli

1 lb. egg pasta dough (techniques chapter)
1 cup egg wash (techniques chapter)

Filling:
2 Idaho potatoes (2 lbs.)
2 bunches leeks, cleaned with white stems chopped (1 1/2 lbs.)
1/2 cup unsalted butter
1/2 cup olive oil
1 teaspoon salt
1/2 teaspoon black pepper
1/2 cup grated Parmesan cheese

Sauce:
2 cups heavy whipping cream
2 cups grated Parmesan cheese
1/4 cup unsalted butter, softened

Serves: 4
Complexity: •••
Preparation Time: 1 Hour, 20 Minutes
Italian Wine: Chardonnay,
Well balanced and buttery,
not barriqued

To prepare ravioli filling, first place peeled potatoes in 6 quarts water with 1 tablespoon salt; lightly boil for 1 hour. Remove potatoes from water and pass through food mill to yield potato puree.

In a large sauce pan, combine butter, olive oil, salt and pepper over low heat; add chopped leeks and saute for 7 minutes. Remove from heat; add potato puree and Parmesan cheese and mix well; set mixture aside.

To prepare ravioli, take refrigerated dough and feed through pasta maker, beginning at #1 setting and graduating to #6. Take sheet of pasta dough and lay flat on lightly floured surface. Place 6 walnut-sized spoonfuls of filling mixture in a row, evenly spaced, along pasta sheet. Brush around each filling pocket with egg wash. Fold pasta sheet over filling, lengthwise, so that crease runs just under the row of fillings. Using fingers, press down around each filling pocket to seal pasta dough and release air bubbles. Using ravioli cutter, cut ravioli, beginning at crease, and make a half-circle around filling pocket, leaving an even frame of dough around each. The ravioli should be lunar or crescent shaped. If necessary, insert needle into pocket to release any air bubbles that may have formed inside. Set ravioli on a floured baking pan.

To prepare sauce, combine cream and Parmesan cheese in small sauce pan over low heat; cook for 8 minutes. Pass contents of pan through strainer into a mixing bowl. Add softened butter and mix well using whisk. Put mixing bowl over pot of boiling water as you mix sauce to keep warmed through.

To cook ravioli, place in salted boiling water for 1 1/2 minutes. Remove from heat and drain. Serve ravioli with warmed cheese sauce.

For this recipe, I would like to thank Guido Alcadi from Da Guido in Costigliole D'Asti. This is the best Italian restaurant in Italy! I love their cooking and great spirit they have created in the restaurant.

Agnolotti Di Carciofi E Pancetta

Artichoke Agnolotti

1 lb. saffron pasta dough (techniques chapter)
1 cup egg wash (techniques chapter)

Filling:
1/4 cup olive oil
1 garlic clove, smashed
3 ounces pancetta
9 fresh artichoke hearts, cleaned, quartered (12 ounces)
1 onion, peeled, finely chopped (1/2 cup)
1/2 cup dry white wine
1 1/2 cups chicken stock (sauces chapter)
1 cup ricotta cheese
1/4 teaspoon salt
1/4 teaspoon black pepper
2 teaspoons fresh Italian parsley, chopped

Sauce:
1/4 cup olive oil
8 fresh sage leaves
1 garlic clove, smashed
1 tablespoon fresh rosemary
1 tablespoon fresh Italian parsley, chopped
2 cups tomato puree
1/2 teaspoon salt
1/2 teaspoon black pepper
1/4 cup unsalted butter

Serves: 4
Complexity: • • •
Preparation Time: 1 Hour
2 Hours Refrigeration
Italian Wine: Arneis,
Delicate white with a good
herbaceous finish.

To prepare filling, in a large saute pan, heat olive oil and garlic over medium heat. When garlic turns brown in color, remove from pan and add pancetta and artichoke hearts. After cooking mixture for 1 1/2 minutes, add onions and cook for 5 1/2 minutes; add wine and chicken stock. Continue to cook over medium heat for 15 minutes and add 1 cup water. After an additional 12 minutes, remove pan from heat and allow mixture to cool completely. When mixture is cooled, transfer to food processor and blend well to achieve artichoke and onion puree. In a medium mixing bowl, combine puree mixture with cheese, parsley, salt and pepper. Mix well and set filling aside.

Take chilled pasta dough and feed through pasta maker, beginning with setting #1 and graduating to the #6 setting. Lay pasta sheet on lightly floured surface and cut into 4" x 4" squares. Place a walnut-sized portion of filling in the center of 1 pasta dough square. Brush along outside edge of square with egg wash (techniques chapter). Fold square, corner to corner, creating a triangle; fold over the very edges of dough and crease to seal the triangle. Next, with the bottom of the triangle facing you, take the two outside corners and fold in, wrapping around the center of the filling pocket. Repeat process for each pasta square.

A nice way to present this dish is to serve with fried artichoke leaves.

Ravioli Di Magro Al Burro E Salvina

Spinach Filled Ravioli

1 lb. egg pasta dough (techniques chapter)
1/4 oz. truffle slices (optional)
1 cup egg wash (techniques chapter)

Filling:
1 lb. fresh spinach, cleaned, drained
8 ounces ricotta cheese
1/3 cup grated Parmesan cheese
1/4 teaspoon salt
1/4 teaspoon black pepper
1 egg
pinch nutmeg

24 quail eggs

Sauce:
1/4 cup unsalted butter
8 fresh sage leaves

Serves: 4
Complexity: • • •
Preparation Time: 1 Hour
Italian Wine: Cortese Di Gavi,
Dry with enough body for the
cream sauce.

To prepare ravioli filling, first cook spinach for 3 minutes in salted boiling water. Drain using colander; press down on spinach leaves to extract excess water. Place drained cooked spinach in large mixing bowl; add remaining filling ingredients and mix well. Place filling in pastry bag.

To prepare ravioli, take refrigerated egg dough and feed through pasta maker, beginning at #1 setting and graduating to #6. Take sheet of pasta dough and lay flat on lightly floured surface. Using a 3 1/4" ring, cut out round pieces of dough. Brush the outer perimeter of the circles with egg wash. Take first round pasta sheet, and using pastry bag, make a ring of filling on top, leaving a hole in center and 1/4" of dough framing along outside edge. Crack quail egg using a knife and place raw egg in center of filling. Take second round pasta sheet and stretch slightly; place over top of filling and, using fingers, press down along perimeter to seal pasta dough. Use prongs of fork to seal ravioli a second time. Using same method, prepare remaining ravioli and set on floured baking sheet.

Cook ravioli in salted boiling water for 2 minutes. Remove and drain.

To prepare sauce, in large sauce pan, saute butter and sage over medium heat; when butter foams, add ravioli and cook for 30 seconds. Serve pasta topped with fresh truffle slices, if desired.

Capelli D'Angelo Alla Marco Polo

Angel Hair "Marco Polo"

1 lb. corn dough (techniques chapter)

Sauce:
1 red onion, peeled (6 ounces)
1 carrot, peeled (3 ounces)
1 turnip, cleaned, peeled (2 ounces)
2 leeks, white stems only, cleaned (2 ounces)
1 red pepper, cleaned, with stem, seeds and veins removed, julienned (3 ounces)
1 yellow pepper, cleaned, with stem, seeds and veins removed (2 ounces)
1 zucchini, cleaned (3 ounces)
1 celery stalk, cleaned (2 ounces)
1 cup olive oil
2 teaspoons salt
1 teaspoon black pepper
1 cup tomato puree

Serves: 4
Complexity: • •
Preparation Time: 25 Minutes
Italian Wine: Cortese Di Gavi,,
Dry white, with a fruity bouquet
and well balanced.

Prepare corn pasta dough. Take chilled dough and pass through pasta maker, beginning at setting #1 and graduating to setting #5. Feed sheet of dough through the angel hair pasta cutting setting. Place cut pasta on floured baking sheet.

To prepare sauce, finely chop vegetables into julienne strips. Heat olive oil in a large sauce pan over medium heat. When oil is hot, add vegetables, salt and pepper and saute for 2 minutes, stirring vegetables as they cook. Add tomato puree and cook an additional 30 seconds.

Cook pasta in salted boiling water for 45 seconds. Remove from heat and drain pasta. Toss pasta with vegetable medley and serve.

Gnocchi Ripieni Alla "Mamma De Chiara"
Stuffed Potato Dumpling

Dumplings:
2 lbs. Idaho potatoes
1 egg
1/4 cup grated Parmesan cheese
pinch nutmeg
1/2 cup all purpose flour
1/2 teaspoon salt

Meat Filling:
4 ounces beef shoulder or neck, ground
5 ounces pork, ground
2 tablespoons olive oil
2 shallots, peeled, finely chopped (1/4 cup)
1 celery stalk, cleaned, finely chopped (1/4 cup)
1 onion, peeled, finely chopped (1/4 cup)
3 sage fresh leaves, finely chopped
1/4 teaspoon fresh rosemary, chopped
1 garlic cloves, smashed
1 1/2 ounces pancetta, ground
1/2 teaspoon salt
1/2 teaspoon black pepper
1/2 cup dry red wine
1 1/4 ounces chicken liver, finely chopped
1 1/2 cups tomato puree
1 tablespoon tomato paste

Sauce:
1 1/2 cups heavy whipping cream
pinch nutmeg
1/2 cup grated Parmesan cheese
1/2 teaspoon black pepper
2 tablespoons unsalted butter
6 ounces mascarpone cheese

Serves: 6
Complexity: ● ● ● ●
Preparation Time: 2 Hour
Italian Wine: Chardonnay,
Barriqued full body, rich
and buttery.

To prepare meat filling, combine olive oil, shallots, celery, onions, sage, rosemary and garlic in large sauce pan; cook over high heat for 4 minutes, stirring as mixture cooks. After 4 minutes, add ground meats, salt and pepper; saute until meat is well browned, 10 minutes, then add wine. Cook until wine is totally reduced. When wine has dissipated, add chicken liver, tomato puree and tomato paste; reduce heat to low. Simmer for 1 1/2 hours, until tomato has reduced to a thick paste. Remove from heat and place in refrigerator to chill.

To prepare dumplings, first place potato on baking sheet and poke the potato before cooking at 325 degrees for 50 minutes. Remove from oven, peel and pass through a food mill to yield potato puree. Set puree aside. In a large mixing bowl, combine warm potato puree, egg, Parmesan cheese, nutmeg, flour and salt; mix well and knead with hands, combining ingredients thoroughly. To test dumpling mixture, take a small piece and place in boiling water; if it holds together, then consistency is correct. If it falls apart, add more flour and blend well. To assemble dumplings, take half of dumpling dough and place on lightly floured surface. Roll dough using floured rolling pin, until dough is 1/8" thick. Cut dough to create a straight, horizontal edge. Brush excess flour off surface of dough. Take meat filling and drop 1 teaspoon of filling 1" from straight edge of dough, leaving 2 1/2" in between each filling pocket. Fold dough over fillings and gently press down to seal dough.

Take 2" ring and place over filling pocket and press down, or use ravioli cutter. Cut all dumplings and place on floured baking sheet.

To prepare sauce, combine ingredients in a medium sauce pan over high heat. When sauce reaches boiling point, reduce heat to low and simmer for 4 minutes; remove from heat.

To cook dumplings, place in salted boiling water. Cook until dumplings rise to top. Remove from water and serve ravioli with cheese sauce.

To make use of leftover dumpling dough, roll dough out into long tube, about 1/2" thick. Cut into 1/4" pieces and press down on each piece lightly with prongs of fork. Cook pasta pieces in salted boiling water until they rise to the top. Serve with meat filling and cheese sauce.

This recipe was taught to me by Mamma DeChiara who was the mother of Enzo DeChiara, the person I came from Italy to work for in 1979. He is the person responsible for my being here. I thank him by putting this recipe in my book..

Paglia E Fieno
Straw and Hay in Gorgonzola Cheese Sauce

1/2 lb. saffron pasta dough (techniques chapter)
1/2 lb. spinach pasta dough (techniques chapter)

Sauce:
2 tablespoons unsalted butter
1/2 tablespoon fresh sage, chopped
6 ounces gorgonzola cheese (3/4 cup)
2 tablespoons heavy whipping cream
1/4 cup grated Parmesan cheese
6 ounces ricotta cheese (3/4 cup)

Serves: 4
Complexity: •
Preparation Time: 15 Minutes
Italian Wine: Barbera D'Asti,
Well balanced red with a hint of
acidity enough to cut down the
gorgonzola cheese.

Take chilled dough and pass through pasta maker, separately, beginning with #1 setting and graduating to #6. Take pasta sheets and feed through pasta cutting setting for fettucine. Set cut pasta aside on floured baking pan.

In a large saute pan, heat butter and sage over medium heat; when butter foams, add gorgonzola and cook for 1 minute, stirring mixture. Add cream, ricotta and Parmesan cheeses; simmer mixture for 4 minutes, stirring to blend cheeses; remove from heat.

Cook pasta in salted boiling water for 45 seconds; remove from water and drain. Toss pasta with cheese sauce and serve.

Tagliatelle Alle Zucchine

Tagliatelle with Zucchini

1 lb. egg yolk dough (techniques chapter)

Sauce:
4 zucchini, thinly sliced (3 lb.)
1 cup olive oil
40 fresh sage leaves
4 garlic cloves, smashed
1 teaspoon salt
1 teaspoon black pepper
16 anchovy fillets
8 plum tomatoes, peeled
3 roma tomatoes, peeled,
  seeded, diced (12 ounces)

Serves: 4
Complexity: •
Preparation Time: 15 Minutes
Italian Wine: Arneis,
Fresh, white, very aromatic.

Take chilled dough and pass through pasta maker, beginning with #1 setting and graduating to #6. Take pasta sheets and feed through pasta cutting setting for tagliatelle. Set cut pasta aside on floured baking pan.

To prepare sauce, heat olive oil over medium heat in large sauce pan. Take garlic cloves and place in center of sage leaves; tie bouquet with cooking twine. When oil is heated, add bouquet and zucchini slices. After 30 seconds, add anchovies, marjoram, salt and pepper; cover pan and reduce heat to low. Stir mixture as it cooks for 8 minutes; remove from heat and discard bouquet.

To cook pasta, place in salted boiling water; cook for 45 seconds and remove from heat. Drain pasta.

Place zucchini sauce back over medium heat and add tomatoes; cook for 45 seconds. Toss drained pasta noodles with zucchini sauce and serve.

Agnolotti Di Coniglio In Salsa Di Vegetali

Rabbit Agnolotti with a Vegetable Ragu

1 lb. tomato pasta dough (techniques chapter)
1 cup egg wash (techniques chapter)

Filling:
5 ounces mild pork sausage, without casing
1/4 cup olive oil
1 onion, peeled, finely chopped (1/4 cup)
1 garlic clove
1/2 teaspoon fresh rosemary
2 fresh sage leaves
12 ounces rabbit meat, cubed
1/3 cup white arborio rice
1/3 cup dry white wine
1 cup veal stock (sauces chapter)
4 ounces fresh spinach, cleaned, drained
1 egg
1 cup grated Parmesan cheese

Serves: 4
Complexity: ● ● ● ●
Preparation Time: 1 Hour, 30 Minutes
Italian Wine: Dolcetto,
Young with good fresh grape flavor.

Sauce:
1 cup rabbit reduction (sauces chapter)
1 carrot, peeled, cut into round balls (2 ounces)
2 turnips, cleaned, peeled, cut into round balls (2 ounces)
1 zucchini, cleaned, cut into round balls (2 ounces)
1/4 cup unsalted butter
1 garlic clove
2 fresh sage leaves
2 beets, cleaned, cut into round balls (2 ounces)

To prepare ravioli filling, heat olive oil in medium sauce pan over medium heat. Add onion, garlic, rosemary and sage leaves and cook for 1 minute; add sausage and rabbit and saute meat for 5 minutes. Add arborio and white wine. When wine has reduced completely add veal stock and 1/2 cup water. After 15 minutes, when there is no moisture left in pan, remove from heat and allow mixture to cool.

Blanch spinach in salted boiling water for 30 seconds and place spinach leaves in strainer, squeezing out excess water by pressing down on leaves. Take spinach and cooled meat mixture and pass through meat grinding attachment on mixer or food processor. Place ground mixture in mixing bowl and add egg and parmesan cheese; mix well and set filling aside.

To prepare ravioli, take refrigerated tomato dough and feed through pasta maker, beginning at #1 setting and graduating to #6. Take sheet of pasta dough and lay flat on lightly floured surface. Drop filling onto dough in 6 walnut-sized portions, leaving 2" in between each. Brush around each filling with egg wash.

Fold dough over, covering filling; place 2" ring over each filling and press down to cut out the ravioli. Press down with fingers to seal dough and release air pockets. Place ravioli on floured baking pan.

To prepare sauce, cook beets in boiling water for 10 minutes and set aside.

In a large saute pan, heat butter, garlic and sage; saute over medium heat until butter foams, then add all vegetables except beets. Cook for 7 minutes and add rabbit reduction and simmer for 2 minutes.

Cook ravioli in salted boiling water for 2 minutes. Remove from water and add to vegetable mix; add beets and toss. Ravioli is ready to serve.

Rabattoni

Potato Swiss Chard Dumplings

1 1/2 lbs. Swiss chard, cleaned, chopped
2 eggs
1/3 cup grated Parmesan cheese
10 ounces ricotta cheese
1/2 cup unseasoned bread crumbs
1 teaspoon salt

Sauce:
1/4 cup unsalted butter
10 fresh sage leaves

Serves: 4
Complexity: • • •
Preparation Time: 50 Minutes
Italian Wine: Primaticcio,
Young, with good acidity.

In a medium stock pot, bring 2 cups water and 1 teaspoon salt to a boil over medium heat. When water boils, add Swiss chard and cook, with lid on, for 9 minutes. Remove from heat and pass through colander lined with cheese cloth. Press down on chard to extract excess water; using cheese cloth, lift out chard and wring cloth, extracting remaining moisture. Place drained Swiss chard in food processor and finely chop. When chard is well blended, add eggs and Parmesan cheese and puree. Pour contents of food processor into mixing bowl and add ricotta cheese, bread crumbs and salt. Mix well and cover bowl with plastic wrap; chill in refrigerator for 30 minutes.

When mixture is chilled, place in pastry tube. On a lightly floured surface, squeeze filling out into 3" long tubes; roll lightly in flour. Place pasta tubes in salted boiling water; when they rise to the top, remove from water.

In a small saute pan, heat butter and sage leaves over medium heat. When butter foams, remove from heat and toss with pasta tubes. To serve, sprinkle pasta with freshly grated Parmesan cheese.

pesci

Piedmont is one region in Italy that does not border the water, but is in close contact with Liguria, located on Piedmont's southern border, which is rich in the fishing industry. I have included recipes in this book that use sweet water fish such as Trout in Barbera Sauce and Dry Cod with Green Sauce as well as recipes I personally learned and developed in the Liguria region along the coast in Italy. These dishes show how to combine delicate fish with the fresh vegetables and sauces of Piedmont.

Fish should always be very fresh. I like to take fish and enhance the flavor and characteristics without covering it with heavy sauces. Very simple preparation reflects the Piedmontese style which brings out the flavor and color of the dish.

Filletto Di Red Snapper Con Finocchio Ed'Aglio

Sauteed Fillet of Red Snapper with Fennel and Garlic

1 1/2 lb. red snapper, cleaned, deboned, scales removed
1 1/2 teaspoon salt
1 teaspoon black pepper
1 cup olive oil
1 teaspoon fresh dill
1 garlic clove, thinly sliced
2 bulbs fennel, including stems, cleaned,
   sliced (1 1/2 lb.)
1/3 cup dry white wine
16 roasted garlic cloves (techniques chapter)

Serves: 4
Complexity: •
Preparation Time: 25 Minutes
Italian Wine: Cortese Di Gavi,
Del Monferrato, fresh white,
fruity with a touch of bitterness
and well balanced.

Cut red snapper fillet into 2" x 3" pieces, 2" thick. Place on baking sheet and season with 1/2 teaspoon each of salt and pepper, 1/8 cup olive oil and dill. Coat fillets with mixture.

Place heavy cast iron skillet over medium heat. When pan is hot, place fillets, skin side up, in skillet and sear for 30 seconds on each side and remove.

In a rectangular baking dish, combine 1 cup olive oil, garlic, fennel, 1 teaspoon salt and 1 teaspoon pepper; mix well. Place snapper on bed of fennel and bake uncovered in oven preheated to 450 degrees, for 15 minutes.

Remove baking dish from oven, remove fish and set aside; place dish back over medium heat. Add white wine and roasted garlic cloves. When wine has completely reduced, remove from heat.

Serve snapper over a bed of fennel dressed with garlic sauce.

If you can get wild fennel, which grows in California, it will make the dish more interesting.

Salmone Alla Salsa Verde

Poached Salmon In Green Sauce

20 ounces salmon fillet, cut into 5-ounce fillets
2 Idaho potatoes, cleaned (1 1/2 lbs.)
8 cups dry white wine
6 tablespoons salt
2 1/2 cups green sauce (sauces chapter)

Serves: 4
Complexity: •
Preparation Time: 1 Hour, 12 Minutes
Italian Wine: Gavi Di Gavi,
White, one year old, well balanced
fruity and fresh.

Bake potatoes with skin on for 1 hour in 450 degree oven, or until fork inserts easily. Remove from oven and slice into 1 3/4" slices approximately 6 ounces each, leaving skin on.

Bring 4 cups of water, wine and salt to a boil and add salmon. Poach salmon in boiling water for 5 minutes and remove. To serve, place salmon over potato slice and top with green sauce.

Hallibut Al Forno Sul Ragu' Di Carciofi Stufati

Sauteed Fillet of Halibut with Artichoke Ragu

1 1/4 lbs. halibut (4-6 ounce fillets)

Marinade:
4 tablespoons fresh rosemary, chopped
2 garlic cloves, thinly sliced
1 teaspoon salt
1 teaspoon black pepper
1 cup olive oil

Ragu Sauce:
1 cup olive oil
16 fresh artichoke hearts, cleaned, sliced (techniques chapter)
4 garlic cloves, smashed, finely chopped
1 carrot, peeled, finely chopped (1 cup)
2 onions, peeled, finely chopped (2/3 cup)
2 cups dry white wine
1 teaspoon fresh thyme, chopped
1 ounce fresh Italian parsley, finely chopped
1 teaspoon salt
1 teaspoon black pepper
1 cup chicken stock (sauces chapter)

Serves: 4
Complexity: ••
Preparation Time: 45 Minutes
Italian Wine: Chardonnay,
Not in barrique, well balanced
and buttery.

Remove skin from halibut; place on baking pan and sprinkle marinade herbs over top, pour olive oil over halibut and herbs. Mix well to coat fillets evenly and allow to marinate for 20 minutes.

In medium sauce pan, saute olive oil, artichoke hearts and garlic over medium heat for 3-4 minutes. Add carrots and onions; saute for 1 minute and cover, bringing heat down to low. After 3 minutes, add white wine, thyme, parsley, salt and pepper. After 5 minutes, add chicken stock and continue to simmer for an additional 17 minutes.

Heat a heavy, cast iron skillet over medium heat. Place marinated fillets, skin side down, in heated pan. Sear the halibut, turning fillets quickly in pan to achieve a light, golden brown color on each side. Transfer fillets to another saucepan and add artichoke ragu. Seal pan with aluminum foil to keep steam from escaping from pan and place over low heat, cooking for 10 minutes.

To serve, place halibut on a bed of artichokes.

Ragu of artichoke can be served by itself as an appetizer or as a pasta sauce with penne or rigatoni. Make sure the pan is very hot when you saute the fish so it will achieve a nice golden crust on top..

Calamari "A Modo Mio"

Stuffed Squid "My Way"

8 squid, cleaned

Stuffing:
1/2 lb. shrimp
1/2 cup prepared porcini mushrooms (techniques chapter)
3 ounces sea scallops
1 teaspoon salt
1 teaspoon black pepper
1/4 cup olive oil
1 garlic clove, thinly sliced
1 cup dry white wine
1 lemon, sliced
quick tomato sauce (sauces chapter)

Serves: 4
Complexity: • • •
Preparation Time: 45 Minutes
Italian Wine: Chardonnay,
Not in barrique, well balanced
and buttery.

To prepare stuffing, combine all ingredients in blender and puree. Pour contents into a pastry tube.

Stuff cleaned squid tubes using pastry bag. Fill each tube about half full with stuffing as fish will shrink as it bakes. After each tube is filled, weave toothpick through top of tube to secure.

In a rectangular baking dish, pour olive oil and add garlic slices. Spread contents with hands to ensure that pan is evenly coated; lay squid in single layer along bottom of coated pan. Pour wine over top and place in preheated oven. Preheat over to 450 degrees. Bake for 15 minutes. Remove from oven and drain juices into small sauce pan and add lemon slices. Bring mixture to a boil over medium heat, 5 minutes. Remove and pass sauce through strainer, removing lemon. Place sauce back over medium heat. Cook for 2 minutes and remove. Add quick sauce and mix well.

Remove toothpick from squid and serve with sauce over each. If you purchase tubes with tentacles, decorate dish with tentacles.

To prepare tentacles for decoration to accompany dish, place in small stock pot. Cover tentacles with water. Add 1 1/2 teaspoons salt and the juice of one lemon. Bring to a boil for 20 minutes. Tentacles will be bright purple in color.

Stuff the calamari only half way; when it cooks, calamari will shrink and will break open. The ingredients can be chopped instead of pureed; but will have a different look and texture. It can be served as an appetizer or main course and is good served over seafood risotto. When buying calamari, make sure they are white and have no smell; meat must be firm. When poaching tentacles, after the water boils for the first time, drain and add fresh water with lemon juice and cook 20 minutes.

Trota Ripiena In Salsa Di Barbera

Stuffed Trout in Barbera Wine Sauce

4 trout fillets, cleaned,
   deboned, butterflied with skin on
1 1/2 teaspoons salt
1/2 teaspoon black pepper
12 fresh sage leaves, chopped
1/4 cup unsalted butter
2 shallots, peeled, sliced (1/2 cup)
2 cups Barbera wine (sauces chapter)
4 ounces fresh wild mushrooms (1/2 cup)
1/2 cup olive oil
2 fresh rosemary sprigs

Serves: 4
Complexity: ● ● ● ●
Preparation Time: 55 Minutes
Italian Wine: Barbera D'Asti,
Red, well balanced,
with a sharp, fruity edge.

Stuffing:
3/4 cup olive oil
3/4 cup pancetta, diced (6 ounces)
4 shallots, peeled, sliced (3/4 cup)
3 teaspoons fresh rosemary, chopped
1 lb. shiitake mushrooms, cleaned, sliced (5 1/4 cups)
1/2 teaspoon salt
1 teaspoon black pepper
2/3 cup Madeira wine
1 teaspoon dried marjoram
2 teaspoons tomato paste

To prepare stuffing, heat olive oil in a medium sauce pan over medium heat. When oil is hot, approximately 30 seconds, add pancetta, shallots and rosemary and saute for 2 minutes. Add mushrooms, pepper, salt, marjoram, tomato paste and Madeira; cook for 3 minutes and remove from heat.

Take uncooked fillets and sprinkle with sage and 1/2 teaspoon each of salt and pepper, on top of fillets only. Stuff fillet with stuffing mixture; fold fillet in half and set aside any extra stuffing. In a small, oven-proof saute pan, heat butter and shallots over low heat for 2 minutes and remove from heat, allowing mixture to cool. Place trout fillets in butter/ shallot mixture and add Barbera wine. Cover pan with aluminum foil, to keep steam from escaping, and cook over high heat, approximately 1 1/2 minutes, until wine comes to a boil. Remove from heat and place fish in original pan in preheated, 450 degree oven to bake for 10 minutes.

After 10 minutes, remove pan from oven; remove trout and set aside. Put pan back over high heat, adding extra stuffing. Cook until sauce loses strong alcohol taste, approximately 2 minutes. Remove from heat and pour contents of pan into blender; puree until smooth. The sauce should have a heavy, dense consistency. If it is too thick, place pureed mixture in saucepan and add chicken stock to dilute slightly.

In a separate sauce pan, saute wild mushrooms, 1 teaspoon salt and rosemary in olive oil over medium heat for 1 minute; remove rosemary sprigs. Peel skin from trout and place fillet over bed of sauteed mushrooms. Serve with barbera sauce.

You can peel the skin off the trout with a fork, being very careful so that the fish is smooth and white. This is a classic dish of Piedemont because it combines red wine with fish.

Cappesante Con Pancetta Al Balsamico

Pancetta Wrapped Sea Scallops in Balsamic Vinegar Sauce

12 seas scallops (3 ounces each)
12 strips pancetta
1 cup olive oil
4 bruciolo (techniques chapter)
1 teaspoon salt
1 cup balsamic vinegar
4 tablespoons veal reduction (sauces chapter)

Serves: 4
Complexity: ••
Preparation Time: 40 Minutes

Take each sea scallop and wrap one strip of pancetta around circumference, securing with toothpick.

In large saute pan, heat olive oil over high heat, adding salt and bruciolo. After 2 minutes, place scallops in pan, cooking 1 1/2 minutes on each side to brown lightly. When all scallops are evenly browned, place on baking sheet in oven preheated to 450 degrees; bake for 4 1/2 minutes. Remove scallops from oven and discard toothpicks.

Take saute pan and discard olive oil. Add balsamic vinegar and return pan to medium heat to deglaze. Heat until vinegar is reduced by half, stirring with wooden spoon to loosen any juices and meat particles. Add veal reduction and heat through, 1 minute. Remove from heat.

To serve, arrange scallops on plate and top with veal reduction sauce.

You can substitute pancetta with strips of bacon, but it will give dish a more smoky flavor.

Brodetto Aromatico Di Cappesante

Little Neck Clams in an Herbed Broth

60 littleneck clams, in shell
1 cup olive oil
4 garlic cloves, smashed
1 ounce fresh Italian parsley, chopped
1 ounce fresh basil, chopped
1 teaspoon freshly ground black pepper
1 cup dry white wine

Serves: 4
Complexity: •
Preparation Time: 25 Minutes
Italian Wine: Arneis,
White delicate, fresh
and strong herbal flavor.

In medium sauce pan, combine olive oil, garlic, parsley, basil and clams and cook over medium heat. When mixture comes to a boil, add white wine and pepper. Cover pan and allow mixture to cook over medium heat for 7 minutes. Remove from heat. Use only the clams with opened shells and discard others as they are unsafe for consumption.

Rotolo Di Salmone Alle Olive Nere

Sauteed Fillet of Salmon Over Swiss Chard in Black Olive Sauce

18 ounces salmon fillet, butterflied, bones and skin removed
1 shallot (1 1/2 ounces)
1 1/2 ounces porcini mushrooms
6 ounces black Calamata olives
1 1/4 cups olive oil
2 cups chicken stock (sauces chapter)
6 ounces plum tomatoes, peeled, seeded
3 tablespoons balsamic vinegar
1 1/4 teaspoons salt
1 1/4 teaspoons black pepper
1 teaspoon fresh rosemary, chopped
4 garlic cloves, smashed
12 ounces Swiss chard

Serves: 4
Complexity: • • •
Preparation Time: 45 Minutes,
12 Hours to Rest
Italian Wine: Chardonnay,
Not in barrique, well
balanced and buttery.

Take shallots and porcini mushrooms and saute in 2 tablespoons olive oil over medium heat for 4 minutes. Take sauteed mushrooms and shallots and place in blender with 2 tablespoons olive oil, olives, chicken stock, tomatoes and vinegar; puree until very smooth. Pour contents of blender into sauce pan and cook over medium heat for 5 minutes; remove from heat.

Take salmon fillet and butterfly meat. Sprinkle rosemary and 1/2 teaspoon each of salt and pepper evenly over fillet. Place one sheet of plastic wrap under and one sheet over salmon fillet and pound using meat mallet, or back of a heavy pan, to flatten meat. Tightly roll salmon, with plastic wrap still on, from side to side, creating a long, thin roll. Cover both ends with plastic wrap and store in refrigerator for 12 hours.

After 12 hours, remove salmon roll from refrigerator and cut into 2 1/2" slices, keeping plastic attached. In a large saute pan, heat 1/2 cup olive oil. When oil is hot, place salmon rolls, end side down, in pan to saute. When salmon is browned evenly on both ends, remove from pan and drain oil. Place salmon rolls back into pan and place in preheated oven. Bake for 7 minutes.

To prepare Swiss chard, wash like spinach leaves, removing stems and using only leaves. Set cleaned Swiss chard aside.

In a large saute pan, heat 1/2 cup olive oil over medium heat. Add garlic and saute until garlic becomes lightly browned. When garlic takes color, remove cloves and add Swiss chard, salt and pepper. Saute for 30 seconds and remove from heat.

After 7 minutes, remove salmon from oven and unwrap plastic wrap. Serve salmon over base of Swiss chard with Calamata olive sauce.

From the picture it may look like a difficult operation to prepare Swiss chard, but it is very easy. It is worth preparing because not only does it make a wonderful presentation at the table, it also tastes good. You can use a nice, round cut of fish instead of a fillet, if you desire.

Medaglioni Di Pesce Spada Con Peperonata E Bagna Cauda

Swordfish Medallions with Stewed Peppers

2 lbs. swordfish loin cut (4 1/2 lb. 1 1/2" fillets, 2" thick)

1/4 cup olive oil
4 tablespoons bagna cauda sauce (sauces chapter)

Marinade:
1 tablespoon fresh Italian parsley, chopped
1/2 teaspoon fresh tarragon, chopped
1/4 teaspoon fresh dill, chopped
1 tablespoon fresh basil, chopped
1/2 teaspoon fresh marjoram
1/2 teaspoon black pepper
1/2 teaspoon salt
1/2 cup olive oil

Serves: 4
Complexity: • •
Preparation Time: 35 Minutes,
2 Hours for Marinade
Italian Wine: Grignolino,
Dry red with a slightly bitter finish.

Pepperonata/Stewed Peppers:
1 onion, peeled, chopped (1 cup)
3 red peppers, cleaned, deveined, chopped (2 1/2 cups)
3 yellow peppers, cleaned, deveined, chopped (2 1/2 cups)
1/4 cup olive oil
3 fresh thyme sprigs, leaves only
1 garlic clove, smashed
1 teaspoon salt
1 teaspoon black pepper
1 teaspoon sugar
2 dried bay leaves
5 plum tomatoes, blanched, seeded, quartered (approximately 1 lb.)

To prepare swordfish, remove fat and skin from fillets. Mix marinade ingredients and pour over fillets in a rectangular dish. Cover and allow fish to marinate for 2 hours in the refrigerator.

To make pepperonata, heat olive oil in a large sauce pan; when oil is heated, add onions, thyme and garlic. Cook over high heat until onions become translucent. Add peppers, bay leaves, salt, pepper and sugar. Cover pan and reduce heat to low. After 13 minutes, add tomatoes and continue to cook mixture for an additional 3 minutes. Remove from heat.

Heat olive oil over medium heat in large, oven-proof saute pan. When oil is hot, add marinated swordfish, lightly browning each side, approximately 2 minutes each side. Remove from heat and place pan in oven preheated to 450 degrees; bake swordfish for 20 minutes.

To serve, place swordfish over bed of pepperonata and crown each fillet with 1 tablespoon of warmed bagna cauda sauce. The pepperonata can be served as a vegetable side dish with many recipes. It is a wonderful complement to pork dishes.

Merluzzo Al Verde

Dry Cod in a Green Herb Sauce

1 1/4 lbs. dry cod
1 1/4 cup olive oil
1 cup all purpose flour
1 ounce fresh spinach, cleaned
1 ounce Swiss chard, cleaned
1 ounce whole fresh Italian parsley
1 ounce fresh Italian parsley, finely chopped
2 yellow peppers, cleaned, deveined, rough cut (7 ounces)
4 leeks, white stems only, cleaned, rough cut (4 ounces)
1 1/2 ounces celery leaves, cleaned
1 tablespoon garlic, chopped
4 fresh sage leaves, finely chopped
1 cup tomato puree
1 tablespoon capers
1 cup milk
1/2 teaspoon black pepper
1 teaspoon salt
polenta (techniques chapter)

Serves: 4
Complexity: • •
Preparation Time: 20 Minutes,
24 Hours for Soaking
Italian Wine: Pinot Bianco,
Dry white, very austere,
good with the tomato.

Dry cod is packaged in its own salt. Before working with the fish, soak in cold water for 24 hours to eliminate or reduce some of the salt.

Take dry cod fillets and coat in thin layer of flour. In a large, non-stick saute pan, heat 1 cup olive oil. When oil is hot, add fish fillets and saute until lightly browned on both sides. Remove and place on baking sheet layered with paper towels to absorb oil.

Thoroughly wash spinach and Swiss chard and leaves, removing stems. In food processor, combine spinach, Swiss chard, whole parsley, yellow pepper, leeks, celery leaves and 1/8 cup olive oil; puree until smooth.

In a large sauce pan, heat 1/2 cup olive oil over medium-high heat. When oil is hot, add chopped garlic, chopped parsley and sage; after 30 seconds, add pureed vegetable mixture. Place fish fillets into pan and add tomato puree, capers and milk and cook for 30 seconds. Add salt and pepper and turn heat to low, simmering mixture. After 8 minutes, turn fillets. Cook for an additional 4 minutes and remove from heat.

Serve cod over 2 cakes of polenta, garnished with sauce.

Dried cod is packaged in salt. You can also buy cod stocafisso, just air dried with no salt, or use fresh cod fish for the recipe. If using dry cod, if you do not set under running cold water for 24 hours, at least soak fish in water for 24 hours and place in the refrigerator until ready to use.

Tonno Ai Porcini Con Salsa Di Barbaresco

Sauteed Tuna With Porcini Mushrooms In Barbaresco Wine Sauce

2 lbs. tuna cut into 4 equal cubes, approximately 2"x 2"
3/4 lb. prepared porcini mushrooms (techniques chapter)
8 fresh anchovy fillets or 4 salted anchovies
1 1/2 tablespoon fresh rosemary, chopped
1 teaspoon salt
1 teaspoon black pepper
3/4 cup olive oil
1 1/2 cup Barbaresco sauce (sauces chapter)
1 bruciolo
3 shallots, sliced (1/2 cup)
1/2 ounce fresh Italian parsley, chopped
3/4 cup Barbaresco wine

Serves: 4
Complexity: ● ● ● ●
Preparation Time: 35 Minutes
Italian Wine: Barbaresco,
Four years old, dry red, full body,
plenty of acidity and well balanced.

To prepare tuna, take fillet and remove dark burgundy area, or bloodline, which contains impurities from fish and can alter taste of the meat. Trim the tuna into equal cubes or leave fillet whole, according to preference. Using a boning knife, make 8 pockets in fish, inserting knife, straight down into fillet. The pocket should be the length and width of the knife's blade. Take anchovies and make a center cut through each. Pull out the bones and separate the two fillets. Take all 8 fillets and stuff into pockets in tuna meat.

Place the stuffed fillets on a baking sheet and sprinkle with salt, pepper, rosemary and 1/2 cup olive oil. Roll each fillet in mixture to coat evenly with herbs and oil. Allow tuna to marinate for 20 minutes.

In a large saute pan, heat olive oil and rosemary/garlic clove for one minute over medium heat. Remove garlic and rosemary. Add tuna fillets and saute, turning until they are browned lightly on all sides, approximately 45 seconds each side; drain oil from pan and set tuna fillets aside.

In the same sauce pan, saute shallots and porcini mushrooms in 1/4 cup olive oil over medium heat for 2 1/2 minutes, or until mushrooms begin to brown. Add Barbaresco wine, let reduce completely and put tuna fillets back in pan over low heat with Barbaresco sauce; cover pan. Cook for 2 minutes, tuna will be cooked medium-rare.

Serve tuna with Barbaresco and mushroom sauce.

Filletto Di Branzino Ai Pomodori Arrostiti

Fillet of Sea Bass with Oven-Roasted Tomato

20 ounces sea bass
1/2 teaspoon salt
1/2 teaspoon black pepper

Marinade:
4 tablespoons olive oil
12 fresh thyme sprigs

Oven Roasted Tomato Sauce:
8 oven roasted tomatoes, quartered (techniques chapter)
20 fresh basil leaves, finely chopped
2 ounces Calamata olives, pitted, quartered
1/4 cup olive oil
2 cloves garlic, thinly sliced
1/4 teaspoon salt
1/4 teaspoon black pepper

Serves: 4
Complexity: • • •
Preparation Time: 1 Hour , 30 Minutes
Italian Wine: Pinot Bianco,
Dry white, very austere,
good with tomato.

Mix marinade in medium mixing bowl and marinate bass for 1 hour.

Mix sauce ingredients and let set for 20 minutes.

Remove fillets and thyme from marinade and set on baking sheet. Sprinkle with salt, pepper. Pour olive oil from marinade over top. Remove from baking sheet, one at a time, and saute fillets in a heated cast iron skillet, 20 seconds on each side. Remove from skillet and place back on original baking sheet. Bake in preheated oven for 4 minutes. Remove from oven and place fillets on baking sheet layered with paper towels to absorb oil.

Place tomato mixture over low heat to warm.

To serve, place fillets over bed of dried tomato mixture with olives.

Cozze Ripiene Ai Vegetali Con Zafferano

Stuffed Mussels In Saffron Vegetable Sauce

2 lbs. mussels in shell (48 mussels)
4 shallots, peeled, sliced (4 ounces)
2 cups dry white wine

Stuffing:
1 1/4 lbs. button mushrooms, cleaned (6 3/4 cups)
1 1/2 lbs. shallots, peeled, chopped (4 3/4 cups)
1 cup olive oil
2 tablespoons salt
2 tablespoons black pepper

Sauce:
4 carrots, peeled, finely chopped (2 cups)
8 celery stalks, cleaned, finely chopped (2 cups)
4 yellow peppers, cleaned, de-veined, finely chopped (2 cups)
4 red peppers, cleaned, deveined, finely chopped (2 cups)
4 zucchini, cleaned, finely chopped (4 cups)
6 shallots, peeled, finely chopped (2 cups)
8 fresh thyme sprigs, leaves only
2 teaspoons saffron threads
4 cups dry white wine
4 cups chicken stock (sauces chapter)
4 cups scallop broth (sauces chapter)
1 cup olive oil

Serves: 4
Complexity: • • • •
Preparation Time: 1 Hour
Italian Wine: Chardonnay,
Not in barrique, well
balanced and buttery.

To prepare mussels, place mussels in large stock pot. Add white wine, and 4 shallots, and cook over high heat until mussels open, approximately 2 minutes. Remove from heat; mussels are cooked. Discard those which still have a closed shell as they are unsafe to eat. Filter broth and set aside.

To prepare stuffing, heat olive oil in a medium saute pan over medium heat. When oil is hot, add shallots and saute for 2 minutes. Add mushrooms, salt and pepper and saute until mushrooms sweat, approximately 2 minutes. Remove pan from heat and pour contents into food processor. Puree until smooth. Take open steamed mussels and stuff each with stuffing mixture; tie each shell securely closed with cooking twine.

In a medium sauce pan, heat olive oil and add carrots, celery and shallots; saute for 4 minutes. Add thyme, saffron, half of filtered broth from steamed mussels and 4 cups white wine. Allow to cook for 12 minutes, then add peppers, zucchini, chicken stock and scallop broth.

Place stuffed and tied mussels inside pot with sauce and cook for 15 minutes over medium heat. Remove from heat and cut twine from each mussel.

Serve mussels in shell over bed of vegetable mixture.

Gamberetti Alla "Santarelli"

Sauteed Shrimp "Santarelli" Style

2 lbs. shrimp in shells, heads on
1 cup olive oil
5 ounces unsalted butter, sliced in 1/4" pieces
4 garlic cloves, smashed
4 lemons, thinly sliced

Sauce:
1 1/2 teaspoons salt
3 teaspoons black pepper
1 teaspoon Hungarian paprika
3 teaspoons Tabasco sauce
1 tablespoon dried, red hot, crushed pepper flakes

Serves: 4
Complexity: •
Preparation Time: 10 Minutes
Italian Wine: Chardonnay,
Not in barrique, well balanced
and buttery.

In a large saute pan, saute garlic in heated olive oil, over medium-high heat for 2 minutes. Add butter, cook for 1 minute, then add lemons. After 30 seconds, add shrimp and sauce ingredients. Cook over medium heat for an additional 2 1/2 minutes. Remove from heat and serve.

I want to thank Senor Santarelli for showing me this recipe at the beginning when opening Galileo; I thank him for the wonderful days we spent talking about food, and I appreciate his support and respect his knowledge about Italian cuisine. That is why I dedicate this dish to him.

Seppie Al Nero

Cuttlefish In Black Sauce

2 lbs. cuttlefish fillets, julienned
3/4 cup olive oil
1 onion, peeled, finely chopped (2 cups)
2 celery stalks, cleaned, finely chopped (1 cup)
1 carrot, peeled, finely chopped (1 cup)
4 garlic cloves, smashed
2 cups tomato puree
2 tablespoons basil puree (techniques chapter)
2 tablespoons black ink from cuttlefish

Serves: 4
Complexity: • •
Preparation Time: 35 Minutes
Italian Wine: Arneis,
White delicate fresh and
strong herbal flavor.

Heat olive oil in a large saucepan over high heat. Add onion, celery, carrots and garlic and reduce heat to low; saute mixture. After 7 1/2 minutes, add tomato puree and basil puree; mix well, cooking for 1 minute. Add cuttlefish and cover pan. After 25 minutes, add black ink. Increase heat to medium and remove lid; bring mixture to a boil. After it reaches the boiling point, remove from heat and serve. If the sauce is too thin, puree vegetable in the sauce.

Razza Al Barolo Con La Testa Di Portobello Al Forno

Skate Wing with Portobello Mushroom In Barolo Wine Sauce

2 lbs. skate wing

Marinade:
1/2 cup olive oil
1 teaspoon fresh thyme, chopped
2 teaspoons fresh rosemary, chopped

4 portobello mushrooms, cleaned (1 1/4 lbs.)
2 teaspoons salt
2 teaspoons black pepper
8 teaspoons fresh parsley, chopped
4 tablespoons basil puree (techniques chapter)
4 garlic cloves, smashed, finely chopped
1 cup olive oil
1/2 cup unsalted butter
1 cup Barolo sauce (sauces chapter)

Serves: 4
Complexity: •••
Preparation Time: 35 Minutes
Italian Wine: Barilot,
Red full body, a blend of
barbera grape and nebbiolo.

To prepare skate fish, peel off outer layer of skin; cut center piece into 2 pieces. Take fish fillets and season with 1 teaspoon each of salt and pepper, coating all sides of fish evenly. Set skate fish aside.

To prepare marinade, combine olive oil, thyme and rosemary. Place fish in marinade and allow to set for 20 minutes.

To prepare mushrooms, take mushrooms and remove stems. The stems can be used in stuffing or as flavoring for stocks. To clean mushrooms, use a damp towel to wipe only the top of the mushrooms. Do not immerse in water. If water gets to the underside of mushrooms it will be absorbed, making the mushrooms soggy. Using a sharp, thin-blade knife, make eight 3/4" incisions into the underside of mushrooms. This will allow them to soak up the oil and herbs, giving them rich flavor.

Take mushrooms and sprinkle undersides with 1 teaspoon of salt and pepper. Place in baking dish, underside up. In a separate bowl, combine parsley, basil puree, garlic, olive oil and butter. Pour mixture over top of mushrooms. Place under broiler for 6 minutes.

Heat a heavy cast iron skillet over medium heat. When pan is hot, add fillets, along with marinade and saute until browned lightly on both sides, cooking approximately 1 minute each side.

Remove fillets and place on baking sheet coated with olive oil. Bake in preheated oven, at 400 degrees, for 8 minutes. Heat Barolo sauce in small sauce pan over medium low heat.

After fish is baked, remove from oven and, using a sharp knife, carefully cut fillets away from bone. Serve over roasted portobello mushrooms and top with Barolo sauce.

Stufato D'Aragosta E Polipo Al Tartufo Nero

Lobster and Octopus Stewed with Black Truffle

1 1/2 lbs. octopus, cleaned
5 teaspoons salt
1/3 cup red wine vinegar
2 lobsters, steamed (1-2 pounds each, techniques chapter)
24 asparagus spears
5 shallots, peeled, chopped (1 1/8 cups)
4 garlic cloves, smashed
8 plum tomatoes, peeled, seeded, halved (24 ounces)
4 teaspoons fresh thyme, chopped
1 ounce whole black truffle, thinly sliced
1 cup black truffle juice
1 cup olive oil
2 teaspoons salt
1 cup dry white wine
1 1/3 cups lobster stock (sauces chapter)
1 wine bottle cork

Serves: 6
Complexity: ● ● ●
Preparation Time: 1 Hour
Italian Wine: Arneis,
White, delicate, fresh
and strong herbal flavor.

To prepare octopus, place cleaned octopus in large stock pot and cover with water; add 3 teaspoons salt and wine vinegar. To tenderize the octopus, place a wine cork in the water. Place over high heat until mixture comes to a boil. After it reaches the boiling point, reduce heat to medium and simmer for 20 minutes. Remove pot from heat and allow octopus to sit in water until water has completely cooled, this will allow octopus to continue to cook while cooling. When octopus is cooled, remove tentacles. Take octopus and slice thinly. Take lobster claw and lobster tail meat and set aside with octopus.

Wash asparagus spears; cut off bottom 2 inches of spears, cutting remaining stems into 1/4 inch pieces. Set aside.

In a medium saute pan, heat olive oil first, adding garlic, shallots, thyme, truffles and salt. Saute over medium heat for 30 seconds. Add white wine and continue to cook over medium heat until wine reduces by half its original amount. Add lobster and octopus meat, asparagus, tomatoes and black truffle juice. Add lobster stock and cook until liquid has reduced by half, approximately 2 minutes. Add 2 1/2 tablespoons olive oil. Mix well and serve.

Branzino Al Sale
Salt Baked Rockfish

4 lbs. rockfish, cleaned, scaled with heads (4-1 lb. fish)
12 lbs. rock salt
1 1/2 cups water
2 teaspoons black pepper
1 ounce fresh dill
1 ounce fresh mint
1 ounce fresh basil

Salmoriglio Sauce:
1 cup olive oil
1/2 teaspoon salt
1/2 teaspoon black pepper
1/4 cup lemon juice
1 teaspoon dried oregano
2 tablespoons fresh mint, chopped
2 tablespoons fresh Italian parsley, chopped

Serves: 4
Complexity: ••
Preparation Time: 45 Minutes
Italian Wine: Gavi Di Gavi,
white, full and fruity.

Take each fish and sprinkle inside with pepper; divide dill, mint and basil, placing 1/4" ounce of each herb inside each fish.

Mix salt and water in mixing bowl, using hands, until mixture achieves a thick, pasty consistency. In a large, heavy casserole dish, cover bottom of pan with 1/4" of rock salt paste. Place fish on top of salt bed and cover with remaining salt paste, completely covering each fish. Bake in preheated oven, at 400 degrees uncovered for 30 minutes.

Meanwhile, in a medium mixing bowl, combine sauce ingredients and mix well using a whisk. Set aside.

When fish is baked, remove from oven. Remove each fish from salt. Take the fish and remove the skin, head and herb stuffing from inside. Be careful not to place any salt on fish meat.

To serve, place fillet on plate and top with sauce.

This recipe is one of my specialties. Make sure to pack down salt over fish so it does not crack when it cooks. Check fish every 10 minutes. When it begins to cook making sure there are no cracks. If there are, apply more of the salt paste and pack down well. Clean the fish very carefully, breaking off the salt crust, then brush away excess salt. Place on a clean dish before peeling away skin with fork.

Spiedino Di Cozze "Alla Ted"

Mussel Skewers "Ted" Style

3 lbs. mussels (approximately 78 mussels)
4 shallots, peeled, sliced (4 ounces)
2 cups dry white wine
4-8" skewers (soak wooden skewers in water for 2 hours)

Breading:
1 cup unseasoned bread crumbs
1 teaspoon dried marjoram
1 teaspoon garlic, chopped
1 1/2 teaspoons dried oregano
2 tablespoons fresh Italian parsley, chopped
1/2 teaspoon dried red hot crushed pepper flakes
1/4 cup olive oil
1/2 teaspoon salt
1/2 teaspoon black pepper
6 fresh basil leaves, finely chopped

Serves: 4
Complexity: ••
Preparation Time: 25 Minutes
2 Hours for Marinade
Italian Wine: Gavi Di Gavi,
White, one year old,
well balanced, fruity and fresh.

To prepare mussels, place mussels in large stock pot. Add white wine, shallots, and cook over high heat until shells open, approximately 2 minutes. Remove from heat; mussels are cooked. Discard those which still have a closed shell as they are unsafe to eat.

Remove mussel meat from opened shell and place approximately 18 mussels on an 8" skewer. Make sure to pierce mussel meat in the center and compact mussels as you assemble on skewer. Assemble four skewers and set aside.

In a medium mixing bowl, combine breading ingredients, mixing well. Place skewers in bread crumb mixture, one at a time, and coat evenly pressing mixture to mussels to achieve a thin layer of coating.

Place skewers on a preheated grill and cook for 2 1/2 minutes on each side. If using wooden skewers, soak in water for 2 hours, before assembling, to keep skewers from burning.

I included this recipe in the book because Ted really likes it and I couldn't avoid putting it in the book; actually, I personally like it too. This recipe is dedicated to Ted because he shows so much interest and energy and happiness when I prepare this dish for him. I have to call it "spiedino alla Ted."

This recipe can be used as a main course or can be adapted as a soup if you do not stuff the mussels. Make the broth as the recipe indicates and serve with fresh mussels.

Dentice Brasato Ai Funghi Selvaggi
Braised Grouper with Mushrooms

4 12 ounce grouper fillets
1/2 lb. shiitake mushrooms, cleaned, sliced (3 ounces)
1/2 lb. portobello mushrooms, cleaned, sliced (3 ounces)
1/2 lb. button mushrooms, cleaned, sliced (3 ounces)
1/2 lb. chanterelle mushrooms, cleaned, sliced (3 ounces)
2 garlic cloves, halved
1/2 cup olive oil
2 tablespoons fresh sage, chopped
2 tablespoons fresh rosemary, chopped
2 cups dry white wine
2 cups chicken stock (sauces chapter)
1/2 teaspoon salt
1/2 teaspoon black pepper

Serves: 4
Complexity: •
Preparation Time: 20 Minutes
Italian Wine: Gavi Di Gavi,
White, one year old,
well balanced, fruity and fresh.

Season grouper fillets with salt and pepper, coating evenly on both sides; set aside.

In a large saute pan, heat olive oil and garlic over medium heat until garlic is lightly browned; add mushrooms, sage and rosemary. Saute for 2 minutes and add wine and chicken stock. Bring mixture to a boil; remove from heat and add grouper. Place pan in preheated oven, baking for 10 1/2 minutes. Serve grouper over bed of mushroom medley.

pollame e volatili

We use all feather birds in this chapter. I suggest purchasing farm-raised chicken over store-bought chicken because farm-raised chickens have better flavor and less fat. Farm-raised chickens are not yellow like store-bought chickens because they eat a much better diet. When you buy the chicken, press down underneath the wing with your finger; if it is tender there, then the meat will be very juicy. If it is firm or dry, the chicken will be tough or dry. Make sure all birds are washed inside and out before use with running cold water and then pat dry with a towel. It is always better to cook meat on the bone unless the recipe calls for another preparation.

I would like to thank D'Artagnan, Inc. in New York for importing wild game like pheasant, partridge and squab. They are much like the birds we get in Italy. We have duck legs and chicken legs in this book because I want people to buy more than just breast meat; you can buy legs and prepare a beautiful dish. I did not include a recipe for Chicken Marengo because while most people see it as a traditional Italian dish, I wanted to leave room for some new dishes that people may not be familiar with.

Cosce D'Anatra Alla Vercellese

Duck Leg "Vercelli" Style

4 duck legs, deboned (9 ounces each)
1 ounce whole black truffle
1 piece caul fat

Stuffing:
12 ounces pancetta
16 ounces veal
1/2 cup Madeira wine
2 teaspoons salt
2 teaspoons black pepper

Serves: 4
Complexity: ● ● ● ●
Preparation Time: 1 Hour, 50 Minutes
Italian Wine: Sizzano,
Red, four or five years old with a
ruby color with enough acid to cut
the fat of the dish.

1/2 cup olive oil
28 cippolini onions, 16 ounces (vegetables chapter)
2 ounces salted pork, cubed (techniques chapter)
4 garlic cloves, smashed
4 tablespoons fresh Italian parsley, chopped
4 cups dry white wine
3 teaspoons sugar
1 cup balsamic vinegar
1 cup veal reduction (sauces chapter)

To prepare stuffing, grind veal and pancetta using meat grinding attachment on mixer or use hand grinder. Combine ground meat with salt, pepper and Madeira. Mix well with hands.

Take duck legs and season inside with a pinch of salt and pepper; insert 1/4 ounce black truffle inside each; stuff each leg with stuffing mixture and wrap leg with caul fat. Set aside.

In a large, oven-proof sauce pan, heat olive oil over medium heat. When oil is hot, place duck legs, seam-side down in pan; add salted pork. Saute for 2 minutes and add, onions, garlic and parsley; cook an additional 3 minutes. Add wine, cover and remove from heat. Place in oven preheated to 400 degrees and bake for 30 minutes.

After 30 minutes, remove pan from oven and place duck and onions aside. Place pan back over medium heat and reduce for 10 minutes. Remove pan from heat and pour contents through strainer. Discard fat and cooked herbs; reserving juice. Combine parsley, sugar, balsamic vinegar, veal reduction and cippolini; heat until warmed through.

Serve duck legs with cippolini onions and balsamic vinegar sauce.

Petto Di Piccione Impanato Con Zucchine Al Balsamico

Fried Breast of Squab

12 boneless, skinless squab breasts
1 cup all purpose flour
1 egg, beaten
1 1/2 cups unseasoned bread crumbs

Zucchini tart:
2 zucchini, sliced thinly in rounds (12 ounces)
2 garlic cloves, halved
2 tablespoons olive oil
4 tablespoons balsamic vinegar

4 tablespoons squab reduction (sauces chapter)
1 pinch salt
1 pinch black pepper
1 cup olive oil
1 bruciolo (techniques chapter)

Serves: 4
Complexity: ● ● ●
Preparation Time: 1 Hour, 35 Minutes
Italian Wine: Barolo,
Red, five or six years old with
enough fruitiness remaining.

To prepare squab breasts, season each breast lightly with a pinch of salt and pepper. Lay breasts in flour, then dip in egg, then transfer to bread crumbs, coating evenly with breading. Set breaded breasts aside.

To prepare zucchini tarts, use a 7 1/2" non-stick saute pan. Rub bottom of pan with half garlic clove, cut side down. Layer zucchini slices in single layer in bottom of pan, cover 1/4 pan completely; season with pinch of salt and pepper. Place pan over medium heat; drizzle a teaspoon of olive oil over top and cook zucchini on one side, for 1 1/2 minutes. Carefully slide the tart from the saute pan onto an oiled baking pan, large enough to hold 4 tarts. Bake tarts in oven preheated to 400 degrees for 6 minutes.

In a medium saute pan, heat olive oil with bruciolo over medium heat. When oil is hot, add breaded squab breast, reducing heat to low. Saute each breast for 1 minute on each side. Remove from pan one at a time and place on baking sheet. Bake for 3 minutes.

Remove zucchini tarts from oven after 6 minutes and drizzle 1 tablespoon balsamic vinegar over each tart. Place back in oven and bake for 1 minute.

Place squab reduction in small sauce pan; heat until sauce reaches a boil and remove from heat.

To serve, place zucchini tart on serving plate, top with squab and pour squab reduction around tart.

I use only squab breast for this recipe but you can take the legs and stuff with sausage and saute with salt, black pepper and hot pepper to serve as appetizer or finger food; can use the bones to make squab glaze for soup

Pollo Arrostito Con L'Uva

Roasted Chicken with Grape Sauce

1 whole roaster chicken, cleaned (6 lb.)
1 teaspoon salt
1 teaspoon black pepper
3 garlic cloves
1 fresh rosemary sprig
3 fresh sage leaves
2 dried bay leaves
1/2 cup olive oil

Stuffing:
7 ounces chicken liver
1/2 cup unsalted butter
3 ounces salted pork (techniques chapter)
2 onions, peeled, finely chopped (1 1/2 cups)
1 ounce fresh Italian parsley

Serves: 4
Complexity: • •
Preparation Time: 1 Hour, 30 Minutes
Italian Wine: Barolo,
Red, five or six years old with
enough fruitiness.

Sauce:
1 onion, peeled, finely chopped (1/2 cup)
1 carrot, peeled, finely chopped (1/2 cup)
1/3 cup olive oil
2 garlic cloves
2 cloves
1 1/2 tablespoons, fresh Italian parsley, chopped
1 1/2 cups chicken stock (sauces chapter)
2 egg yolks
1/2 cup heavy whipping cream
4 ounces peeled white grapes

To prepare chicken, wash inside and outside of bird and dry thoroughly. Season inside of chicken with 1/2 teaspoon salt and peppers. Place garlic cloves, rosemary, sage and bay leaves inside chicken. Set chicken aside.

To prepare stuffing, combine ingredients in food processor and puree until smooth. Pour contents into pastry bag; stuff chicken with stuffing mixture. Using cooking twine, tie chicken legs together, then wrap twine around base of chicken, securely wrapping bird. Using remaining 1/2 teaspoon each of salt and pepper, season outside of chicken; place on baking pan and coat evenly with olive oil, including base. Bake in oven preheated to 400 degrees oven 1 hour and 10 minutes. Baste with juices in pan every 10 minutes, as chicken bakes.

To prepare sauce, combine onions, carrots, olive oil, garlic, cloves and parsley in medium sauce pan and cover; saute over low heat for 12 minutes. Add chicken stock and cook 8 minutes. Remove sauce from heat, remove cloves and pour contents into blender; puree until smooth. Place pureed mixture back into pan and add egg yolks and cream; place over medium heat and mix well with a whisk. Allow mixture to come to a boil and remove from heat when the sauce will coat the back of a spoon; add grapes and mix well. Remove chicken from oven and carve meat. Serve chicken topped with grape sauce and spoon stuffing on the side.

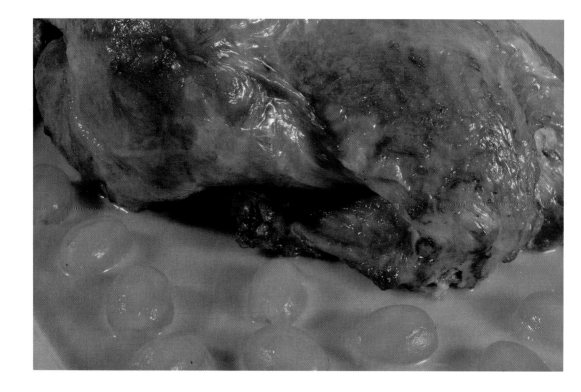

Bocconcini Di Pollo Alla Grappa

Chicken With Grappa

1 whole roasting chicken, cleaned
3 ounces pork sausage link, cut into 1/2" pieces
3 gold potatoes, diced 1/2" thick (6 ounces)
1/4 cup olive oil
3 fresh rosemary sprigs
2 garlic cloves
1 cup chicken stock (sauces chapter)
2 ounces grappa
3 ounces veal reduction (sauces chapter)

Serves: 4
Complexity: •
Preparation Time: 1 Hour, 25 Minutes
Italian Wine: Barbera Del Monferrato, Red, one or two years young full of tannin, refreshing.

Take chicken and split legs, breasts, and thighs into 2" pieces. Heat large sauce pan over medium heat and add olive oil. When oil is heated through, add chicken, potatoes and sausage; saute 6 minutes. Add herbs and garlic, saute until chicken becomes light brown in color. Add chicken stock, a bit at a time to keep pan from burning. Cover and place pan in preheated 350 degree oven for 9 minutes.

Remove pan from oven and place back over heat. Add grappa and allow to reduce by half. Add veal reduction and cook for 10 minutes and remove mixture from heat and spoon onto serving plates.

Quaglie Ripiene Al Fegato D'Anatra

Stuffed Quail with Duck Liver

8 semi-boneless quail
1/2 cup olive oil

Marinade:
4 pinches salt
4 pinches black pepper
2 teaspoons fresh sage, chopped
2 teaspoons fresh rosemary, chopped
1/2 cup Madeira wine

Serves: 4
Complexity: • • •
Preparation Time: 1 Hour, 45 Minutes
2 Hours for marinade
Italian Wine: Carema,
Red ruby color with orange reflecting
in the color, light rose perfume.

Stuffing:
2 boneless, skinless chicken breasts (16 ounces)
8 ounces duck liver
1 cup heavy whipping cream
3 egg whites
1 teaspoon salt
1 teaspoon black pepper
black truffle sauce (sauces chapter)

Place marinade ingredients in baking pan; season quail with salt and pepper and place in marinade; allow to marinate for 2 hours in the refrigerator.

To prepare stuffing, combine chicken breast and duck liver in food processor; blend well and add cream and egg whites; continue to blend until ingredients are incorporated well. Add salt and pepper and blend again until smooth; do not over mix.

Remove quail from marinade and stuff inside of each bird. Set stuffed birds aside.

Heat olive oil in oven-proof saute pan over medium heat. Place stuffed birds in hot oil and saute until golden brown on each side, adjust seasoning with a pinch of salt and pepper, if desired. Remove pan from heat and place in preheated 400 degree oven. Bake quail for 10 minutes.

Remove and serve quail with prepared black truffle sauce.

Hector Guerra, who worked with me for 5 years, previously worked for Yannick Cam, a French chef in Washington D.C. Hector showed me this recipe for stuffing.. I want to thank Hector and Yannick for it. When making stuffing, put an ice cube in the stuffing to keep it cold. It will make stuffing soft and airy and will prevent it from breaking down with the cream. Do not stuff bird too full, as stuffing will expand inside bird as it cooks.

Pernice Al Forno Con La Salsa Di Fegato D'Anatra

Wild Partridge with Duck Liver Sauce

4 whole partridge, cleaned, reserve livers and hearts (1 lb. each)
4 bruciolo (techniques chapter)
8 fresh sage leaves
8 fresh thyme sprigs
1/2 cup olive oil
1 teaspoon salt
1 teaspoon black pepper
1 cup duck liver sauce (sauces chapter)

Serves: 4
Complexity: ••
Preparation Time: 1 Hour, 25 Minutes
Italian Wine: Barberesco,
At least 6 years old, fully developed
to meet the red meat of
the partridge.

Clean partridge and remove livers and hearts, set aside for use in sauce. Take partridge and insert into each bird, 1 bruciolo, 2 sage leaves and 2 thyme sprigs. Season inside and outside of birds evenly with salt and pepper. Set aside.

In a large, oven-proof sauce pan, heat olive oil; place partridge in hot oil and brown both sides, approximately 3 minutes. Remove pan from heat and cover. Place in preheated 400 degree oven and bake for 13 minutes. Remove birds from pan and set aside.

Place pan back over medium heat and add duck liver sauce; chop partridge livers and hearts; add to sauce. Bring mixture to a boil and remove from heat.

To serve, slice partridge into quarters; serve 2 breasts and 2 wings, topped with duck liver sauce.

Wild partridge is dark meat; regular partridge (white meat) can be used as well, however it should be cooked medium-rare or the meat will be dry. The legs will take longer to cook than the breast on the white partridge. After the breast meat is cooked, pull off breast meat and set aside. Place the carcass with legs back in the oven to bake for an additional 3 minutes.

Petto Di Tacchino Farcito

Stuffed Breast of Turkey

1 turkey breast, butterflied (16 ounces)
1/2 teaspoon salt
1/2 teaspoon black pepper
1/2 teaspoon fresh thyme, chopped
3 1/2 ounces prosciutto, thinly sliced

Crepes:
1 onion, peeled, finely chopped (1 cup)
4 tablespoons olive oil
2 eggs
1 tablespoon basil puree (sauces chapter)
3/4 teaspoon salt
3/4 teaspoon black pepper

4 ounces salted pork, diced
(techniques chapter)
1 bruciolo (techniques chapter)
1 1/2 cups dry white wine
1 lb. button mushrooms, sliced
2 cups Madeira wine
1 cup veal reduction (sauces chapter)

Serves: 4
Complexity: • • •
Preparation Time: 1 Hour, 40 Minutes
Italian Wine: Barolo,
Red, at least ten years old in order
to be velvety with a full bouquet.

Place butterflied turkey breast, opened, over long sheet of plastic wrap, fold sheet of plastic over top of turkey, so meat is in between 2 plastic sheets. Pound with meat mallet until turkey is approximately 8" x 10" and 1/4" thick. Season with salt, pepper and thyme. Place prosciutto slices over top.

To make crepes, saute onions in 2 tablespoons olive oil over low heat for 10 minutes; remove from heat and allow to cool. Combine cooled onion mixture, salt, pepper, eggs and basil puree in mixing bowl; mix well until ingredients are blended.

Heat an 11 1/2" non-stick saute pan over medium heat. The size of pan is important to achieve correct size for finished crepe. Add 2 tablespoons olive oil and allow oil to heat through. When oil is hot, add egg mixture, turning pan to coat evenly. Cook each side for 40 seconds and place lightly browned crepe on top of prosciutto layer. Starting on one side, roll turkey, width to width, using plastic to pull roll. When turkey is completely rolled, tie with twine (techniques chapter). Season roll with 1/2 teaspoon each of salt and pepper. Set roll aside.

In a medium stock pot, place salted pork and bruciolo. Saute over medium heat for 30 seconds and add turkey roll. Saute until roll is evenly browned. Add white wine and cover pot. Transfer to oven preheated to 400 degrees and bake for 27 minutes.

After turkey is baked, remove from oven and set roll aside. Place pan back over medium heat and add Madeira wine; when wine has reduced by half, add veal reduction. Cook for 1 minute and remove from heat.

Cut twine from roll and slice. To serve, place turkey roll slices on bed of Madeira sauce.

In place of the Madeira wine sauce, saute 1 lb. of button mushrooms in 1/4 cup olive oil for 30 seconds; add 3 cups tomato puree, 2 tablespoons basil puree and 1 teaspoon each of salt and black pepper over medium heat for 8 minutes. Serve sauce over turkey roll.

Giambonetti Di Pollo

Stuffed Chicken Legs

4 chicken legs, de-boned, 16 ounces
1/4 teaspoon salt
1/2 teaspoon black pepper

Stuffing:
4 fresh artichoke hearts, thinly sliced (5 ounces)
1/4 cup olive oil
1 1/2 teaspoons salt
1 1/2 teaspoons black pepper
2 garlic cloves
1 ounce prosciutto, julienned
2 tablespoons olive oil

Sauce:
1 onion, peeled, sliced (1 cup)
4 garlic cloves grated Parmesan cheese
4 fresh sage leaves
1 cup Madeira wine
1 cup veal reduction (sauces chapter)

Serves: 4
Complexity: ● ● ● ●
Preparation Time: 1 Hour, 40 Minutes
Italian Wine: Barbera Del Monferrato, Red, one or two years young, full of tannin, refreshing.

To prepare stuffing, heat olive oil in medium sauce pan; when oil is hot, add artichokes, garlic, salt and pepper. Saute until garlic turns golden brown in color, approximately 5 minutes; remove from heat and drain oil. Strain contents and allow to cool. Take cooled mixture and combine with prosciutto in mixing bowl; blend well.

Take chicken leg and season inside with 1 teaspoon pepper and 1 teaspoon salt. Stuff leg with mixture; tie leg with cooking twine.

In a medium, oven-proof sauce pan, heat olive oil over medium heat; when oil is hot, add chicken leg. Season with 1/4 teaspoon each of salt and pepper. Saute leg 1 minute each side and add onions, garlic and sage; cook 1 minute. Add Madeira and cook until alcohol is completely reduced. When alcohol has burned off, remove pan from heat and add veal reduction. Place pan in oven preheated to 400 degrees and bake for 20 minutes.

After 20 minutes, remove pan from heat and remove chicken from pan; set chicken aside. Place pan back over medium heat and bring contents to a boil; remove from heat and transfer to blender; puree until smooth.

Remove cooking twine and slice stuffed leg; serve over bed of sauce.

Leftovers are very good served cold and thinly sliced with a green sauce as an appetizer.

Galletto Alla Boscaiola

Cornish Hen with Shiitake Mushrooms

4 cornish hens, cleaned (1 lb. each)

1 cup olive oil
20 garlic cloves
8 fresh rosemary sprigs
4 potatoes, boiled, peeled, 1/8" slices, (28 ounces)
32 shiitake mushroom heads
1 1/3 cups dry white wine
4 teaspoons fresh Italian parsley, chopped

Stuffing:
4 fresh rosemary sprigs
4 garlic cloves
20 fresh sage leaves
2 teaspoons salt
2 teaspoons black pepper

Serves: 4
Complexity: • • •
Preparation Time: 1 Hour, 45 Minutes
Italian Wine: Dolcetto DidianoD'Alba,
Red, dry and fruity, very lively.

Place all ingredients for stuffing in blender and puree for 10 seconds. Stuffing should be chopped, not in liquid stage. Divide stuffing into 4 parts.

Take hens and insert rosemary, garlic and sage. Cut off wings and tie hens with cooking twine; season outside with salt and pepper.

In an oven-proof large sauce pan over medium heat, saute olive oil, garlic and rosemary; when garlic turns brown in color, add hens, breast side down in pan. Saute for 2 minutes.

Remove from heat and set hens aside. Add potato slices, mushrooms, 1/2 teaspoon salt and place hens back in pan, breast side up. Place pan in preheated 400 degree oven. Bake for 30 minutes.

After 30 minutes, remove from oven and remove potatoes, herbs and mushrooms; set aside.

Place pan back over medium heat and add wine; deglaze pan, scraping meat particles with spatula; add parsley. Continue to cook until wine has reduced by half. Remove from heat, turn hen breast side up and add potatoes, mushrooms and salt to pan.

To serve, place hens over potato mixture; dress with reduction sauce.

Tie hen with kitchen twine and use regular needle. When making sauce, make sure wine is reduced by half. It is important that you cook sauce until you do not smell any alcohol. It is a light sauce which is easier to digest and lets you taste the flavor of the ingredients in the dish.

Pollo All'Albese

Alba Style Chicken

4 boneless chicken breasts, remove skin (5-8 ounces each)
1/2 tablespoon salt
1 teaspoon black pepper
2 quarts chicken stock (sauces chapter)

Meatball mixture:
1 ounce Italian bread, without crust
1/4 cup milk
2 ounces ground beef
2 ounces pork sausage meat, without casing
2 fresh sage leaves, chopped
1 tablespoon fresh Italian parsley, chopped
1/2 teaspoon fresh rosemary, chopped
1/4 tablespoon basil puree (sauces chapter)
1 egg
3 tablespoons
1/2 cup olive oil

Dijon sauce:
6 anchovy fillets, chopped
1 tablespoon Dijon mustard
2 tablespoons lemon juice
1/2 teaspoon white truffle oil
2 tablespoons olive oil

2 cups potato puree (vegetables chapter)

Serves: 4
Complexity: • • •
Preparation Time: 30 Minutes
Italian Wine: Barolo,
Red, at least ten years old in order to
be velvety with a full bouquet.

Put chicken stock in sauce pan large enough to hold 4 chicken breasts. Bring chicken stock to boil over medium heat; after stock reaches a boil, reduce heat and simmer stock. Season chicken breasts with salt and pepper; add to stock. Poach chicken breasts for 12 minutes and remove.

Using meat grinding attachment on a mixer or a hand grinder, grind together bread soaked in milk, beef, pork, herbs and pinch of salt and pepper. In mixing bowl combine ground mixture with egg and Parmesan cheese; blend well. Using wet hands, form mixture into marble-sized meat balls. Set meatballs aside.

In a large sauce pan, heat olive oil over high heat. When oil is hot, add meatballs and saute by turning the pan in a circular motion to brown them evenly. After 2 minutes, place sauteed meat balls on baking sheet layered with paper towels to absorb oil.

In a blender, combine ingredients for Dijon sauce and blend well.

Slice chicken breasts and serve with meatballs over potato puree; top with Dijon sauce.

If sauce breaks down or separates in blender, add 3 tablespoons hot chicken stock or hot water; continue to blend until sauce achieves a creamy consistency.

Petto Di Fagiano Ai Marroni Con Il Suo Sugo

Pheasant Breast with Chestnut Stuffing

4 pheasant breasts, boneless
1 piece caul fat
4 fresh sage sprigs
4 fresh rosemary sprigs

Filling:
4 ounces chicken
4 ounces duck liver
1/2 cup heavy cream
2 egg whites
1/4 cup olive oil
4 ounces chestnuts, peeled
1 ounce pancetta, diced
1 teaspoon salt
2 teaspoon black pepper

Marinade:
2 fresh rosemary sprigs
2 fresh sage sprigs
2 tablespoons olive oil
1 teaspoon salt
1 teaspoon black pepper

Serves: 4
Complexity: • • • •
Preparation Time: 30 Minutes
Italian Wine: Barolo,
Red, at least ten years old in
order to be velvety and have
a full bouquet.

To prepare filling, combine chicken and duck liver and blend in food processor. When meat is blended, add cream and egg white and puree. Place mixture in covered bowl and place in refrigerator.

In a medium saute pan, heat olive oil, pancetta, chestnuts, salt and pepper over medium heat; cook for 4 minutes, until chestnuts are lightly browned. Remove from heat and allow mixture to cool. After it has cooled, add to refrigerated chicken mixture.

Combine ingredients for marinade; place breasts in mixture and allow to marinate for 2 hours. After pheasant is marinated, place breasts on flat surface, skin side down. Take chilled chicken mixture and spread 1/3" thick on 1 breast; take other breast and place on top, skin side out. Wrap breast package with caul fat.

Heat a medium saute pan over medium heat and add olive oil. When oil is hot, add pheasant. Saute for 2 minutes each side, until lightly browned. Remove from pan and place in baking dish and place 2 sprigs of rosemary and sage on each breast; bake for 12 minutes in oven preheated to 400 degrees.

Remove from oven and allow meat to rest for 5 minutes before serving.

Faraona Alla Monferrina

Stuffed Guinea Hen

8 guinea hen breasts, with skin
1 cup olive oil
8 fresh rosemary sprigs
8 fresh sage leaves
4 pieces caul fat

Marinade:
16 fresh rosemary sprigs
16 fresh sage leaves
1 cup olive oil

Stuffing:
8 ounces sweetbreads, diced into 1/4" pieces
4 ounces pork sausage, without casing
4 ounces porcini mushrooms, diced into 1/4" pieces
4 tablespoons shallots, finely chopped
1/2 teaspoon salt
1/2 teaspoon black pepper

Serves: 4
Complexity: • • • •
Preparation Time: 35 Minutes
Italian Wine: Barolo,
Red, at least ten years old in
order to be velvety with a full
bouquet.

Prepare marinade; add guinea hen breasts and allow to set for at least 2 hours in refrigerator.

In a medium sauce pan, heat 1/2 cup olive oil over medium heat; when oil is warmed thoroughly, add mushrooms and shallots; saute until shallots are lightly browned. Add sweetbreads and saute until mixture is golden color. Remove from heat and place contents of pan on large cookie sheet to cool. When mixture has cooled, place in bowl and add sausage with spoon until completely mixed.

Place marinated breasts on flat surface, skin side down. Take sausage mixture and divide mixture on each of 4 breasts; spread evenly over top of each breast. Take remaining 4 breasts and place one on top of each, skin side out. Wrap breast package with caul fat.

Heat a medium saute pan over medium heat and add 1/2 cup olive oil. When oil is hot, saute guinea breasts for 2 minutes on each side, until lightly browned. Remove from pan and place in baking dish and placing 2 sprigs of rosemary and 2 sage leaves on top of each breast; bake for 16 minutes in oven preheated to 450 degrees.

Remove from oven and allow meat to rest 5 minutes before serving.

Petto D'Anatra Con I Cavoli

Breast of Duck with Cabbages

Sauce:
24 ounces boneless duck breast, with skin

16 ounces green cabbage leaves
8 ounces pancetta, diced
1 cup olive oil
4 teaspoons salt
4 teaspoons black pepper
1/4 cup unsalted butter

2 cups duck reduction (sauces chapter)
1/4 cup unsalted butter

Serves: 4
Complexity: ••
Preparation Time: 1 Hour, 25 Minutes
Italian Wine: Boca,
Red ruby color with a full
perfume of violets.

Blanch cabbage in boiling water for 30 seconds; remove from water and drain leaves. Julienne cabbage and set aside.

In a large saute pan, heat 1/2 cup olive oil and pancetta over medium heat for 30 seconds. Add blanched cabbage, 2 teaspoons salt and pepper, cook for 1 minute; reduce heat to low and add butter. Continue to stir as mixture cooks for 4 minutes and remove from heat.

In a separate pan, heat 1/2 cup olive oil over medium high heat. Place duck breasts, seasoned with 2 teaspoons salt and black pepper in heated oil, skin side down; after 1 minute reduce heat to medium. Saute for 3 minutes; turn breasts and cook an additional 3 minutes until breasts are golden brown on both sides. Remove breasts from heat and set aside for 5 minutes.

For the sauce, heat duck reduction and butter in small sauce pan until mixture reaches a boil; remove from heat. To serve, place duck breast over bed of cabbage and top with duck sauce.

Make sure that the cabbage is not overcooked or it will lose green color; blanch leaves quickly and cook panchetta quickly over very high heat.

contorni

Side dishes in Piedmontese cuisine are in great numbers and include almost all vegetables. Many of the vegetables originally came from America like potatoes, polenta and beans. For this book, I took the most important vegetable dishes as they related to the fish, meat and poultry recipes; I like to combine vegetables with the food; I like to serve vegetables not as a side dish but as a part of a main dish or as a dish by themselves. The selection, while it is good, represents only a small sample of the vegetable dishes from Piedmont. I picked the most unusual recipes, which may not be found in other books, like the Butternut Squash with Cacio Cheese and Tortino.

The Piedmont region is rich in vegetables. Most of the cuisine is based on vegetables; based on what is fresh. You can use these recipes by themselves and they will be very successful.

Carciofi All'Acciuga

Braised Artichokes

5 fresh artichokes, cleaned
2 garlic cloves, thinly sliced
5 anchovy fillets
1/2 teaspoon dried oregano
3 tablespoons olive oil
2 tablespoons red wine vinegar
1/4 teaspoon salt
1/4 teaspoon black pepper
3/4 cup dry white wine

Serves: 2
Complexity: • •
Preparation Time: 1 Hour
Italian Wine: Barbera Del Monferrato,
Red young with a fragrant
grape flavor.

Remove tough, outer leaves and stems of artichokes; place in water with lemons. Take remaining portion and cut off 1/4" from end and scoop out inside using melon scoop.

Place artichokes, scooped side down, in bottom of medium sauce pan. Add garlic, anchovies, herbs, spices, olive oil, vinegar and 1/4 cup of white wine. Place over low heat and allow to cook slowly. As sauce reduces, add the remaining 1/2 cup of wine. After 30 minutes, artichokes are cooked.

Remove artichokes from pan and place on serving platter, pour sauce over top and serve.

Patate A Tocchetti

Diced Potatoes

4 potatoes, peeled, cubed (2 1/4 lbs.)
1 cup olive oil
1 teaspoon salt
1 teaspoon black pepper
8 garlic cloves
8 ounces Swiss cheese, julienned

Serves: 4
Complexity: •
Preparation Time: 25 Minutes
Italian Wine: Barbera D'Alba,
Red with tannin and well balanced.

In a medium sauce pan, heat olive oil and potatoes over medium heat. After 1 1/2 minutes, add spices and garlic cloves. After 6 minutes, drain oil and remove garlic cloves. Peel skin off garlic cloves and slice in half.

Place sauteed diced potatoes in baking dish; add garlic cloves and top with Swiss cheese. Bake in oven preheated to 400 degrees for 5 minutes. Remove from oven and serve.

Make sure that the potatoes are cooked; although the recipe indicates 6 minutes, it may take longer to cook depending on the thickness of the potato. If you prefer, you can substitute fontina, American or cheddar cheese for the Swiss cheese.

Zucchine Al Balsamico

Zucchini With Balsamic Vinegar

8 zucchini, sliced (1 1/2 lbs.)
1 cup olive oil
8 garlic cloves, chopped
1 teaspoon salt
1 teaspoon black pepper
8 tablespoons fresh mint, chopped
1 cup red wine vinegar

Serves: 4
Complexity: •
Preparation Time: 20 Minutes

In a large saute pan, heat olive oil; add zucchini slices and saute over medium heat; add garlic, salt and pepper. Cook zucchini 1 minute on each side, until lightly golden brown; remove from heat and drain oil from pan.

Add mint and vinegar to zucchini mixture and mix well. Remove zucchini slices and line up in rows on serving plate. Pour sauce from pan over top.

This dish can be served cold as an antipasti and can be covered with plastic and refrigerated for up to 5 days.

Purca Di Patate All'Aglio Dolce

Potato Garlic Puree

8 large potatoes, baked, peeled (4 lbs.)
1 garlic head, roasted (techniques chapter)
1/4 cup unsalted butter
1/4 cup grated Parmesan cheese
1/4 cup heavy whipping cream
1/4 cup veal meat juice (sauces chapter)

Serves: 4
Complexity: •
Preparation Time: 10 Minutes
Italian Wine: Dolcetto di Dogliani,
Dry red, not too acidic,
slightly bitter finish.

Bake potatoes in 350 degree oven for 1 hour. Take baked potatoes and peel; puree using a food mill or press.

In a large mixing bowl, combine pureed potatoes, butter, cheese and cream. Remove 24 cloves of roasted garlic; peel and add to mixture.

Serve with 1 tablespoon meat juice over each serving.

Bake the potato in the oven to get a stronger potato flavor and avoid having too much moisture in puree. You may leave some of the potato skin on if you wish.

Cipolle Ripiene Al Cioccolato

Stuffed Onion with Chocolate

4 onions (20 ounces)
1 teaspoon salt
2 dried bay leaves
3 cloves
2 cups dry white wine

Stuffing:
1 garlic clove
1/4 cup grated Parmesan cheese
8 amaretto cookies
1/2 teaspoon salt
1/2 teaspoon black pepper
2 tablespoons cocoa powder
1/4 cup unsalted butter

Serves: 4
Complexity: • •
Preparation Time: 40 Minutes
Italian Wine: Cortese Dei Colli Tortonesi,
White with a light bitter line and an
almond flavor that will pick up the
flavor of amaretto.

Take onions and cut off top 1/4". Using a melon scoop, clean out inside of onions, leaving outer 3 layers of onion intact. Set aside, separately.

In a medium stock pot, combine 4 cups water, salt, bay leaves, cloves and wine. Place over medium heat and bring mixture to a boil. When it reaches boiling point, add onion shells; reduce heat to low and simmer for 10 minutes. Remove shells from water, and remove any pieces that may have fallen off while cooking.

To prepare stuffing combine ingredients, along with inner onion layers, in food processor; puree until smooth. Set aside.

Take a baking dish and coat bottom and sides generously with butter. Place onion shells in bottom of pan, using excess onion pieces to cover any holes at base of onion. Spoon stuffing into onion shells and bake in preheated oven at 400 degrees for 25 minutes.

Remove from oven and serve.

This is a recipe that shows the creativity of Piedmontese cooking. The onions can also be stuffed with a mixture of ground sausage mixed with chocolate, if you prefer.

Tortino Di Costine

Swiss Chard Torte

1 1/2 lbs. Swiss chard, cleaned, chopped
1/2 cup olive oil
1 teaspoon salt
1 teaspoon black pepper
1 egg
1 cup grated Parmesan cheese
1/4 cup all purpose flour
1/2 cup red wine vinegar

Serves: 4
Complexity: • •
Preparation Time: 25 Minutes
Italian Wine: Grignolino,
Light red with a nice freshness,
good with the dish.

Heat large saute pan over medium heat. When pan is hot, reduce heat to low and add olive oil, Swiss chard and salt and pepper; saute, stirring contents for 2 1/2 minutes. Remove from heat and set aside.

In a large mixing bowl, combine 1 egg, cheese, flour and red vinegar. Mix well and add sauteed Swiss chard; continue to mix well until blended.

Take baking rings, 3" wide by 1" high, and coat inside with oil; place on baking dish. Pour Swiss chard mixture into rings and bake in preheated oven at 400 degrees for 10 minutes.

Remove from oven and allow to cool for 2 minutes. Place ring with mixture on serving plate; remove form and serve.

Tortino Di Tapinambur

Jerusalem Artichoke Torte

5 artichokes, cleaned (techniques chapter)
2 garlic cloves, thinly sliced
5 anchovy fillets
1/2 teaspoon dried oregano
3 tablespoons olive oil
2 tablespoons red wine vinegar
1/4 teaspoon salt
1/4 teaspoon black pepper
3/4 cup dry white wine

Serves: 4
Complexity: •
Preparation Time: 45 Minutes
Italian Wine: Barbera D'Alba,
Red with tannin and well balanced.

Place cleaned artichokes, scooped side down, in bottom of medium sauce pan. Add garlic, anchovies, herbs, spices, olive oil, vinegar and 1/4 cup of white wine. Place over low heat and allow to cook slowly. As sauce reduces, add the remaining 1/2 cup of wine. After 32 minutes, artichokes are cooked.

Remove artichokes from pot and place on serving platter; pour sauce from pot over top and serve.

Polpettone Di Patate

Potato Loaf

6 potatoes, peeled (1 lb.)
2 eggs
1 cup Parmesan cheese
1/4 cup olive oil
2 onions, peeled, finely chopped (1 1/2 cups)
1 garlic clove, smashed
1/2 ounce fresh Italian parsley, finely chopped
6 fresh basil leaves, finely chopped
1 teaspoon salt
1 teaspoon black pepper
1 cup tomato puree
2 tablespoons unseasoned bread crumbs, sifted

Serves: 4
Complexity: • •
Preparation Time: 1 Hour, 10 Minutes
Italian Wine: Dolcetto D'Ovada,
Nice red with a round finish,
very vivacious.

Clean and peel potatoes and place in boiling water for approximately 30 minutes. When potatoes are cooked, they should be tender, remove from water and set aside.

Heat olive oil in a medium saucepan over medium heat. When oil is hot, add onions, garlic, parsley, basil, salt and pepper; saute for 15 minutes. Add tomato puree and continue to cook over medium heat for an additional 4 minutes; remove pan from heat.

Take boiled potatoes and puree using a food mill, do not use a food processor. In a separate bowl, puree the tomato mixture, again using the food mill. In a large mixing bowl, combine both pureed mixtures. Add eggs and cheese and mix well.

Brush the inside of a small loaf pan with melted butter. Add bread crumbs and turn the pan, coating the bottom and all sides equally with bread crumbs. Pour potato puree mixture into the coated pan. Next, brush the back of a large, flat spoon with olive oil and use it to spread and flatten the mixture in the pan.

Bake the loaf for 10 minutes at 450 degrees then reduce heat to 350 degrees for an additional 11 minutes. Remove from oven and allow to cool for 5 minutes. Remove from pan and slice to serve.

Cipolline All' Aceto Rosso

Pearl Onions in Sweet and Sour Sauce

30 ounces pearl onions, cleaned
4 teaspoons sugar
1/3 cup red wine vinegar
10 fresh sage leaves, finely chopped
1/4 cup olive oil

Serves: 4
Complexity: •
Preparation Time: 45 Minutes

In a baking or casserole dish, combine ingredients and mix well, coating cippollini evenly. Bake in preheated oven set at 450 degrees for 35 minutes.

Blanch the cipolline in boiling water for 2 minutes, remove the pan from heat, leaving cipolline in water, and the skin will peel off easily.

Torta Di Zucca Al Cacio

Butternut Squash Torte Filled with Cacio Cheese

2 butternut squash (3 1/4 lb.)
3/4 cup olive oil
2 garlic cloves, smashed
2 1/2 teaspoons grated Parmesan cheese
3 ounces cacio cheese

Serves: 4
Complexity: ● ● ●
Preparation Time: 55 Minutes
Italian Wine: Dolcetto D'Ovada,
Nice red with a round finish
and very vivacious.

Wash squash under cold water and, using a large knife, cut off bulb, removing it from the "trunk" of the vegetable. Take the trunk and cut into thin slices.

In a large saute pan, heat olive oil. Add garlic and cook until garlic is golden brown; remove garlic cloves. Add squash slices in single layer and saute lightly until golden brown, 1 minute on each side. After cooked on both sides, remove squash slices from pan and place on a baking sheet layered with paper towels to absorb the oil. Sprinkle lightly with salt.

To prepare as a side dish, place a 4" round mold or form in the bottom of a small saute pan. Cut squash slices in half and build one layer at the bottom of the baking form. Next, slice cacio cheese very thin; layer 1 ounce of cheese on top of squash. Top with 1 teaspoon Parmesan cheese. Repeat three layers: squash, cacio and Parmesan cheese. Again, repeat three layers and lightly press down on mixture in form. Add a final layer of squash and top with Parmesan cheese. Do not add top layer of cheese if baking in a convection oven.

Place pan in 450 degree oven for 15 minutes. Remove from oven and let sit. Slide form off of baking sheet to serve. Each 4" tart serves one person.

To make this recipe without a mold, use a 7 1/2" saute pan. Melt butter in bottom of pan and spread to coat bottom and sides. Follow the steps outlined above, but use whole slices of squash. Layers should consist of 1 ounce cacio cheese and 1 tablespoon Parmesan cheese. Bake at 450 degrees for twenty minutes.

To make the single serving tarts, use a tuna can with top and bottom removed in place of a mold or form.

The torte should have a nice brown edge all around. After baking, the torte can go back on the oven for a minute or so to achieve the golden brown color.

carni e selvaggina

This chapter was the most intricate for me to work on, but was the most exciting and interesting. Working with meat in Piedmontese recipes is very different today than it was 60 years ago, because meat was preserved in so many different ways, as there was no refrigeration. I wanted to take the original recipes and cook the meat in the proper way as it is eaten today, while keeping the origin and history of the recipe. The flavors and inventiveness of the recipes are very interesting and represent the level of Piedmontese cuisine; it can be simple but still rich and good. Dishes like Bollito Misto and Fritto Misto are traditional foods of this region that represent the richness of food that they used to eat. We use very good parts of the meat such as loins, but we also use other parts of the meats.

Petto Di Vitello Ripieno In Salsa Di Vino Bianco

Stuffed Veal Breast

2 1/2 lbs. veal breast, boneless
3/4 lb. veal stew meat
3/4 lb. salted pork (techniques chapter)
3 garlic cloves
1 bruciolo (techniques chapter)
1 ounce fresh Italian parsley
2 eggs
3 ounces Italian bread, without crust
2 3/4 teaspoons salt
2 3/4 teaspoons black pepper
1/4 cup heavy whipping cream
1 piece caul fat
1/4 cup olive oil
2 cups dry white wine
1 cup veal stock (sauces chapter)

Serves: 4
Complexity: ● ● ● ●
Preparation Time: 1 Hour, 20 Minutes
Italian Wine: Lesona,
Red made with nebolo grapes.
The bouquet is like violets. Dry and strong in tannin.

Have your butcher cut a pocket in the veal breast or, to prepare yourself, take veal breast and, using a long, thin-blade knife, cut a pocket in veal. Slide knife in carefully at one side of meat and slowly drag across, leaving opening at top end of veal.

To prepare stuffing, take veal meat, salted pork, garlic, parsley and bread and grind together using meat grinding attachment on a mixer or food processor. After mixture is ground, add eggs, whipping cream and 1/4 teaspoon pepper; mix well with hands, combining all ingredients. Take veal breast and sprinkle 1/4 teaspoon of salt and pepper inside. Using stuffing mixture, stuff breast. Using a common needle and thread, sew up the edge of the veal breast along the very tip of the meat. Stitch in 1/2" increments. Wrap the stuffed breast in caul fat and set aside.

In a large saucepan, heat olive oil over medium heat. When oil is hot, add bruciolo. Allow to saute for 1 1/2 minutes and add meat; cover and reduce heat to low. After 5 minutes, carefully turn meat. Add 1 teaspoon salt and pepper and turn meat again after an additional 5 minutes. Add wine and veal stock. Cover pan and place in preheated oven set at 375 degrees Bake for 44 minutes.

Remove from oven after baked. Remove veal and pass sauce through a strainer. Put sauce back over medium heat to warm until served.

Trim off stitches at the end of veal pocket; slice stuffed veal breast and serve with veal sauce.

Depending on the cut of meat, you may have stuffing left over. If you do, use the stuffing to make meatballs.

Involtini Di Fegato Alla Canavesana

Sausage Roll "Canavesana" Style

11 ounces calves liver, finely chopped
9 ounces mild pork sausage, casing removed
1/3 cup grated Parmesan cheese
1/2 cup raisins
2 juniper berries, smashed, finely chopped
1/2 teaspoon black pepper
1/2 teaspoon salt
1/2 ounce fresh Italian parsley, chopped
1 tablespoon unsalted butter
1/2 shallot, peeled, chopped (1/4 cup)
1 teaspoon fresh rosemary, chopped
1/2 cup dry white wine
3/4 cup tomato puree
1 tablespoon fresh basil, chopped
1 piece caul fat

Serves: 4
Complexity: ● ● ●
Preparation Time: 35 Minutes
Italian Wine: Lesona,
Red made with nebolo
grapes. The bouquet is like violets.
Dry and strong in tannin.

Soak raisins in warm water for 30 minutes. In a large mixing bowl, combine calves liver, sausage, cheese, soaked raisins, juniper berries, salt, pepper and parsley. Mix well using hands. Take caul fat and roll out, stretching piece until flat. Cut if necessary to make 5" x 10" sheet of caul fat. Place 1/4 of mixture in center of sheet and wrap sides around mixture, beginning with width and then folding in length sides of sheet, forming a sausage roll. Prepare rolls and set aside.

In a large sauce pan, heat butter over medium heat. When butter foams, add sausage, shallots and rosemary. Saute sausage until lightly browned on each side, approximately 1 minute each side. Add wine and cook until completely reduced. When wine has dissipated, add tomato puree and basil. After a total cook-time of 15 minutes, remove from heat. Slice sausage and serve over bed of sauce.

Piccolo Fritto Misto Alla Piemontese

Fried Mixed Meat, Vegetables and Fruit

1 ounce fresh yeast
12 ounces beer

8 cups oil canola or peanut oil
4 ounces veal fillet, 4 slices
4 ounces leg of rabbit, pounded
4 ounces sweetbreads
6 ounces calf's liver, sliced into 8 pieces
10 ounces mild Italian sausage
4 ounces apple, peeled, cored, sliced into 8 pieces
2 bananas, sliced into 8 pieces
12 amaretto cookies
8 ounces semolina (techniques chapter)
1 cup all purpose flour
2 eggs
1 cup unseasoned bread crumbs
2 lemons

Serves: 4
Complexity: ••
Preparation Time: 35 Minutes
Italian Wine: Grignolino,
Red, light, with a touch
of acidity and slightly bitter.

To prepare batter, dissolve yeast in beer; heat slightly, bringing beer to body temperature, or 90 degrees. Add flour and mix well. Cover batter and allow to sit at room temperature for 30 minutes. After 30 minutes, place batter in refrigerator and keep cold until ready to use.

Heat oil in large stock pot over medium-high heat.

To bread meats, first place eggs in small mixing bowl and beat well. Take veal fillets and coat in flour; then dip in egg; and finally roll in bread crumbs. After meat is breaded, pound with broad side of a knife or meat mallet to compact breading. Follow process for veal fillets, sweetbreads, rabbit and semolina cakes.

When oil is hot, fry breaded meats until golden brown, approximately 30 seconds. Remove from oil and place on baking sheet layered with paper towels to absorb oil.

One at a time, place apple slices, bananas and cookies into batter, coating each thoroughly and evenly. Place in hot oil to fry until golden brown, approximately 15 seconds. Remove and place on paper towels to absorb oil. Place calf's liver in oil and fry for 10 seconds; remove.

Sprinkle lightly with salt and pepper and serve with lemon slices.

Allow fried foods to set in warm area while frying other foods to accompany the dish. You may want to place them on a plate, set on the opened door of a warm oven.

This recipe got its name because there are only nine ingredients. A large fritto misto could contain up to 18 ingredients and could include oranges, calf brain, porcini mushrooms, lamb chop, cock's comb, lamb brain, zucchini flowers and eggplant. All these ingredients are fried and served as an appetizer. Good luck to you.

Costolette Di Cinghiale Con Salsa Di Vegetali Stufati

Roast Rack of Wild Boar

36 ounces wild boar (rack of 8 chops)
1/4 cup olive oil
1 garlic clove, smashed

Marinade:
4 garlic cloves, smashed, finely chopped
1 teaspoon fresh rosemary, chopped
8 fresh sage leaves, chopped
2 juniper berries, smashed, finely chopped
1/4 teaspoon dried marjoram
1/2 teaspoon dried cumin
1/2 teaspoon ground cinnamon
1/2 teaspoon salt
1/2 teaspoon black pepper
1/4 cup olive oil
1/4 teaspoon lemon zest, finely chopped

Sauce:
1 onion, peeled, chopped (1/2 cup)
1 carrot, peeled, chopped (1/2 cup)
2 celery stalks, chopped (1/2 cup)
1/2 cup dried porcini mushrooms
1/2 teaspoon fresh rosemary, chopped
1/2 teaspoon fresh thyme, chopped
2 fresh sage leaves
1 clove
1 juniper berry, smashed
1/2 teaspoon cinnamon
1/2 teaspoon salt
2 cups light, dry, red wine
1/2 cup veal reduction (sauces chapter)
1 cup veal stock (sauces chapter)

Combine marinade ingredients, except lemon zest, in large baking pan; mix well. Add rack and massage marinade sauce into meat, rubbing all sides to coat each chop evenly. After all chops are coated, sprinkle lemon zest over top. Marinate for 2 hours at room temperature.

To prepare sauce, in a medium sauce pan, combine olive oil, vegetables and herbs. Saute over medium heat for 3 minutes. Add red wine and salt and continue to cook over medium heat. After 7 minutes, reduce heat to low. After wine is reduced by half, approximately 7 minutes, add veal reduction and veal stock. After 30 minutes, remove mixture from heat. Pour contents of pan into blender and puree on high for 30 seconds; return to pan and warm over low heat until served.

Place a heavy, cast iron skillet over medium heat. When pan is hot, add meat, along with marinade, and saute until meat is browned, turning as it cooks, for 1 1/2 minutes. After meat is browned evenly, place chops back in original baking pan and pour marinade juices over top. Bake in oven preheated to 400 degrees for 20 minutes.

When meat is cooked, remove from oven and cut rack into chops, 2 per serving. Serve boar chops with 3 tablespoons of blended sauce.

Rub the marinade into the meat to remove some of the strong taste and allow the meat to absorb the marinade.

Serves: 4
Complexity: ● ● ●
Preparation Time: 40 Minutes
2 Hours for marinating
Italian Wine: Carema,
Red, dry and supple at least
5 years old, with a bouquet
of fermented rose.

Arrosto Di Vitello Alla Senape

Roasted Veal with Mustard

2 1/2 lbs. veal roast (leg or shoulder), wrapped in cooking twine
1/4 cup red wine vinegar
4 anchovy fillets in oil
1/4 cup olive oil
1 teaspoon salt
1 teaspoon black pepper
1 onion, peeled, finely chopped (1 cup)
1/3 cup Dijon mustard
1/2 ounce porcini or shiitake mushrooms, dried
1/2 cup veal stock (sauces chapter)

Serves: 4
Complexity: ••
Preparation Time: 1 Hour, 15 Minutes
Italian Wine: Bramaterra,
Red with a full body, velvety,
slightly bitter.

Place veal roast in heavy, covered, oven-proof stock pot or pan. Add red wine vinegar, anchovies, olive oil, mustard, onions and mushrooms. After all ingredients are combined, cover pot and cook over medium heat for 5 minutes. When mixture reaches a boil, add veal stock. Place covered pot in oven preheated to 400 degrees. Bake for 1 hour.

Remove pan from oven; take roast out of pan and set aside. Pour contents of pot into food processor and puree until smooth.

Remove twine from veal roast and cut into 1/8" slices. Serve roasted veal over a bed of blended sauce.

Rognone Di Vitello Al Madera

Veal Kidneys with Madeira Sauce

Serves: 2
Complexity: ••
Preparation Time: 15 Minutes
Italian Wine: Barolo,
Red at least 15 years old with full body, good tannin.

1 piece veal kidney (20 ounces)
12 pancetta slices
1/4 cup olive oil
1 cup Madeira sauce (sauces chapter)

Wrap pancetta slices around kidney, covering the entire piece. Secure with a toothpick.

Heat large, oven-proof cast iron skillet over medium heat. Add olive oil and allow oil to become hot. Place wrapped kidney in oil and saute for 30 seconds. Remove pan from heat and place in oven preheated to 450 degrees; bake for 6 minutes. Remove kidney from pan and roll in towel to remove blood. Allow kidney to rest in towel for 5 minutes.

Remove kidney from towel; discard toothpick. To serve, cut into slices and arrange over top of warmed Madeira sauce.

Make sure veal kidneys are extremely fresh, they should be a purplish brown, lively color; nice and firm to the touch. Buy the meat with the fat still around the kidneys and you can trim it yourself. If you buy kidneys with fat, the fat should be white in color, not yellow. The whiter the fat, the healthier the animal was when it was alive.

Filetto Di Vitello All'Aceto Balsamico

Fillet of Veal in Balsamic Vinegar Sauce

24 ounces veal fillet, cut into 12 medallions

1 lb. Swiss chard, cleaned, stems removed, julienned
1/2 cup olive oil
4 garlic cloves, smashed
4 ounces salted pork, julienned (techniques chapter)
1 teaspoon salt
1 teaspoon black pepper

Marinade:
1/2 cup olive oil
1/2 teaspoon salt
1/2 teaspoon black pepper
1 fresh rosemary sprig,
   leaves removed, finely chopped

Serves: 4
Complexity: • • •
Preparation Time: 35 Minutes

Sauce:
1/2 cup olive oil
4 bruciolo (techniques chapter)
1/2 cup balsamic vinegar
1 cup veal stock (sauces chapter)
4 ounces dark raisins (soaked in warm water for 20 minutes)
4 ounces toasted pine nuts

To prepare marinade, combine ingredients in baking pan and add veal fillet. Allow meat to marinate for 20 minutes at room temperature.

To prepare Swiss chard, in a large saute pan, warm olive oil and garlic over medium heat. When oil is hot and garlic turns light brown in color, add salted pork; after 20 seconds, add Swiss chard and salt and pepper; saute for 1 1/2 minutes and remove from heat.

To prepare sauce, heat olive oil and bruciolo in a medium sauce pan over high heat. When oil is hot, add veal medallions and saute 1 minute each side. Remove pan from heat; discard bruciolo and drain oil. Remove fillet and roast in oven preheated to 400 degrees for 4 minutes. Remove from oven; add balsamic vinegar and place pan back over heat, cooking until vinegar reduces by half its original amount; add veal stock, raisins and pine nuts. Continue to cook until sauce reduces by half.

Serve veal medallions with sauce, surrounded by sauteed Swiss chard.

For this recipe I like to put only half of the pine nuts and raisins in while cooking and add the remaining nuts and raisins at the end to keep the light color of the pine nuts.

Stufato Di Lepre Alla Frutta Fresca

Hare Stewed with Fresh and Dry Fruits

1 hare
1 teaspoon salt
1 teaspoon black pepper
5 ounces salted pork, finely chopped (techniques chapter)
1/3 cup olive oil
1 bruciolo (techniques chapter)
3 ounces raisins
2 ounces chestnuts
4 ounces prunes, pitted
1 onion, peeled, finely chopped (1/2 cup)
5 ounces dried porcini mushrooms
4 ounces shiitake mushrooms, julienned
5 ounces fresh porcini mushrooms
4 Bartlett pears, peeled, quartered
2 dried bay leaves
1 ounce fresh Italian parsley, chopped
1 teaspoon fresh thyme
2 cloves
1 1/2 ounces black truffle peelings (optional)
2 cups dry red wine
1 cup veal stock (sauces chapter)
1 cup rabbit stock (sauces chapter)

Serves: 4
Complexity: • • •
Preparation Time: 55 Minutes
Italian Wine: Bramaterra,
Four or five years old with intense
bouquet, dry and velvety.

To prepare hare, have butcher cut off legs of hare and cut each into 3 equal parts; French cut the ribs (techniques chapter); cut shoulder into 2 equal parts; from neck and above, cut into 2 equal parts; and cut loin into 4 slices.

Place meat in baking dish and season with salt and pepper; mix well to coat meat. Set aside.

Heat large sauce pan over high heat. When pan is hot, add olive oil, salted pork and bruciolo; saute for 1 1/2 minutes. Add hare meat and saute, turning meat as it cooks to lightly brown evenly on all sides, approximately 3 minutes; remove bruciolo and remove pan from heat.

In a heavy, large stock pot, place sauteed rabbit, along with oil from pan. Add raisins, chestnuts, prunes, mushrooms, pears, onions, red wine, veal stock, herbs and black truffle peelings, as desired. Place pot over high heat and cover. When mixture reaches a boil, approximately 6 minutes, reduce heat to low; replace cover. Continue to cook for 32 minutes and remove from heat.

Remove meat and set aside. Place pot, with sauce, back over medium heat. Add rabbit stock, as needed; bring mixture to a boil, approximately 2 minutes and remove from heat. Serve hare over mushroom sauce, garnished with pear slices.

This dish can be served with a garnish of the vegetables that were used in the dish to cook with. If you want to make it fancier, use pureed sauce and serve sauce on the bottom of the dish with hare on top. You can also substitute duck for hare, cooking it the same way.

Medaglioni Di Vitello All'Agresto Piemontese
Veal Medallions in a Sweet and Sour Sauce

24 ounces veal filets, cut into 12 medallions
1 teaspoon salt
1 teaspoon black pepper
1/4 cup olive oil
1 bruciolo (techniques chapter)

Sour Sauce:
1/2 ounce dried porcini mushrooms
1/2 cup Marsala wine
1 leek stem, cleaned, quartered lengthwise (1 ounce)
1 shallot, peeled (1 ounce)
1 tablespoon celery leaves
2 tablespoons lemon juice
3 fresh sage leaves
1/4 cup olive oil
1 ounce fresh Italian parsley
2 garlic cloves
4 anchovy fillets
1 tablespoon red wine vinegar
1/4 cup capers, drained
1/2 cup veal stock (sauces chapter)
1 tablespoon veal reduction (sauces chapter)

Serves: 4
Complexity: ••
Preparation Time: 25 Minutes
Italian Wine: Bramaterra,
Four or five years old with
intense bouquet, dry and velvety.

To prepare sour sauce, soak porcini mushrooms in Marsala wine for 20 minutes. Combine celery leaves, sage, shallot and leek and chop finely together. Drain mushrooms from Marsala; chop finely and add to mixture.

In a medium sauce pan, heat olive oil over medium heat; add chopped mixture and saute for 4 minutes. Combine parsley, garlic and anchovies; chop finely and add to saute pan. Cook for 1 minute and add red wine vinegar, capers, lemon juice, veal stock and veal reduction. Continue to cook, stirring mixture until it reaches a boil, approximately 10 minutes; remove from heat.

Sprinkle veal filets with salt and pepper evenly on both sides and set aside.

In a large saute pan, heat olive oil with bruciolo. When oil is hot, add medallions and saute, 2 1/2 minutes each side, until veal is lightly browned. Remove from heat.

Serve veal medallions over sauce.

Filetto Di Manzo All'Ortolana

Filet of Beef with Eggplant in Gorgonzola Cheese Sauce

20 ounces beef tenderloin
4 eggplant, sliced into 1/4" pieces (1 lb.)
8 plum tomatoes, sliced into 1/4" pieces
1 1/4 cups olive oil
1 teaspoon salt
1 teaspoon black pepper
2 bruciolo (techniques chapter)
6 fresh basil leaves

Sauce:
2 tablespoons unsalted butter
8 fresh sage leaves, chopped
1 1/2 ounces gorgonzola cheese
1/2 cup veal reduction (sauces chapter)

Serves: 4
Complexity: ••
Preparation Time: 30 Minutes
Italian Wine: Barbaresco,
Red, four or five years old, still full
of energy and well balanced.

In an extra-large saute pan, heat 1 cup olive oil over medium-high heat. When oil is hot, place eggplant slices in a single layer in the bottom of pan. Cook until eggplant is golden brown; then turn and cook other side. When both sides are evenly browned, remove eggplant from pan and place on a sheet pan layered with paper towels to absorb the oil.

In same pan, saute tomatoes, as above. Cook-time should be approximately 10 seconds per side for each tomato slice. Place sauteed tomato slices on a sheet pan layered with paper towels to absorb the oil.

Beef filet should be carved into 1/2"slices. Using one teaspoon each of salt and pepper, season both sides of filet. Set aside.

Heat 1/4 cup olive oil and bruciolo in a large sauce pan over high heat. When oil is hot, add filet slices. Saute for 30 seconds on each side; remove from heat and keep warm.

To prepare sauce, in a small sauce pan, cook butter and sage leaves over low heat until butter foams. Add gorgonzola and veal reduction and increase heat to high until cheese melts completely.

To serve, stack beef filets with sauteed eggplant and tomatoes, creating colorful layers. Add a basil leaf in between layers to add color and flavor. Pour gorgonzola sauce over top.

For this dish, I want to thank Chef Sergio May who came to Galileo four years ago to cook for the Olive Oil Consortium. He showed me the dish; I just changed the sauce slightly but it has his same excellent result.

Coniglio Al Civet

Braised Rabbit In White Wine

1 rabbit, including kidneys and liver
1/2 cup olive oil
4 garlic cloves, smashed

Marinade:
1 onion, peeled, chopped (1 cup)
1 carrot, peeled, chopped (1 cup)
2 celery stalks, cleaned, chopped (1 cup)
2 cloves
3 dried bay leaves
2 1/2 cups dry white wine
1 tablespoon black peppercorns
8 fresh thyme sprigs
4 fresh sage leaves
1 tablespoon fresh rosemary, chopped

Serves: 4
Complexity: ● ●
Preparation Time: 1 Hour
Marinate for 24 Hours
Italian Wine: Bricco Dell'Uccellone,
Red full and fruity, aromatic bouquet.

To prepare marinade, combine ingredients in large mixing bowl. Take rabbit and remove kidneys and liver; set aside. Place rabbit in marinade and allow to set for 24 hours in refrigerator. After 24 hours, remove vegetables and set aside. Remove rabbit and herbs; season rabbit with 1 teaspoon each of salt and pepper.

In a large saute pan, heat olive oil and garlic over high heat; when garlic turns light brown in color, add rabbit and herbs and saute for 4 minutes, turning rabbit to brown meat evenly. Add vegetables set aside from marinade and continue to saute over high heat for 2 minutes. Transfer contents into sauce pan with lid; cook on medium-low heat, covered, for 40 minutes.

Remove pan from heat and discard bay leaves; remove meat and set aside. Pour contents of pan into blender; add rabbit kidneys and liver; puree until smooth. Pass pureed mixture through sieve to yield smooth sauce.

To serve, place rabbit over bed of sauce.

Filletto Di Manzo Al Barolo
Filet of Beef in Barolo Wine Sauce

25 ounce beef filet tenderloin
1/2 cup veal reduction (sauces chapter)
1/2 cup olive oil
1 teaspoon salt
1 teaspoon black pepper

Marinade:
1 onion, peeled, finely chopped (1/3 cup)
1 carrot, peeled, finely chopped (1/3 cup)
1 celery stalk, cleaned, finely chopped (1/3 cup)
1/2 teaspoon cinnamon
2 cloves
2 dried bay leaves
2 garlic cloves, cut in half
1 fresh rosemary sprig
6 fresh sage leaves
4 fresh thyme sprigs
2 cups Barolo wine
10 black peppercorns

Serves: 4
Complexity: ••
Preparation Time: 25 Minutes,
24 Hours for Marinade
Italian Wine: Barolo,
Red at least 8 years old, fully
developed to have the roundness
of old wines.

Combine marinade ingredients in an oblong fruit bread or loaf pan. Place beef tenderloin in marinade and cover with plastic wrap. Allow meat to marinate in the refrigerator for a minimum of 24 hours and a maximum of 36 hours.

Remove meat from marinade and season with salt and pepper; set aside. Using a colander, strain marinade, separating vegetables and extracting juices.

In a medium sauce pan, heat 1/4 cup olive oil over high heat. Add vegetables from marinade and saute for 6 minutes. Add juices from marinade and continue to cook for 20 minutes. Remove bay leaves and garlic and reduce heat to medium. When sauce has reduced to half, add veal reduction. After 3 minutes, empty contents of sauce pan into blender. Puree until smooth. Place in pan and return to stove over low heat to keep sauce warm.

In a large saute pan, heat 1/4 cup olive oil over medium-high heat. Place filet in pan, searing each side of fillet for 3 minutes. Turn meat to brown each side. After meat is seared, remove from pan and place on broiling pan. Bake for 8 minutes in preheated oven at 450 degrees.

Remove filet from oven and slice. Serve with marinade sauce.

This recipe shows a change of technique can only improve the flavor and presentation. It used to be that we would marinate beef for 2-3 days and cut it in cubes and stew it for a long time and overcook the beef. Now, we marinate the meat and saute and roast it and serve it medium rare, not overcooked, bringing out the flavor of the meat. The sauce has all of the same old-style flavor of beef with Barolo from 100 years ago. For this recipe you can also use marinated strip loin, rib eye or part of a beef shoulder.

Costoletta Alla "Galileo"

Grilled Rib Rack of Veal "Galileo" Style

42 ounces rack of veal (4-12 ounce chops)

Marinade:
14 fresh sage leaves
6 fresh rosemary sprigs
6 garlic cloves, sliced
2 fresh thyme sprigs
1/4 cup olive oil

Mushroom Ragu:
1 teaspoon salt
1 teaspoon black pepper
8 ounces shiitake mushrooms, sliced
2 portobello mushrooms, sliced (3 ounces)
6 button mushrooms, sliced (3 ounces)
1/2 cup olive oil
3 garlic cloves, smashed
2 shallots, peeled, chopped (2/3 cup)
1/2 tablespoon salt
1/2 tablespoon black pepper
1/3 cup fresh Italian parsley, chopped
rosemary sauce (sauces chapter)

Serves: 4
Complexity: ••
Preparation Time: 40 Minutes,
24 Hours for marinade
Italian Wine: Barbaresco,
Red, dry, full body, robust,
velvety and well balanced.

In a baking pan, mix ingredients for marinade, reserving 4 sage leaves, 2 rosemary sprigs and 2 garlic cloves; set these herbs aside. Place chops in a single layer over the top of the marinade bed and turn chops to coat evenly. On top of each chop, place one sage leaf, 1/2 sprig of rosemary and 1/2 garlic clove. Cover pan and allow meat to marinate in refrigerator for a minimum of 24 hours and a maximum of 48 hours.

To prepare mushroom ragu, saute olive oil, garlic and shallots in a large sauce pan over high heat. After shallots become translucent, add mushrooms, salt and pepper. Add parsley and continue to saute. After vegetables and herbs have cooked down, discard garlic and remove from heat.

Remove chops from marinade and place on a preheated grill. Grill until chops are browned and lightly crispy.

Remove chops from grill and serve over a bed of mushroom ragu. Complement with rosemary sauce.

This dish has been the most requested dish in the history of Galileo. It is a simple dish and I hope everyone at home will enjoy as we do at Galileo.

Carre Di Maiale Al Latte Con Patate Al Forno

Braised Loin of Pork with Potato

32 ounce pork roast, bound in twine
3 fresh rosemary sprigs
2 teaspoons salt
2 teaspoons black pepper
1/2 cup olive oil
2 garlic cloves, smashed
1 onion, peeled, finely chopped (1 cup)
3 1/2 cups milk

Serves: 4
Complexity: ••
Preparation Time: 1 Hour, 40 Minutes
Italian Wine: Dolcetto Di Dogliani,
Red and dry, not too acidic, slightly
bitter but agreeable.

Take pork roast, still bound in twine, and weave rosemary sprigs underneath twine. In a large, heavy sauce pan, heat olive oil, garlic and salt and pepper over medium heat. Add pork roast and cover pan. As the roast cooks, còntinue to turn to keep meat moist. After approximately 20 minutes, the roast should be lightly browned; add onion and reduce heat to low. Remove garlic and cook for an additional 5 minutes. Add 3 cups of milk and cover pan. Continue to turn roast as it cooks over low heat for a total cook-time of 1 hour and 10 minutes. Remove meat and set aside.

Add 1/2 cup milk to mixture in the pan and bring back to a boil over medium heat. Blend mixture using a hand blender, to achieve a thicker, frothy sauce.

Slice pork roast and serve with sauce.

Agnello Al Forno Nella Crosta Di Patate

Roasted Leg of Lamb Wrapped in Potato Shell

1 leg of lamb
6 Idaho potatoes, peeled (3 lbs.)
2 tablespoons corn starch
2 1/2 tablespoons salt
2 tablespoons black pepper
1 tablespoon fresh thyme
6 cloves garlic, finely chopped
5 fresh rosemary sprigs, finely chopped
2 tablespoons olive oil

Serves: 8
Complexity: ••••
Preparation Time: 1 Hour, 10 Minutes
Italian Wine: Bricco Della Bigotta,
Red, full body with a rich bouquet.

Boil peeled potatoes for 32 minutes and remove from water. Using a cheese grater, shred potatoes into a medium mixing bowl. Add 2 tablespoons of corn starch and 1 tablespoon each of salt, pepper and thyme. Mix well and set aside.

In a separate bowl, combine garlic and rosemary. Coat lamb leg with the mixture then season with 1 1/2 tablespoons salt and 1 tablespoon pepper. Place the coated leg of lamb on a baking sheet coated with olive oil.

Coat lamb with potato mixture, spreading crust evenly over the entire leg. Bake in preheated oven set at 350 degrees for 45 minutes. Remove from oven, allow to cool for 10 minutes and remove the potato shell. To serve, slice the lamb meat along with the potato shell.

You can use half of the leg of lamb or use deboned loin of lamb in this recipe. Always use fresh American lamb; do not buy frozen lamb imported from other countries.

Salsiccia Di Maiale Con Il Fegato Di Vitello

Pork Sausage with Calf's Liver

5 ounces pork sausage
2 tablespoons olive oil
1 shallot, peeled, chopped (1/3 cup)
1 teaspoon fresh rosemary, chopped
1 cup Barbera wine
1/2 teaspoon salt
1/2 teaspoon black pepper
2 ounces calf's liver
4 fresh sage leaves
3 teaspoons unsalted butter

Serves: 4
Complexity: • •
Preparation Time: 1 hour
Italian Wine: Gabbiano,
Red, well balanced
with an intense bouquet.

Take sausage and poke holes the length of the meat, inserting knife straight into side of sausage link.

In a small saute pan, saute sausage in olive oil; add shallots and rosemary. When shallots become translucent, add Barbera wine, salt and pepper; cook for 12 minutes and remove sauce from heat.

In a medium saute pan, heat 1 tablespoon butter and sage leaves over high heat. When butter foams, add liver, salt and pepper. Sear the liver for 10 seconds on each side and remove pan from heat, leaving livers in pan.

Using a colander, strain the Barbera wine sauce, extracting the juice. Put the juices back over high heat for 2 minutes. Add 1 teaspoon butter making a "butter sauce."

To serve, slice sausage in 1/4" slices and pour barbera wine over top. Remove liver from pan and top with butter sauce. Serve with Polpettone di Patate (vegetables chapter).

You can use pork lungs and hearts to make this dish and cut down the amount of liver, making the dish richer. Most people use the liver because it is easier to find.

Ossobuco D'Agnello Ai Carciofi

Braised Lamb Shanks with Artichokes

4 lamb shanks (13 ounces each)
1/3 cup olive oil
2 garlic cloves, smashed
4 fresh thyme sprigs
8 shallots, peeled
2 carrots, peeled, cubed to 1/4" pieces (5 ounces)
8 fresh artichoke hearts, cut into 6 pieces (techniques chapter)
4 teaspoons salt
4 teaspoons black pepper
2 cups dry white wine
2 cups veal stock (sauces chapter)
1/3 cup fresh Italian parsley, chopped

Serves: 4
Complexity: • • •
Preparation Time: 1 Hour, 20 Minutes
Italian Wine: Boca Novarese,
Red, well balanced, velvety with a
violet bouquet.

Preparing the meat: Starting at the top or thin end of the shank, carefully carve away meat from the bone, cutting tendons and ligaments. Using only the tip of a flexible knife, carve away the meat and pull down, revealing the clean bone left behind. Continue to work your way down, forming a ball-shaped base of meat at the end of the bone. The meat base should be approximately 3" high. Clean the bone, as needed, removing any tendons or meat particles. Cut off the knuckle bone at the base with a cleaver, if necessary, to allow shank to sit up straight, with the bone sticking straight up from the center of the meat base. Using cooking twine, tie the meat base around its mid-section to secure.

In a heavy, cast iron sauce pot, combine 2 tablespoons olive oil, garlic, thyme, shallots, carrots, artichoke hearts, salt and pepper and saute over medium high heat for 4 1/2 minutes. Remove from heat.

Prepare lamb shanks as outlined above. Taking 2 teaspoons each of salt and pepper, season each shank. In a separate saucepan, heat 1/4 cup olive oil and saute shanks until meat is browned, approximately 5 1/2 minutes.

After shanks are browned, place on top of vegetable mixture in sauce pot and pour wine and veal stock over top. Cover pot and bake in preheated 450 degree oven for 55 minutes, turning meat after 25 minutes. Check meat as it cooks; if meat becomes dry, add veal stock as needed to keep moist.

Before serving, remove garlic and thyme. Add parsley and stir. Serve lamb shanks over artichoke mixture.

Spalla D'Agnello Ripiena Brasata Con Le Cipolle

Braised Stuffed Lamb Shoulder with Onion Sauce

4 lb. lamb shoulder with bone

Stuffing:
3 ounces salted pork, cubed
   (techniques chapter)
2 garlic cloves
1/4 ounce fresh Italian parsley, whole
2 fresh thyme sprigs, remove leaves
3 ounces scrap lamb meat
2 teaspoons black truffles
1 ounce white bread

2 tablespoons dark rum
1 egg
1/4 cup fresh Italian parsley, chopped
1/4 cup Bechamel sauce (sauces chapter)
2 teaspoons salt
1/3 cup heavy whipping cream
1/2 teaspoons cumin
1 teaspoon dried marjoram
2 tablespoons olive oil
2 garlic cloves, smashed
2 onions, peeled, finely chopped (2 cups)
1 cup dry white wine
1/2 teaspoon red wine vinegar

You may request that your butcher chop through the neck bone of the lamb shoulder. If the end of the rack is attached, use a large cleaver to remove it.

To prepare shoulder meat, carefully remove spatula bone, or the long, flat bone that runs the length of the shoulder meat, using a thin, flexible blade knife. Scrape the meat from the bone from inside, peeling meat away and rolling it down as you go. Cut the tendons and ligaments, not the meat, continuously pulling. Proceed slowly; the knife blade should always be within sight to ensure that you are cutting what is intended. Continue to cut slowly toward the bone, never cutting the meat itself. When you have removed the bone, you should have a long pocket-shaped cut of meat that is ready to be stuffed. If you have a knuckle at the end of the meat, carefully remove it before continuing. Note: always keep meat cool; if it begins to feel warm, return it to the refrigerator to cool.

Using the meat grinding attachment on a mixer or food processor, mix stuffing ingredients. Pass through a second time to ensure that ingredients are well mixed. In a large mixing bowl, add to the stuffing mixture, rum, egg, Bechamel sauce, cream, cumin, marjoram and salt. Mix well using a wooden spoon. Continue to mix until all ingredients are well blended, forming a dense mixture. Set aside.

Take lamb meat and cut off flap of meat along the side; butterfly the meat and place inside, covering the hole left from where the knuckle bone was removed. Stuff the meat with the stuffing mixture. Be careful not to overstuff as the stuffing will shrink while it cooks, causing it to fall apart.

Using a needle and thread, sew the large, open end of the shoulder meat closed in 1/4" intervals. Be careful to sew only along the very edge of the meat. After the meat is cooked, the stitches can be trimmed off. When the meat is stuffed, season the outside of the meat with 2 teaspoons each of salt and pepper.

In a medium sauce pan, heat olive oil over high heat. When oil is hot, add meat and garlic cloves. Turn the meat to achieve a golden color on all sides; be careful not to break the skin of the meat. Add onions and wine and cook for 2 minutes. Cover and remove from heat; place in preheated 450 degree oven and bake for 50 minutes, rotating pan in oven every 15 minutes.

Remove from oven and set meat aside, allowing it to cool for 10-15 minutes before serving. Return pan back to stove over medium heat. Add red wine vinegar and cook for 3 minutes. Remove from heat and pour contents of pan into blender. Puree until smooth.

Slice the stuffed lamb and serve over bed of sauce.

Serves: 6
Complexity: ● ● ● ●
Preparation Time: 2 Hours, 15 Minutes
Italian Wine: Barolo,
Six or seven years old with a full body
and tannin in full force.

Carre' D'Agnello Al Forno Con Purea Di Melanzane
Roasted Leg of Lamb with Eggplant Puree

1 rack of lamb, 8 French cut chops
4 eggplants, halved lengthwise (31 ounces)
1/2 teaspoon salt
1/4 teaspoon black pepper
4 teaspoons grated Parmesan cheese
3/4 teaspoon cumin
5 bruciolo (techniques chapter)
2 fresh thyme sprigs
1 cup Barbaresco wine
1/2 cup veal reduction (sauces chapter)
2 ounces salted pork, cubed (techniques chapter)
1/4 cup honey
2 tablespoons olive oil

Serves: 4
Complexity: • • •
Preparation Time: 45 Minutes
Italian Wine: Darmagi,
Red, full bodied and aromatic.

Place eggplants face up on cookie/baking sheet in a single layer. Bake for 15 minutes in preheated oven set at 450 degrees. Eggplants should be soft to the touch and slightly browned. Scoop out the pulp of eggplants, discarding skin. Put pulp eggplant in blender or food processor; puree for 30 seconds. Add Parmesan cheese and a pinch of cumin; puree an additional 15 seconds. Set mixture aside.

Trim fat from lamb and season evenly with 1/2 teaspoon salt and 1/4 teaspoon pepper. Set meat aside.

In a medium saute pan, combine thyme and 1 bruciolo with wine and cook over medium heat. Alcohol will flame. Allow the alcohol to burn off and liquid to reduce by half; add 1/2 cup veal reduction. Let mixture reduce again. After liquid is again reduced by half, add salted pork and allow it to cook down. Remove from heat.

In a small mixing bowl, combine honey and cumin. Warm over medium heat for approximately 20 seconds. Set aside.

In a large sauce pan, saute olive oil with 4 bruciolo for 2 minutes over medium heat. Add meat; when meat begins to brown, brush honey/cumin mixture over top and turn meat. After meat is browned evenly, remove from pan and place in broiling pan. Pour remaining honey sauce over top and bake in 450 degree oven for 9 minutes. Remove meat from oven every 3 minutes while meat is cooking to brush with honey mixture. The honey will help to form a crust on the meat.

Remove meat from pan and cut into chops. Top serve, place chops over bed of eggplant puree. Top with Barbaresco sauce.

Eggplant puree can be served as a vegetable side dish with many recipes. It is a wonderful complement to lamb.

Carbonada

Braised Beef with Onions and Red Wine

26 ounces of beef, cubed in 1" pieces
1/2 cup olive oil
2 ounces salted pork, cubed (techniques chapter)
2 dried bay leaves
1 1/2 onions, peeled, julienned
1 teaspoon salt
1 teaspoon black pepper
10 fresh sage leaves, finely chopped
1 bottle dry red wine
1/2 tablespoon tomato paste

Serves: 4
Complexity: ••
Preparation Time: 50 Minutes
Italian Wine: Fara,
Red, from nebbilo grapes, vespolina
and bonarda; a good blend
full body, dry and sapid.

This recipe makes good use of pieces of beef left over from other recipes. Cuts of meat used in this instance are scraps from a beef tenderloin filet.

In a large sauce pan, heat 1/3 cup olive oil; when oil is hot, add salted pork and saute over medium-high heat. When pork becomes golden brown, add onions and continue to cook for 3 minutes; reduce heat to medium. Cook until onions become golden, not brown. Remove pan from heat.

In a separate pan, heat 2 tablespoons olive oil over medium high heat. In a small mixing bowl, combine chopped sage leaves and salt and pepper. When oil is hot, add beef and herbs, including sage mixture and bay leaves. Saute until meat is browned; drain fat from pan.

Add drained meat and bottle of wine to onion mixture. Increase heat to high until mixture boils. After it reaches the boiling point, reduce heat to medium and add tomato paste. Cook for an additional 3 minutes. Remove from heat and drain meat through a colander. The flavorful meat can be served over polenta, potatoes or arborio.

Costolette D'Agnello Alla Piemontese

Rib Chop of Lamb "Piedmontese" Style

12 lamb loin chops

Marinade:
1/2 fresh rosemary sprig, finely chopped
1/2 garlic clove
2 tablespoons olive oil

Gherkin Sauce:
8 gherkins, cubed (1 1/2 ounces)
2 fresh tarragon sprigs
4 fresh basil leaves
1 fresh dill sprig
1 fresh thyme sprig, leaves only
1 teaspoon fresh Italian parsley
2 tablespoons olive oil
1 1/2 ounces prosciutto, cubed
1/4 cup unsalted butter
1 teaspoon black pepper
1 teaspoon salt
1/4 cup lemon juice

Serves: 4
Complexity: ••
Preparation Time: 15 Minutes
2 hours for Marinade
Italian Wine: Freisa Di Chieri,
Red, very dry with a bouquet
of raspberry and violets.

Combine ingredients for marinade and pour over chops in a small loaf or bread pan. Cover with plastic and allow meat to marinate for 2 hours in the refrigerator.

Combine all herbs and one tablespoon olive oil in food processor and blend on high for 1 minute. Set aside.

In a medium saute pan, melt butter over medium heat. When butter is melted, add ingredients for gherkin sauce. Simmer for 2 minutes and add lemon juice and 3/4 teaspoon each of salt and pepper. Stir sauce and remove from heat.

In a separate saute pan, heat 1 tablespoon olive oil. Using 1/4 teaspoon each of salt and pepper, season chops and place in pan. Saute chops over high heat for 15 seconds on each side. Discard oil and add gherkin sauce. Return pan to medium heat and simmer for an additional 15 seconds.

Serve chops topped with sauce.

Carre Di Cervo Al Forno Con La Salsa Di Ciliege Secche

Rib Rack of Venison with Dry Cherry Sauce

1 venison rack, cut into 8 French-cut chops (approximately 36 ounces)

Marinade:
2 tablespoons fresh rosemary
16 fresh sage leaves
1/4 cup olive oil
1 teaspoon salt
1 teaspoon black pepper

Dry Cherry Sauce:
4 ounces dried cherries
  (soaked in 1 cup port wine for 30 minutes)
1 shallot, peeled, chopped (1/4 cup)
1/4 cup olive oil
1/4 cup veal reduction (sauces chapter)

Serves: 4
Complexity: ● ● ●
Preparation Time: 1 Hour
Italian Wine: Carema,
Five or six year old red, with a
flowery bouquet, dry, velvety
and soft to the palate.

Place venison chops in bottom of baking pan; place marinade ingredients over top of chops; allow to marinate at room temperature for 20 minutes.

Heat cast iron skillet over medium heat. When pan is hot, add venison chops with marinade; saute each side for 1 minute and place back in baking pan with marinade. Bake in oven preheated to 400 degrees for 25 minutes.

In a medium sauce pan, saute olive oil and shallots over medium heat for 1 1/2 minutes. Add cherries and port; cook until wine is reduced by half, approximately 6 minutes. Add veal reduction and cook an additional 5 minutes and remove from heat.

Slice venison chops, two per serving, and serve over bed of cherry sauce.

Carre Di Maiale Brasato Alle Nocciole

Pork Loin Braised With Hazelnut Sauce

4 1/2 lbs. pork roast
1/4 cup olive oil
2 bruciolo (techniques chapter)
3 dried bay leaves
1 teaspoon salt
1 teaspoon black pepper
3 cups chicken stock (sauces chapter)
1 1/2 cups heavy whipping cream
8 ounces hazelnuts, chopped

Serves: 6
Complexity: ● ●
Preparation Time: 2 Hours, 25 Minutes
Italian Wine: Barbera D'Alba,
Red with a light almond
finish and aroma.

Place heavy, ceramic baking pan or dish over high heat; add olive oil. When oil is hot, add bruciolo, bay leaves and pork roast. Saute pork, turning as it cooks, until it is evenly browned. While the meat browns, season with salt and pepper. After cooking for 7 minutes, add chicken stock and heavy cream.

Continue to cook mixture until it reaches a boil; cover and remove from heat.

Bake in oven at 400 degrees for 2 hours.

Place hazelnuts in a small saute pan and cook over medium heat; stir nuts as they cook, until a golden brown color, approximately 4 minutes. Remove from heat and set aside.

When roast is baked, remove pan from oven and set meat aside. Strain sauce through colander. Pour sauce back into pan and place over high heat; bring to a boil. After mixture boils for 6 minutes, add 1/2 cup cream and hazelnuts; cook an additional minute. Remove from heat.

Costine Di Maiale Alla Griglia

Grilled Marinated Baby Pork Ribs

1 whole baby back pork rib slab (3 lbs.)

Marinade:
1 onion, peeled, thinly sliced
3 garlic cloves, sliced
2 fresh rosemary sprigs, broken into pieces
6 fresh sage leaves, rough cut
1/3 cup red wine vinegar
2 cups dry red wine
2 teaspoons salt
2 teaspoons black pepper

Serves: 4
Complexity: • • •
Preparation Time: 1 Hour
12 Hours for Marinating
Italian Wine: Ghemme,
Five or six years old, dry and slightly
bitter with a violet bouquet.

Cut rib into thirds, or 6-rib slabs. Lay 3 slabs flat along the bottom of an oblong container. Combine ingredients for marinade and pour over top. Cover and place in refrigerator. Marinate meat for 12 hours, turning them after 6 hours.

After 12 hours, remove meat and season with salt and pepper on both sides. Place on preheated grill. Grill until ribs are crusty on the outside.

The marinade can be saved and used over the next 5-6 days on other meats.

Do not expect to have soft, tender meat. Instead, you will have firm but very tasty meat. I do not boil the ribs beforehand, I just marinate and grill them. This way, the fat stays on the meat and cooks with the meat, giving it flavor.

Scaloppine Di Ghiandole Di Vitello Alla Mario Sobbia

Sweetbreads "Mario Sobbia Style

2 lbs. prepared sweetbreads (techniques chapter)
8 ounces shiitake mushrooms, julienned
4 ounces prosciutto, julienned
1 cup unsalted butter
8 fresh sage leaves
1 teaspoon salt
1 teaspoon black pepper
2 teaspoons fresh rosemary, chopped
1 cup Marsala wine
2 cups black truffle sauce (sauces chapter)

Serves: 4
Complexity: • • •
Preparation Time: 20 Minuites
Italian Wine: Barilot,
Red, full body, a blend of
barbera grape and nebbiolo.

In a large saute pan, heat butter and sage leaves over high heat; when butter foams, add sweetbreads, seasoned lightly with salt and pepper on both sides. Saute sweetbreads, 1 minute on each side; remove sweetbreads and sage and put breads on towel to absorb oil.

Put saute pan back over medium heat and add mushrooms, prosciutto, salt, pepper, rosemary and Marsala. Cook until wine reduces completely and add black truffle sauce. Bring to a boil, then remove from heat.

To serve, place sweetbreads over bed of mushroom ragu.

Mario Sobbia was my favorite teacher at the cooking school in Torino, and remains a dear friend. Because of the great confidence Mario had in me, I am thankful that today I am able to achieve a different level of professionalism.

Bollito Misto

Mixed Boiled Meat with Vegetables

2 lbs. lean short ribs of beef
4 lbs. bottom round of beef
1 lb. beef hocks
1 1/2 lbs. lamb shoulder
1 lb. veal breast
1 calf foot, parboiled for 15 minutes
1/2 lb. lean pork fat belly

Aromatic Vegetables:
1 onion, peeled, sliced
1 garlic clove
2 carrots, peeled, sliced
2 turnips, peeled, sliced
2 tomatoes, blanched (techniques chapter)

Serves: 4
Complexity: • • •
Preparation Time: 1 Hour
Italian Wine: Barilot,
Red, full body, a blend of
barbera grape and nebbiolo.

Bouquet Garni:
2 fresh thyme sprigs
2 fresh Italian parsley sprigs
1 dried bay leaf

Vegetable Garnish:
1 lb. of six different types of vegetables in season (cabbage, peas, zucchini, etc.)
1 lb. new potatoes, cleaned, peeled
12 white onions, peeled
2 quarts chicken stock (sauces chapter)
3 cups green sauce (sauces chapter)
1 teaspoon salt
1/2 teaspoon black pepper

Place meat in a large stock pot and cover with cold water. Bring to a boil over low heat, skimming impurities off the top as the mixture cooks. When mixture reaches boiling point, add garlic clove and aromatic vegetables. Tie ingredients for bouquet garni securely with cooking twine. To stock pot, add the bouquet garni, salt and pepper and simmer for 1 1/2 to 3 hours. When meat has become tender, remove and keep warm. The veal and lamb will cook in approximately 1 1/2 hours, while the beef will be fully cooked in approximately 3 hours.

To prepare the vegetable garnish, place vegetables, excluding potatoes and onions, in stock pot with chicken stock and cook until tender. Cook potatoes and onions in water until tender.

To serve, arrange the meat on a platter and cover with strained broth. On a separate platter, arrange the vegetable garnish and serve with green sauce on the side.

Filetto Di Maiale Con Lenticchie

Baked Stuffed Pork Fillet Wrapped In Phyllo Dough

1 pork tenderloin
18 chestnuts, peeled
2 ounces roasted almonds, finely chopped
1 onion, peeled, chopped (2 ounces)
5 fresh sage leaves, finely chopped
1 fresh rosemary sprig, finely chopped
2 garlic cloves, finely chopped
1 teaspoon unsalted butter
1 juniper berry, smashed
1 dried bay leaf
1/2 cup Madeira wine
Crepinette (enough to wrap 4 pieces of pork)
8 ounces shredded phyllo dough
4 ounces fine cornmeal
1 teaspoon salt
1 teaspoon black pepper

Lentils:
8 ounces green lentils, cleaned
2 garlic cloves, smashed
1/2 cup olive oil
1 fresh rosemary sprig
4 ounces salted pork (techniques chapter)
1 carrot, peeled, cut into balls (3 ounces)
1 turnip, peeled, cut into balls (3 ounces)
8 baby leeks, cleaned
1 quart chicken stock (sauces chapter)
1/2 teaspoon dried hot red pepper flakes
1 cup Madeira wine
1/2 cup beef reduction (sauces chapter)

1/2 cup olive oil
4 garlic cloves
2 fresh rosemary sprigs
2 quarts grapeseed oil

Serves: 2
Complexity: ● ● ●
Preparation Time: 30 Minutes
2 Hours for Marinating
Italian Wine: Dolcetto Di Dogliani,
Red, dry, not too acidic, slightly bitter
but agreeable.

To prepare pork fillet, cut fillet into 8 slices 1/2" thick. Place in a small container and season with chopped garlic, rosemary, sage, juniper berry and bay leaf. Add Madeira, salt and pepper; allow to marinate for 2 hours.

Cook chestnuts in boiling salted water until tender. Drain and press through a food mill; add almonds and mix well. In a small saute pan, saute onions in olive oil until onions become tender. Add chestnut mixture and butter and mix well; remove from heat and set aside.

Remove the bay leaf from the marinated fillet and break it into four pieces; set aside. Take two slices of pork and make a sandwich with two teaspoons of chestnut mixture in the middle and one piece of bay leaf. Wrap each "sandwich" in crepinette and roll in corn meal. Set coated sandwiches aside. Saute sandwich in olive oil with garlic and rosemary over medium heat until pink. Remove from the saute pan and place on a sheet pan layered with paper towels to absorb oil. Wrap each sandwich in shredded phyllo dough and fry in grapeseed oil until phyllo dough is crispy and golden in color.

To prepare lentils, place olive oil in small saute pan with garlic, hot pepper, rosemary and blanched salted pork cut into small cubes. Saute over medium heat until garlic takes a golden brown color. Add vegetables and lentils and cover with chicken stock. Let simmer for 10 minutes. Add wine and allow to reduce by half, then add beef reduction and reduce by half again.

To serve, place the crispy pork sandwich wrapped in phyllo dough on top of braised lentils and serve hot.

Coniglio Ripieno Al Prosciutto

Stuffed Rolled Rabbit

1 rabbit, deboned, liver and heart aside, (20 ounces)
8 strips pancetta
3 tablespoons olive oil
1 bruciolo (techniques chapter)
1 cup dry white wine
1/2 cup rabbit sauce (sauces chapter)
1/2 teaspoon salt
1/2 teaspoon black pepper

Frittata Batter:
3 eggs
1 tablespoon fresh Italian parsley, chopped
1 tablespoon fresh tarragon
1 tablespoon grated Parmesan cheese
1/2 teaspoon salt
1/2 teaspoon black pepper
1 tablespoon all purpose flour
1/3 cup milk

Serves: 4
Complexity: ● ● ●
Preparation Time: 1 Hour
Italian Wine: Grignolino,
Red, dry and with a slightly
bitter finish.

Flatten rabbit meat using a meat mallet. Lay strips of pancetta lengthwise, with strips slightly overlapping meat. Set aside.

To prepare frittata batter, in a medium mixing bowl, combine ingredients. Mix well, then transfer to a blender and puree mixture until smooth. In a medium, non-stick saute pan, heat 1 tablespoon olive oil over medium heat. Add 1/2 cup of frittata mixture and allow to cook 2 minutes on one side; remove from heat and flip quickly; the consistency will be similar to a crepe. Remove from pan. The frittata cake should be light brown on one side and white on the other.

On top of rabbit meat layered with pancetta slices, add a single layer of frittata cakes. Fold the rabbit meat, surrounding the pancetta and frittata, in half lengthwise. Tie the meat every 1/2 inch using cooking twine, forming a long roll. Cut roll in half, as needed, the meat roll will need to fit in a large saute pan. Season rabbit roll(s) with 1/2 teaspoon each of salt and pepper.

In a large saute pan, heat 2 tablespoons olive oil over medium heat; add bruciolo and saute for 30 seconds. Add rabbit roll(s) and saute until meat becomes lightly browned on each side. After meat is browned evenly, remove pan from heat and place in preheated oven set at 450 degrees for 13 1/2 minutes.

Remove meat from pan and set aside. Return original pan to medium heat and add white wine; allow to reduce almost completely and then add rabbit sauce. Chop rabbit liver and heart and add to sauce; saute for 2 minutes. Remove from heat and pour contents of pan into blender. Puree until smooth.

Unwrap cooking twine from rabbit rolls. Cut into 1/4" slices and serve with sauce.

If you do not want to use the frittata inside, you can just use prosciutto and spinach.

dolci

Desserts are part of the social life of the Piedmontese family. Dessert is not eaten at the end of meal, but as an outside part of the meal, late in the afternoon between lunch and dinner or after dinner as a small part of the meal. After dinner, we use seasonal fruit in our recipes in Piedmont such as figs, apples, cherries and pears. During the day we have beautiful cakes and fruit tarts. Piedmontese serve very sophisticated desserts. I want to thank my chef mentors who introduced me to pastry preparation. I always remember making Creme Caramel. Just before midnight before we went to sleep, we would put it in the wood-burning oven and take off the ashes. The oven would be hot enough to cook it and in the morning at 5:00 a.m. we would pull it from the oven and have warm creme caramel for breakfast. I would like to thank my brother-in-law's mother who gave me the pudding recipe for this chapter.

Pere Arrostite In Salsa Di Barolo

Roasted Pear in Barolo Wine Sauce

8 Bosc pears (Anjou or Bartlett)
2 cups Barolo wine
1 cup sugar
2 tablespoons unsalted butter

Serves: 8
Complexity: •
Preparation Time: 50 Minutes
Italian Wine: Freisa D'Asti Amabile,
Red with a sweet, dry, fruity,
grape flavor.

Place peeled pears in buttered baking dish with sugar and wine. Bake in preheated oven at 350 degrees for 35 minutes, basting pears often with wine syrup.

Remove from oven and set pears aside. Reduce pear syrup to a dense consistency by cooking over medium-low heat until mixture coats the back of a spoon. Using an apple corer, remove core from each pear from the bottom. To serve, place baked pears on serving plate topped with pear reduction sauce.

Krumiri Di Casale Monferrato

Corn Cookies

1 cup cornmeal, very finely ground (+ 2 tablespoons to coat pan)
1 cup unsalted butter (+ 2 tablespoons to coat pan)
3/4 cup all purpose flour
1/2 cup + 2 tablespoons sugar
1/2 teaspoon baking powder
4 eggs
1 teaspoon vanilla

Serves: 4
Complexity: • •
Preparation Time: 1 Hour
Italian Wine: Moscato D' Asti,
White sparkling, sweet and fresh.

Combine all ingredients and mix well, using dough hook attachment on mixer, at medium speed. When butter is completely incorporated into mixture, remove dough and wrap in plastic wrap; do not over mix dough. Place wrapped dough in refrigerator for 30 minutes.

Coat bottom of baking sheet first with butter and then flour. Remove chilled dough and transfer into pastry bag with a star tip. Squeeze dough out to form small, 2" curved tubes onto prepared baking sheet.

Bake at 375 degrees for 20 minutes.

Crostata Di Prugne In Salsa Di Grappa

Plum Tart with Plum Ice Cream in Grappa Sauce

Dough for Crust (pasta frolla):
1 1/2 cups + 2 tablespoons pastry flour
1/2 cup sugar
3/4 cups unsalted butter
4 eggs
1 tablespoon honey
1/2 lemon rind
1/2 orange rind
1 teaspoon vanilla
1 pinch salt
1 tablespoon baking powder

Plum Jam:
3 lbs. Italian prune plums, pitted, quartered
1 cup sugar
juice of 1 lemon

Plum Base for Gelato:
1 cup Italian prune plums
1 cup water
3/4 cup sugar
1 cinnamon stick
1/2 vanilla bean
2 cups vanilla gelatin

Vanilla Gelato:
1 1/2 cups milk
1/2 cup sugar
1 vanilla bean
9 egg yolks
1 1/2 cups cream

Grappa English Cream:
1 cup milk
1 cup heavy whipping cream
1/4 vanilla bean
1/2 cup sugar
5 egg yolks
3 tablespoons grappa

To Top Tart:
1 lb. Italian prune plums,
remove pit and cut in half
(to place on top of tart)

Serves: 8
Complexity: •••
Preparation Time: 1 Hour, 10 Minutes
Italian Wine: Malvasia D'Asti,
white, sweet and rich.

To prepare marmalade, place 3 lbs. plum quarters into small mixing bowl; add lemon juice and sugar and mix to coat. Allow mixture to sit until juices extract from plums; transfer contents into sauce pan and cook over low heat to reduce and thicken juices. Cooking time will be 1 to 2 hours, cooking slowly over very low heat. When cooking is almost complete, taste juice and add sugar to adjust sweetness and lemon juice to adjust tartness. Pour contents into shallow pan and allow to cool at room temperature.

To prepare pasta frolla, mix flour, sugar, salt and grated rinds of orange and lemon. Add remaining ingredients and mix well using a spoon. Stir mixture rapidly to avoid butter becoming warm and melting. Do not mix with hands as body temperature will melt butter. Wrap dough in plastic wrap and place in refrigerator for 2 hours. Roll chilled dough to fit a 10" tart ring. Grease tart ring and place dough inside, trimming dough 1/2" above ring edge. Place in refrigerator to chill.

Roll a second piece of pasta frolla dough to 12" circle and place on tray; put in refrigerator to chill. After dough is chilled, cut the 12" round piece into 1/2" strips for the tart lattice top.

Fill the chilled tart shell with cooled plum marmalade. Cover the top with a layer of plums cut in half. Brush the edge of the tart shell with egg wash, using 1 egg and 1 tablespoon water; also brush lattice strips while they are still on tray. Working quickly, lay strips across tart in a criss-cross pattern. Preheat oven to 425 degrees.

While the oven is heating, return tart to refrigerator to keep cool. Sprinkle tart with sugar just before baking; bake at 425 degrees for 10 minutes, then reduce heat to 350 for an additional 20 to 25 minutes. Bake until tart is dark golden brown and the filling bubbles.

To prepare plum gelato, take plums, quartered, and place in small sauce pan with water, sugar, cinnamon stick and half vanilla bean; cook over low heat until plums are very tender. Remove cinnamon stick and vanilla bean; pour contents into blender and puree; pass through strainer to yield smooth puree.

To prepare vanilla grappa sauce, combine milk, cream, sugar and vanilla bean in small saucepan over medium heat; cook until the mixture boils. Add egg yolks and cook until thickened. Strain into container and chill mixture in an ice bath; remove vanilla bean and add grappa; mix well.

To prepare vanilla ice cream, bring milk and cream to a boil with vanilla stick. When mixture reaches a boil, remove from heat and cover; allow to set for 2 hours. Remove vanilla stick mix egg yolk and sugar until mixture becomes light yellow; add milk and place back over low heat until mixture becomes thick enough to coat the back of a spoon. Cool the mixture. Measure amount of plum puree and add equal amount of vanilla gelato base and process in ice cream mixture until it reaches proper consistency.

To assemble, place a slice of plum tart in the center of a serving plate with 3 tablespoons of sauce; top with a scoop of ice cream.

Bunet Alla Moda Della Mamma Di Silvano

Chocolate Pudding "Silvano's Mother's Style"

5 eggs
6 tablespoons sugar
3 tablespoons bitter cocoa powder
1 tablespoon grated sweet chocolate
1/4 cup fernet or rum
8 ounces amaretto cookies, chopped
2 cups milk, warmed

Caramel:
1/3 cup sugar
3 tablespoons water

Serves: 8
Complexity: ••
Preparation Time: 2 Hour, 10 Minutes
Italian Wine: Brachetto D'Acqui,
Red sparkling with a fresh fruity flavor.

Mix eggs and sugar for 5 minutes using a mixer at medium speed, until mixture becomes pale yellow. Add cookies, cocoa powder, grated chocolate and fernet. If you want dessert to be very sweet, use rum instead. When mixture is blended, add milk and mix again. Set mixture aside.

Prepare caramel by cooking sugar and water over low heat until it becomes dark golden in color. Pour mixture into bottom of 8" x 4" loaf pan. Allow to cool until caramel is set.

Top caramel mixture with prepared custard; bake in water bath at 375 degrees for 35 minutes. Remove from oven and allow to cool completely. To serve, turn pan over onto serving platter. The caramel will melt into a syrup and coat the dessert.

I want to thank Silvano's mother for this beautiful recipe. She used to make this every October when our families met at an annual reunion to eat white truffles. We used to save money all year long. When October would come, Silvano's father would find the white truffles in Araban. We would buy truffles and both families would cook dishes and everything had white truffles on top, of course. The highlight of this meal for me, was the chocolate pudding that Silvano's mother used to make.

Torta Di Nocciole Con Lo Zabaglione Di Moscato

Hazelnut Cake In Moscato Wine Zabaglione

Torte:
3/4 cup + 2 tablespoons all purpose flour
3/4 cup + 2 tablespoons sugar
5 ounces hazelnuts, peeled and finely chopped
1/3 cup unsalted butter, softened (set out of refrigerator for 2 hours)
3 eggs
1 lemon juice
1 tablespoon baking soda
1 tablespoon olive oil
6 tablespoons milk

Moscato Zabaglione:
4 egg yolks
6 tablespoons sugar
1/2 cup Moscato wine
1/2 cup heavy whipping cream

Serves: 8
Complexity: ••
Preparation Time: 1 Hour, 5 Minutes
Italian Wine: Moscato D'Asti,
White sparkling, sweet and fresh.

Chocolate Sauce:
1 1/2 ounces bittersweet chocolate
2 tablespoons sugar
1 tablespoon unsalted butter
1/2 cup water

To prepare torte, lightly butter and flour 9" cake pan and set aside. Combine torte ingredients in a bowl and mix well at medium speed until well blended. Pour contents into cake pan and bake in oven preheated to 350 degrees for 45 minutes. Remove from heat and allow to cool upside down on cooling rack.

To prepare muscato zabaglione, place egg yolks, sugar and wine in small mixing bowl and place over pot of boiling water. Whip until mixture becomes foamy and thick to form a ribbon. Remove from heat and place mixture in refrigerator until it cools. When mixture has cooled completely, fold in whipping cream which has been whipped to form stiff peaks.

To prepare chocolate sauce, combine water and sugar in small sauce pan over low heat; cook until sugar is dissolved, 3 minutes. Add butter and chocolate and continue to stir until ingredients are well blended, 5 minutes.

Serve cake warm with a zabaglione and chocolate sauce.

Bavarese Al Marsala E Cioccolato Con I Marroni

Bavarian Cream of Marsala Wine and Chocolate

Zabaglione Bavarian Cream:
10 egg yolks
1/2 cup + 2 tablespoons sugar
2 tablespoons Marsala wine
2 cups heavy whipped cream
3 gelatin sheets
3 ounces bittersweet chocolate

Gianduia Sauce
3 ounces Gianduia chocolate
4 tablespoons sugar
2 tablespoons unsalted butter
1 cup water

Maron Glasse:
12 ounces fresh chestnuts, peeled
1 1/2 cups roasted pear syrup

Tulip Cookie:
4 egg whites
1/2 cup + 3 tablespoons powdered sugar
1/4 cup + 1 tablespoon cake flour
1/4 cup + 1 tablespoon unsalted butter

Serves: 8
Complexity: • • • •
Preparation Time: 45 Minutes
12 Hours to Rest
Italian Wine: Malvasia D'Asti,
White sweet and rich.

To prepare zabaglione, place egg yolks, sugar and wine in mixing bowl and set bowl over pot of boiling water; mix well using whisk until mixture reaches ribbon stage. When the whisk is lifted from the mix, the mixture will fold down from the whisk like a "ribbon." Remove mix from hot water and add gelatin sheets, which have been pre-soaked in cold water for 3 minutes to soften, then drained; set aside to cool at room temperature, do not cool in the refrigerator. When mix has completely cooled, fold in cream. Set aside 1/4 of mixture for Bavarian cream. Fill Bavarian molds 3/4 full with zabaglione cream.

Take the remaining 1/4 of mixture and add chocolate, which has been melted by placing it in bowl over a pot with hot water, or bain marie. Place chocolate mixture in pastry bag with a round tip. Using the pastry bag, inject the chocolate mixture into the zabaglione cream, placing walnut-sized portions in the center of the mold.

To prepare gianduia sauce, combine sugar and water in small pan over low heat; stir until sugar has melted; add chocolate and butter. Continue to stir over low heat until mixture is thoroughly melted and well blended.

To prepare tulip cookies, preheat oven to 375 degrees. Whip egg whites to a barely soft peak. Sift together sugar and flour, then add to whipped egg whites. Add melted butter and stir. On the back of a very flat sheet pan that has been buttered and floured, spread mixture in a very thin, even layer. Bake until lightly brown. Shape into a leaf form upon removal from oven.

To prepare glasse, blanch fresh chestnuts and peel. Use roasted pear syrup to cover chestnuts in a small sauce pan. Cook over low heat and simmer until chestnuts are tender; remove from heat. Allow chestnuts to cool in pear syrup for 12 hours.

To assemble, place zabaglione mold in warm water for a few seconds; with a firm move of the wrist, release the zabaglione on the center of a serving platter. Place the cookie in back, leaving it standing up. Pour two spoonfuls of gianduia sauce around zabaglione and decorate with chestnuts in syrup.

Tiramisu Croccante "Alla Michel Richard"

Crunchy Tiramisu

1 teaspoon ground espresso beans
1 tablespoon rum

Mascarpone Cream:
4 egg yolks
1/2 cup sugar
1 container mascarpone cheese
1/2 cup heavy cream
1/3 tablespoon dark rum

Pan Di Spagna:
1/3 cup powdered sugar
3 tablespoons all purpose flour
2 tablespoons cornstarch
3 egg whites
3 egg yolks
1 tablespoon vanilla

Crunchy Phyllo:
1 box phyllo, 1 lb.
1/2 lb. unsalted butter, melted
3/4 cup powdered sugar

Baking Pan:
1 ounce butter
1 ounce all purpose flour

Serves: 8
Complexity: • • •
Preparation Time: 40 Minutes
6 Hours Refrigeration
Italian Wine: Moscato D'Asti,
White sparkling, sweet and fresh.

To prepare mascarpone cream, whip egg yolks and sugar in a small mixing bowl; blend until mixture becomes thick with a pale yellow color. Add mascarpone cheese and fold until smooth. In a separate bowl, whip cream and rum to a soft peak, then add to mascarpone mixture and blend ingredients. Set aside in refrigerator.

To prepare pan di spagna, rub 1/2 sheet pan with butter and dust lightly with flour; set pan aside. Mix flour and cornstarch in a small mixing bowl. In a separate bowl, mix sugar and the egg yolks until mixture becomes foamy. In a large mixing bowl, whip egg whites until they form a stiff peak; fold egg yolk mixture, one spoonful at a time. Next, fold flour mixture, passing through a sifter. Add vanilla and blend well. Spread batter onto prepared sheet pan no more than 1/4" thick, using a spatula. Bake in oven preheated to 350 degrees for 10 minutes, or until golden in color.

Loosen pan di spagna from pan allow to cool. Place pan di spagna back into pan and soak with espresso and rum mixture. Spread mascarpone mixture evenly over cake; sprinkle with ground espresso beans, wrap tightly and place in freezer. When cake is firm, cut into 2" squares; return to freezer to keep firm.

To prepare phyllo, preheat oven to 350 degrees. Lay one sheet of phyllo on a cutting board, brush with melted butter and dust with sugar. Repeat with two additional sheets of phyllo, ending with sugar on top. Using a knife, trim edges to make even. Cut into 3" squares and place on baking sheet. Bake in preheated oven for 8-10 minutes, or until lightly browned.

To assemble, place phyllo square on serving plate, top with a mascarpone square (place cheese squares in refrigerator prior to assembly to allow them to soften slightly); repeat with phyllo, then cheese, and top with a final phyllo layer.

For this dish, I thank Michel Richard, because I took this idea after working with him one day. Preparing it in the Napolean style is a great idea. I thank him.

Ricotta Fritta Con Le Bugie

Fried Ricotta Balls with Fried Flat Sweet Bread

Ricotta Fritters Mixture:
2 lbs. ricotta cheese
1/4 cup candied orange, finely minced
1 tablespoon orange flower water
3/4 cup sugar
1/4 cup toasted pistachios, chopped

To Cook Fritters:
1 cup all purpose flour
2 eggs, beaten + 2 tablespoons water
1 cup unseasoned bread crumbs, finely ground
1/2 gallon grapeseed oil

Bugie:
1 cup pastry flour
1/2 cup + 2 tablespoons sugar
3/4 tablespoon baking powder
1 lemon, rind only
2 eggs
2 tablespoons unsalted butter

Serves: 8
Complexity: ● ● ●
Preparation Time: 45 Minutes
Italian Wine: Moscato D'Asti,
White sparkling, sweet and fresh.

Raspberry Sauce:
1 1/4 cups fresh raspberries (10 ounces)
1/2 cup + 2 tablespoons sugar
2 tablespoons water
1/2 cup triple sec

To prepare fritters, first drain ricotta. (To completely dry ricotta cheese, allow to drain in cheesecloth overnight). Take dry ricotta and combine in mixing bowl with candied orange, orange flower water, sugar and pistachios. Mix ingredients well, then roll into 1 1/4" balls. Take each ball and roll first in flour, then in egg, and finally in bread crumbs. Place balls in refrigerator until ready for use. Heat grapeseed oil to 375 degrees and place balls in heated oil, frying until golden brown. Remove from oil and place on baking sheet lined with paper towels to absorb oil.

To prepare bugie, combine ingredients and set in refrigerator for an hour or longer. Take chilled dough and roll into thin layer; cut into strips 2" in length. Place strips in hot oil to fry. Remove from oil and place on baking sheet lined with paper towels to absorb oil; dust with powdered sugar.

To prepare raspberry sauce, dissolve sugar in water and place in small sauce pan over medium heat for five minutes. Add berries and cook for 2 minutes; pour mixture into blender and puree. Add triple sec and blend again. Pass sauce through strainer to yield smooth sauce.

To serve, place ricotta fritters and bugie on serving plate and dress with raspberry sauce.

I combined two recipes to make this dish because I wanted to add crunchiness to it. Bugie is usually made at a carnival at the end of February in Italy; the children eat it sprinkled with sugar. I remember I used to eat a lot of them.

Fichi Fritti Con Gelato Al Miele

Fried Figs with Honey Ice Cream

8 black mission figs, washed and quartered
1/2 gallon grape seed oil

Batter:
1/2 cup all purpose flour
1 tablespoon fresh yeast
3/4 cup Italian Proscecco champagne

Honey Ice Cream:
1/2 quart milk
1/2 quart heavy cream
1/3 cup sugar
1/2 cup + 2 tablespoons honey
12 egg yolks

Serves: 4
Complexity: ••
Preparation Time: 50 Minutes
Italian Wine: Passito Di Caluso,
White with a sweet, dry fruity flavor.

To prepare ice cream, heat milk, cream and honey. Mix egg yolks and sugar together until light yellow. Add to hot milk mixture and cook over low heat until mixture becomes thick, completely coating the back of a spoon. Remove from heat and cool. Place contents in ice cream maker. Process until mixture reaches proper consistency and place in freezer.

To prepare fig batter, dissolve yeast in Proscecco. Sift flour and add to yeast/ proscecco mixture. Allow mixture to rest for 30 minutes. If you do not intend to use immediately, place mixture in refrigerator and remove 30 minutes before use. Heat grape seed oil in large pot. Drop each fig into batter and fry, one at a time, in the heated oil. Remove fried figs and place on a baking sheet lined with paper towels to absorb oil.

Serve figs with ice cream on the side.

Fragole All'Aceto Balsamico

Strawberry with Balsamic Vinegar Dressing

1 lb. strawberries
1/2 cup balsamic vinegar
(vinegar aged 10 years is best,
 but regular balsamic will do)
1/2 cup sugar

Serves: 4
Complexity: •
Preparation Time: 2 Hours

Wash, hull and slice strawberries. Marinate the berries in vinegar and sugar in the refrigerator for 2 hours to allow juices from strawberries to extract into a rich sauce.

Crostata Di Mele Con Il Gelato Di Uvetta Sultanina

Apple Tart With Raisin Ice Cream

Apple Crostata
Flaky Pastry Dough:
2 1/4 cups all purpose flour
1/2 teaspoon salt
1 tablespoon sugar
1/2 cup + 2 tablespoons unsalted butter, cold
1/2 cup cold water

8 apples (Macintosh),
 peeled and cored
juice of 1/2 lemon
1/2 cup sugar

Raisins for Ice Cream:
1 1/2 cups raisins
3/4 cup cognac
1/2 cup water

Raisin Ice Cream:
1/2 cup milk
1/2 cup sugar
1 stick vanilla
9 egg yolks
1/2 cup cream

Serves: 8
Complexity: • •
Preparation Time: 1 Hour
Italian Wine: Malvasia Di
Castelnuovo Don Bosco,
White sweet, slightly dry
with a sharp finish.

To prepare pastry dough, mix dry ingredients in a large mixing bowl; cut in butter in 1/4" pieces, remove from mixer. Add water all at once; toss quickly to coat all ingredients. Add more water, one tablespoon at a time, if too dry, do not over mix. Form dough into disk shape, pressing lightly. Wrap in plastic wrap and place in refrigerator to chill. When dough is chilled, remove and place on lightly floured, flat surface; roll disk into 12" circle. Lay dough on baking sheet and return to refrigerator.

Take peeled and cored apples, slice into wedges. Place wedges in bowl and add lemon juice, sugar; mix well to coat apples. Place apple wedges over top of dough, starting 3" from outside edge. Layer apples until all wedges are placed on dough. Take edge of dough and fold over to cover outside row of apples. Be careful not to break dough, as juice will leak and cause it to bake improperly.

Place pan in refrigerator to chill again before baking. After crostata is chilled, bake at 425 degrees for 15 minutes; reduce heat to 350 degrees and bake for an additional 40 to 50 minutes, until the filling bubbles in the center.

To prepare raisins for ice cream, heat raisins, cognac and water in small sauce pan over low heat to simmer. Cover pot and allow raisins to absorb most of the liquid, then remove from heat.

Take approximately half the raisins and any remaining liquid and place in food processor; puree and allow mixture to cool.

To prepare ice cream, combine milk, sugar and vanilla stick in small saucepan over medium heat; cook until the mixture boils. Add egg yolks and cook until thickened. Strain into cold cream and mix well. Chill mixture in an ice bath and remove vanilla stick. Add raisin puree. Churn the ice cream mixture in an ice cream freezer, folding in remaining whole raisins. Store in freezer until use.

Serve the apple tart warm, with the raisin ice cream and toasted dipped almonds.

Mele Alla "Ca Peo"

Sauteed Apple "Ca Peo" Style

Pear Syrup:
8 pears
1 lb. sugar
3 quarts dry white wine

Sauteed Apple Stick:
4 apples
2 tablespoons unsalted butter
2 ounces raisins
1 ounce toasted pine nuts
1/2 cup kirsch liquor or cherry liquor

Serves: 4
Complexity: ••••
Preparation Time: 40 Minutes,
5 Hours for Pear Juice
Italian Wine: Passito Di Caluso,
white with a sweet, dry fruit flavor.

Chestnut Ice Cream:
2 egg yolks
1/2 cup + 2 tablespoons sugar
1/2 cup milk
1/2 vanilla stick
1/2 lb. chestnuts (boiled in 3 cups of milk for 1 1/2 hours), puree using blender
1/2 cup heavy cream
1 tablespoon dark rum

To prepare pear syrup, wash pears and place in roasting pan; add sugar and wine and roast in preheated oven set at 150 degrees for 5 hours, turning pears every 30 minutes. Remove pan from oven and remove pears, keeping them for another preparation. Set pear syrup aside.

To prepare ice cream, combine milk and vanilla bean in small saucepan over medium heat; cook until the mixture boils. Remove from heat and allow to cool for two hours. In a separate bowl, mix egg yolks with sugar until mixture becomes light golden in color; add milk and cook over low heat until mixture coats the back of spoon. Strain mixture and cool. Stir in cream, chestnut puree and rum. Freeze mixture in ice cream maker.

Peel apples. Using a tube-shaped apple cutter, cut cylinder shapes from apples, avoiding the seeds. Keep apples in lemon water while you continue to peel and cut. Drain apples and saute in butter over low heat; add raisins and pine nuts; when apples turn golden brown, add kirsch and pear syrup; cook 2 minutes.

To serve, place apples in pasta bowl with a scoop of chestnut ice cream, topped with pear sauce.

I want to thank Franco Solari and his wife from "Ca Peo" restaurant in Lelvi Liguira, in Italy. When they came to cook at Galileo a few years ago, they presented this dish to me and I took it from them. I value their friendship. They do a beautiful job at the restaurant in Italy.

Tegoline Alle Mandorle

Thin Almond Cookies

1/2 cup + 2 tablespoons all purpose flour
1/3 cup unsalted butter
2 eggs
1/3 cup sugar
3 ounces sliced roasted almonds
1 ounce butter (for baking pan)
1 1/2 ounces all purpose flour (for baking pan)

Serves: 8
Complexity: ● ● ●
Preparation Time: 35 Minutes
1 Hour Refrigeration
Italian Wine: Passito Di Caluso Liquoroso,
Full flavor with a light, dry, fruity flavor.

Cream butter and sugar together, then slowly add eggs, one at a time. After eggs are blended with mixture, add flour and then almonds.

Let mixture rest in refrigerator for 1 hour.

Coat bottom of baking sheet first with butter and then flour. Remove chilled dough from refrigerator and transfer into pastry bag. Using a 1/4" round tip for the bag, squeeze dough out to form small, 2" tubes onto prepared baking sheet. Bake at 300 degrees until cookies become golden in color.

Brutti Ma Buoni

Almond Cookies

20 ounces peeled almonds
2 cups + 2 tablespoons sugar
7 egg whites
2 tablespoons unsalted butter
1 pinch cinnamon
1 pinch vanilla
1 ounce butter (for baking pan)

Serves: 8
Complexity: ● ● ●
Preparation Time: 1 Hour, 15 Minutes
Italian Wine: Brachetto D' Acqui,
Red, sparkling with a fruity flavor.

Place almonds on baking sheet and bake at 300 degrees for five minutes, turning them several times. Remove toasted almonds from oven and place in food processor; chop almonds very fine, until the consistency resembles coarse flour.

Place egg whites in mixing bowl and whip until firm; using a spatula, fold in almonds, sugar, vanilla and cinnamon. Place mixture in a small sauce pan over low heat; stir continuously with a wooden spoon as mixture cooks for 20 minutes; remove from heat.

Rub the bottom of a baking sheet with butter. Using teaspoons, form almond mixture into small rounds, the size of walnuts, and place on baking sheet. Bake at 250 degrees for 40 minutes. The cookies will turn lightly golden brown; they can be stored in a sealed tin for 3 to 4 weeks.

The name means "ugly but good." Don't worry if they do not look good while you are spooning them. The taste will make up for their looks.

Pere Ripiene Al Gorgonzola E Tartufo Bianco

Stuffed Pear with Gorgonzola Cheese and White Truffle

8 Bosc pears, peeled
4 cups water
2 cups dry white wine
2 cups sugar
1 cinnamon stick
1 star anise
1 dried bay leaf
1 lemon peel

Caluso Wine Zabaglione:
4 egg yolks
4 1/2 egg shell sugar
4 1/2 egg shell passito di caluso
1/2 ounce fresh white truffle

Gorgonzola Stuffing:
2 ounces gorgonzola cheese
2 ounces mascarpone cheese
1/4 cup heavy cream
salt
black pepper

Serves: 4
Complexity: ● ● ● ●
Preparation Time: 1 Hour
Italian Wine: Passito Di Caluso,
White with a sweet, dry, fruity flavor.

In a medium sauce pan, combine water, wine, sugar, cinnamon, anise, bay leaf and lemon peel; cook over medium heat until mixture reaches a boil. Add pears and reduce heat to low; simmer until pears become tender, approximately 25 minutes.

Prepare zabaglione immediately before serving, place egg yolks, sugar and passito wine in mixing bowl and set bowl over pot of boiling water; mix well using whisk until mixture reaches ribbon stage, when the whisk is lifted from the mix, the mixture will fold down from the utensil like a "ribbon". Remove from heat and keep warm until assembling pear.

To prepare stuffing, pass gorgonzola cheese through a sieve and fold in mascarpone cheese and cream; add salt and pepper to taste.

To assemble, using an apple corer, remove core from each pear from the bottom. Fill pears with gorgonzola cheese mixture and place on serving dish. Serve each with a spoonful of hot zabaglione. Using a mandolin, thinly shave white truffles directly over pears.

Food Concepts:
A Unique Resource For Food Industry Professionals

Food Concepts Marketing Corporation combines proven experience in the food industry with true marketing savvy. A full-service marketing and advertising agency, the Cleveland-based firm includes an 800-square-foot professional demonstration kitchen, an expansive photography studio and an in-house, art department.

Food Concepts has carved out its niche in the food industry, offering clients strategic marketing counsel that is grounded in the true understanding of, and passion for, good food and wine.

Established in 1990, Food Concepts manages nationally and internationally renown chefs, putting professional chefs in touch with consumers through personal appearances; television interviews and demonstrations, and cookbook development. Food Concepts recipe tested Charlie Trotter's first cookbook, as well as Jacques Pepin's *Simple and Healthy Cooking* cookbook. Food Concepts negotiates product endorsements for chefs, in addition to the development and marketing of brand endorsements.

Food Concepts has positioned itself as a leader in the marketing arena by combining its creative talent and strategic marketing philosophy with an innovative and invaluable resource for food service professionals. Food Concept's custom, state-of-the-art test kitchen, located in the agency's loft office space, provides clients with newfound capabilities that spark new business ventures, maximize existing operations and improve their bottom line.

Drawing on its experience in the industry, Food Concepts works hand-in-hand with food service professionals to develop and orchestrate new product launches; reposition existing products within the industry to maximize product potential; develop product packaging or repackage existing products to drive sales; identify retail outlets for direct product distribution; and identify sources for product manufacturing and distribution.

Food Concepts also consults on and assists with establishing new restaurant ventures, which may include site selection and funding; menu development and planning; evaluation of food costs and operational budgets; equipment and product supplier leads; and kitchen staff training.

The professional, in-house photography studio stems from the inherent appreciation for and understanding of photography held by Food Concept's president, Ted Boehm, who has worked as a commercial photographer for more than 15 years. Under Mr. Boehm's direction, the photo studio provides clients with a full-range of photographic capabilities for shooting food in a correct and authentic environment by understanding how food is prepared, cooked and presented.

With the assistance of Curtis Newton, heading our design and creative department, the implementation of chef's direction for food styling and presentation becomes a simple task.

In working with chefs around the world, you gain a sense of "food excellence" from their combined knowledge. The intuitiveness of preparation and presentation, their tradition of family and love and passion of food,

I was taught the appreciation and respect of Italian food from my family. While growing up, we would go to visit my Italian relatives and experience course after course, every holiday and special event, making each of them better than the one before. My Grandpa (Boehm) and Nono (Zangrando) love to eat and experience the ethnic foods of Germany and Italy. Many times, they would sit and enjoy a bottle of wine and trade "old stories" of times well remembered. This passion and understanding of food and wine is an ongoing tradition in my family, continuing with our newest member, Joshua Dante.

Roberto truly loves to cook and prepares foods for others to experience. Life could not exist for Roberto without his passion for food, tradition and love of family. I feel honored that he included Food Concepts and myself in this, his first cookbook.

For further information
please contact:
Mr. Ted Boehm, President
Food Concepts
Marketing Corporation
2530 Superior Avenue, 7th Floor
Cleveland, Ohio 44114
216.241.4949
Fax 216.241.4320

"Galileo ... Washington's most popular and sophisticated Italian Restaurant ...Chef Roberto Donna's cooking is delicate, imaginative and satisfying ..."

Thomas Head
Roll Call

"Chef Roberto Donna has practically become a national treasure ..."

Phyllis C. Richman
The Washington Post

Awards and Achievements:

The Insegua del Ristorante Italiano, 1996
One of the 20 finest Italian Restaurants in the world.

The James Beard Award, 1996
Best Chef/Mid-Atlantic Region

The Fine Dining Hall of Fame, 1996
Nation's Restaurant News

Traveler's Choice Award, reader selected, June 1996
Washington Flyer Magazine

Restaurateur of the Year, 1995
Restaurant Assoc. of Metropolitan Washington

Achievement Award, 1992
Italian Wine & Food Institute

President's Humanitarian Award, 1992
American Culinary Federation, Nation's Capital Chef's Association

The Caterina de Medici Award, 1991
Federazione Italiana Cuochi

The Chef of America Award, 1991
Master Chef's Society

One of the Ten Best Chefs in America, 1990
Food and Wine

Galileo
1110 21st Street North West
Washington, D.C. 20036
202.293.7191

Il Radicchio
1509 17th Street North West
Washington, D.C. 20036
202.986.2627

1211 Wisconsin Avenue, North West
Washington, D.C. 20007
202.337.2627

1801 Clarendon Boulevard
Arlington, VA 22201
703.276.2627

223 Pennsylvania Avenue, South East
Washington, D.C. 20003   *(In partnership with Enzo Fargione)*

Arucola   *(In partnership with Mahe Bogdanovich)*
5534 Connecticut Avenue, North West
Washington, D.C. 20015
202.244.1555

Pesce   *(In partnership with Jean Louis Palladin)*
2016 P Street, North West
Washington, D.C. 20037
202.466.3474

Il Pane
1211 Wisconsin Avenue, North West
Washington, D.C. 20007
202.944.9466

I Matti
2436 18th Street, North West
Washington, D.C. 20009
202.462.8844

Cesco   *(In partnership with Francesco Ricchi)*
4872 Cordell Avenue,
Bethesda, MD 20814
301.654.8333

Dolcetto   *(In partnership with George & Mahe Bogdanovic, Arthur Alafoginis)*
3201 New Mexico Avenue, North West,
Washington, D.C. 20016

Barolo   *(In partnership with Enzo Fargione)*
223 Pennsylvania Avenue, South East
Washington, D.C. 20003